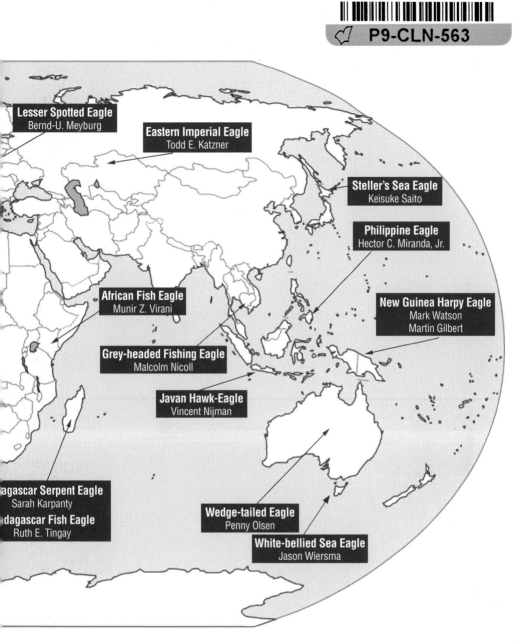

Lesser Spotted Eagle
Bernd-U. Meyburg

Eastern Imperial Eagle
Todd E. Katzner

Steller's Sea Eagle
Keisuke Saito

Philippine Eagle
Hector C. Miranda, Jr.

African Fish Eagle
Munir Z. Virani

New Guinea Harpy Eagle
Mark Watson
Martin Gilbert

Grey-headed Fishing Eagle
Malcolm Nicoll

Javan Hawk-Eagle
Vincent Nijman

agascar Serpent Eagle
Sarah Karpanty

dagascar Fish Eagle
Ruth E. Tingay

Wedge-tailed Eagle
Penny Olsen

White-bellied Sea Eagle
Jason Wiersma

AROUND THE WORLD

THE EAGLE
WATCHERS

THE EAGLE WATCHERS

Observing and Conserving Raptors around the World

EDITED BY
RUTH E. TINGAY
AND TODD E. KATZNER

Foreword by
Keith L. Bildstein
and Jemima Parry-Jones, MBE

Comstock Publishing Associates
a division of
Cornell University Press
ITHACA AND LONDON

First published 2010 by Cornell University Press

Printed in the United States of America

Library of Congress Cataloging-in-Publication Data

The eagle watchers : observing and conserving raptors around the world / edited by Ruth E. Tingay and Todd E. Katzner ; foreword by Keith L. Bildstein and Jemima Parry-Jones.

    p. cm.

  Includes bibliographical references.

  ISBN 978-0-8014-4873-7 (cloth : alk. paper)

  1. Eagles. 2. Eagles—Conservation.   I. Tingay, Ruth E. II. Katzner, Todd E.   III. Title.

  QL696.F32E22 2010

  598.9'42—dc22   2009052785

Cornell University Press strives to use environmentally responsible suppliers and materials to the fullest extent possible in the publishing of its books. Such materials include vegetable-based, low-VOC inks and acid-free papers that are recycled, totally chlorine-free, or partly composed of nonwood fibers. For further information, visit our website at www.cornellpress.cornell.edu.

Cloth printing   10 9 8 7 6 5 4 3 2 1

The editors would like to dedicate this book to the memory of two eagle watchers who came before us, whose work toward the study, protection, and conservation of eagles is an inspiration to us all.

Jeff Watson, one of our contributing authors, passed away before he could see the publication of this book. Jeff was a mentor to many of this book's contributors, and his own book, *The Golden Eagle*, has served as a beacon and set the standard for many who follow in eagle studies.

Leslie Brown was among the most productive of raptor biologists, publishing half a dozen books as he strove to instill in others the wonder he felt for his beloved eagles. A man of drive and passion, topped with a healthy dose of rebellion, Leslie's influence continues unabated.

All royalties accrued by the sales of this book are being donated to the following two raptor conservation organizations:

Hawk Mountain Sanctuary

Hawk Mountain Sanctuary is the largest and oldest raptor conservation organization in the world. Founded in 1934 to stop the slaughter of hawks migrating along the Kittatinny Ridge in the Central Appalachian Mountains of eastern Pennsylvania, USA, the Sanctuary remains focused on its principal mission of protecting both common and endangered migratory birds of prey and the habitats on which they depend. Today, Hawk Mountain maintains the longest and most complete record of raptor migration in existence. In the mid-twentieth century, this invaluable resource was used by conservationists, including Rachel Carson, to document pesticide-era declines in North American populations of raptors. In the 1980s and 1990s, Hawk Mountain strengthened its role as an international center in raptor migration science, and as a global mentor to raptor conservationists, with its successful international internship program. To date, 311 young conservationists from 58 countries on six continents have benefited; many have gone on to leadership positions in conservation science, conservation education, and natural resource management.

Visit http://www.hawkmountain.org

National Birds of Prey Trust

The National Birds of Prey Trust is a charitable, grant-giving organization dedicated to the conservation of all bird of prey species and their habitats. It is based near Cirencester, Gloucestershire, United Kingdom. The Trust is active mainly through the provision of grants to support appropriate projects throughout the world. The work of the Trust is, by definition, restricted to the conservation of raptors, and this will inevitably include the conservation of their habitat. The Trust is not restricted to any specific geographic region or type of habitat; raptors live in all types of habitat, so all of them are of interest in terms of raptor conservation. The Trust's mission encompasses both field and captive areas of work.

Visit http://www.nationalbirdsofpreytrust.net

Contents

Foreword

When we accepted the editors' invitation to write a foreword for *The Eagle Watchers*, we did so with a bit of trepidation. After all, both Ruth Tingay and Todd Katzner had been Leadership Interns at Hawk Mountain Sanctuary, and both have received funding from the National Birds of Prey Trust. Because profits from the sales of this book will be used to support the work by these organizations in raptor conservation, some might think our praise for the book is based on our own self-interest, but this is not the case. The work that follows stands on its own as a significant and substantial contribution, both to raptor science and conservation in general, and to the human spirit in particular.

The 29 essays herein offer genuinely enlightening and, at times, hilarious exposés of the people behind "eagle biology," as well as serious, up-to-date accounts of what makes eagles tick in increasingly human-dominated landscapes. Anyone who reads *The Eagle Watchers* cover-to-cover—and once you have started reading this book we cannot imagine your not finishing it—will discover a newfound appreciation both for eagles and for the people who study them.

We should, however, warn you that the women and men who study large birds of prey—and eagles most certainly are large birds of prey—are cut from a different cloth than those who study other birds or, for that matter, other plants and animals. Although difficult to describe, the distinction is easy enough to see. Eagle watchers, to borrow several lines from the great Klondike poet Robert Service, are among those "That don't fit in," but rather "Break the hearts of kith and kin . . . and roam the world at will. They range the field and they rove the flood, and they climb the mountain's crest; theirs is the curse of the gypsy blood, and they don't know how to rest." These "extreme" field biologists have both literally and figuratively tasted wildlife to its fullest. Eagles themselves, after all, usually are the biggest, baddest, and, in many instances, most difficult-to-study raptors in the neighborhood, and why should those who study them be any different? Simply put, eagle watchers are the people whose lives and stories—while perhaps better not lived by most of us—make for evocative reading.

The Eagle Watchers is a different kind of "science" book. What struck us as we read this book was the passion that comes through from these researchers for their subject. Most of the writing that scientists produce—even that appearing in the popular literature—has been stripped of its humanity. Scientists are "scientists" first and, as such, must be unbiased. Their passion, if it exists at all, must be for science; their personalities should not bias and confound their findings. Fortunately, these instructions were not given to the authors of this work, or if they were, they were summarily dismissed. As a result, the essays that follow offer the unvarnished truth, something far more personal than what eagle watchers typically tell their supervisors and loved ones upon returning from the field.

These 29 essays detail more than one hundred years' worth of detailed fieldwork by many of the most significant contributors to the field and, as such, offer up rich and rewarding contributions to eagle biology and conservation. For the most part, readers will find that although successes outnumber failures, the race to learn more about eagles remains a close one, that the learning curve about eagles still points upward, and that much remains to be understood about these enigmatic birds.

The Eagle Watchers contains a number of tales that involve both the rewards and the difficulties of remote fieldwork: work that takes place far from the Internet, far from Blackberry e-mails, and far from a decent espresso. Traditional approaches to eagle science, including remote fieldwork, are a necessary tool in the eagle watcher's toolkit and, along with the modern techniques of radio and satellite tracking, are depicted accurately and honestly, and both with and without enthusiasm as circumstances merit. These tales are the heart and soul of *The Eagle Watchers*, the part that makes the book so special.

Keith L. Bildstein, PhD
Sarkis Acopian Director of Conservation Science
Hawk Mountain Sanctuary, United States

Jemima Parry-Jones, MBE
Director
The International Centre for Birds of Prey,
United Kingdom

Preface

The idea for this book was conceived on a hilltop on the Isle of Skye in western Scotland in the winter of 2005. Ruth was on the island for five months to conduct a research study on wintering golden eagles, and was having the time of her life, living in splendid isolation in a cottage by the sea, getting her "fix" of eagle sightings on daily treks across the moorland. Her eagle-biologist friends and colleagues understood the attraction without the need for any explanation. Her nonbiologist friends were simply bemused by her occupation.

It was a visit by her parents that created the spark for this book. Keen hill walkers in the Lake District of England for decades, they had rarely encountered an eagle (a sad reflection of the current golden eagle distribution in the United Kingdom). Those they had seen were merely a distant speck on the horizon, and they were never quite certain if it was a buzzard or an eagle. On a gloriously sunny winter's day on Skye, Ruth took them up one of the hills, where they were treated to the most spectacular close-range views of three juvenile golden eagles, wheeling, twisting, and soaring over a ridge just 400 m (440 yd) in front of them. Her parents were spellbound, and at that point Ruth realized just how special this sighting was for them. She had become blasé and almost expected such a good sighting every day. For her parents, and likely for many others, an eagle sighting is often a privileged once-in-a-lifetime experience. They sat watching on the hill for several hours, and by the time they began their descent, the concept for *The Eagle Watchers* book was hatched. The book would be an anthology of tales written by the people who study eagles in the wild, but written for the people who haven't had the chance to experience these magnificent yet often misunderstood creatures, up close and personal.

Eagle biologists are a wild, untamed lot. However, as we have learned through editing their stories, they are also single-minded in their devotion to their work and to their birds. Few are rich, but most are sustained by their desire to do fieldwork and to learn more about eagles. As you will see, several are funny, even downright hilarious, others bleed passion for their work through their words, others have lived through physical or emotional adventures that would have broken less committed souls, and still others have gone seemingly to the ends of the earth for the chance to study one of these rare birds.

During the course of their field trips, the authors have been stalked by grizzly bears, been followed by the secret police, fired mortar rockets over a school gymnasium, tracked eagles from outer space, been guest of honor at a circumcision ceremony, shared an aquatic car with the Khmer Rouge, and been press-ganged into a frenzied tribal death march through the jungle. They have been scientists, pioneers, explorers, and total idiots. Most of all, they have been committed to the conservation of these spectacular birds of prey. As human populations and resource consumption increase, protection of our natural resources becomes more and more critical. Ultimately, more than anything, conservation is the theme that binds this book together, and it is the reason we have put so much effort into creating it. That ethos is also what drove the authors to write about their life's work, while simultaneously hoping that the book sells well, so that large revenues are generated to protect these magnificent species and their kin.

We selected two organizations to benefit from the proceeds of this book. Hawk Mountain Sanctuary in the United States and the National Birds of Prey Trust in the United Kingdom have provided endless encouragement and support for both of us during our fledgling raptor conservation careers, and we hope the funds created from sales of our book can help others in similar positions who are enthralled by the presence of an eagle and wish to contribute to its conservation.

We are indebted to the friends and colleagues who have freely contributed their stories to this book, for their willingness to share their own eagle-watching experiences and particularly for their gracious acceptance of our editorial criticisms. Thank you all. We also thank the photographers who generously sent us their eagle and author images free of charge, especially those people who were not already involved with the book: Mark Anderson, Ruari Beaton, Keith Bildstein, Annelize Crean, Kurt Elmquist, Neil Gray, Elizabeth Hawkes, Gilles Martin, Dom Morgan, Pete Morris, Ryan Phillips, Hannah Thomas, Simon Thomsett, Debbie Thoy, Paolo Torchio, Bas van Balen, Mark Warrillow-Thomson, Vanessa Watson, Linda Wright, and Christian Ziegler. Special thanks to Mike Collopy and Phil Whitfield for their critical reviews of earlier versions of the book. We are also indebted to our editor, Heidi Lovette, and Rachel Post and Candace Akins at Cornell University Press, for their acceptance and vision, but most importantly, for their patience; this project has had to be squeezed in amidst our professional and personal commitments, which resulted in slow progress. Todd appreciates the continued support of his employer, the National Aviary, throughout the writing period.

We hope you enjoy reading these pages. It has been a labor of love for many of us, and we hope that even if we can't take all of you into the field to see our birds, through us you may develop a sense for what it is to sell your life to watching eagles.

RUTH TINGAY (*Scotland*)
TODD KATZNER (*United States*)

THE EAGLE
WATCHERS

1

Eagle Diversity, Ecology, and Conservation

Todd E. Katzner and Ruth E. Tingay

INTRODUCTION

Eagle populations over much of the world are threatened. Of the 75 currently recognized eagle species, at least 30 (approximately 40%) are of conservation concern, and for nearly each of them, populations are declining (see the appendix for listings). The cross-species nature of these declines implies that there are likely group-level characteristics of eagles that make them particularly vulnerable to impacts from growing human populations and increasing resource consumption. In cases where declines have been evaluated, the causes are generally similar to those that threaten other large predators. Eagle populations are most strongly influenced by direct human impacts such as shooting, poisoning, and other persecution, and by indirect impacts such as disturbance at nests and habitat loss. Ironically, eagles are sensitive indicators of the health of our environment, reflecting biodiversity trends across groups of other species. Biodiversity is a vital indicator of the well-being of our planet. Studies have demonstrated that the presence of a top predator (such as an eagle) in a particular area is generally indicative of greater biodiversity than in areas where these predators do not occur. Thus, by protecting eagles, we protect a suite of other, unrelated species that live in the same area, through what is known as the "umbrella effect."

At the same time that some humans persecute eagles and destroy the resources on which they depend, other humans revere these birds, regularly using them as symbols of strength and unity. In early history, the Greeks believed that the eagle was the messenger of Zeus, the King of the Gods. The Romans traditionally released a live eagle at the funeral of a fallen emperor, believing that it would provide safe passage to heaven for the emperor's soul. More recently, a multitude of countries—the United States, Kazakhstan, the Philippines, Russia, Germany, Indonesia, Mexico, Armenia, Egypt, Romania, Austria, Panama, Serbia—have used eagles either as a national emblem or as a sign of regal power and authority. Likewise, many native peoples in

North America revere eagles, placing special value on their feathers. The Buryats near Russia's Lake Baikal and tribesmen in Papua New Guinea place similar totemic symbolism on eagles.

There is something special about eagles, that worldwide they simultaneously inspire both such respect and hatred from humans. Something about these remarkable animals projects majestic stature and generates visceral fear. Something elemental in them seems to bring out the best and the worst in human nature.

This book documents the experiences of one group of humans—eagle biologists—with eagles, through personal narratives of their encounters with eagles in the wild. This chapter focuses on the basics of eagle biology, ecology, and conservation, to provide a perspective and a context for the stories that follow.

WHAT IS AN EAGLE?

Eagles are large predatory birds found nearly worldwide. From a taxonomic perspective, as birds they are members of the Kingdom Animalia, the Phylum Vertebrata, and the Class Aves. Within the Aves, they are members of the Order containing diurnal predatory birds—the Falconiformes (some authors have split Falconiformes into two separate orders, one of the same name composed of the falcons and caracaras and the other named the Accipitriformes, composed of the hawks, eagles, and vultures). Diurnal birds of prey are characterized by having a hooked bill, strong eyesight, and exceptionally powerful feet, which are their primary weapons used for killing prey and for defending territories. There are no flightless members of this group, but there are multiple families—the Falconidae (falcons and caracaras), Accipitridae (the hawks, eagles, kites, and Old World vultures), Pandionidae (osprey), Sagittariidae (the secretarybird), Cathartidae (New World vultures and condors), and perhaps others yet to be recognized.

Most eagles are among the largest of the diurnal birds of prey, although some are small in relative terms. The term "eagle," though, is not a technical scientific term, and there is not complete agreement as to what is and what is not an eagle. Certainly from a scientific perspective there are multiple groups with different scientific names that, in English, we refer to as eagles. There are a few generalities that we can draw about eagles though. First and foremost is their size—eagles are among the largest of land birds that take live prey. They have a wide wingspan, huge feet, and a big bill. These characteristics distinguish them from other birds of prey. Like other raptors, eagles have sharp beaks and talons and exceptionally good eyesight (similar to a human looking through 10-power binoculars). Eagles are generally long-lived species with low reproductive rates. Some of the larger eagles may produce only one chick every one or two years, and if the chick survives, it can take up to five years for it to become sexually mature and breed. This trait makes eagles particularly vulnerable to population decline, as, if many individuals die, it can take years for a population to rebound and approach its former size.

DIVERSITY WORLDWIDE

Eagles comprise a remarkably diverse group of species. Although our interpretation of their taxonomy regularly changes (Bill Clark touches on this in chapter 16), there are 75 species of eagles currently recognized (see the appendix). These 75 species are broken down into five major groups, with several species that don't fit well into other groups. The taxonomy we use here is generally derived from that of Lerner and Mindell (2005).[1] Where we differ from their analysis, we do so for simplicity and we note those cases below.

I. Sea or Fish Eagles (10 species)

The sea or fish eagles are a group of eagles most frequently found near water. For reasons that are not well understood, all members of this group have a fused joint in their middle toe. Some of the sea eagle species have highly specialized diets, but in general terms the group usually eats fish taken either dead or alive from the water. Many are also opportunistic and will take waterbirds, seabirds, land birds, mammals, reptiles, amphibians, and carrion. For the most part sea eagles nest in trees or on cliffs close to water. This group is exceptionally widespread, with members found across most of the Northern Hemisphere and throughout southern Eurasia, including Australia and the Pacific islands, and much of sub-Saharan Africa. The only continents where it is rare to see a sea eagle are South America and Antarctica.

There are two genera in this group; *Haliaeetus* (8 species) and *Ichthyophaga* (2). Among the most famous of the *Haliaeetus* eagles is the bald eagle

[1] Lerner, H., and D. Mindell. 2005. Phylogeny of eagles, Old World vultures, and other Accipitridae based on nuclear and mitochondrial DNA. *Molecular Phylogenetics and Evolution* 37: 327–346.

(*Haliaeetus leucocephalus*), the national symbol of the United States. Also of note are Eurasia's white-tailed sea eagle (*Haliaeetus albicilla*) and the massive Steller's sea eagle (*Haliaeetus pelagicus*). This genus includes the world's most poorly studied Northern Hemisphere eagle, Pallas's fish eagle (*Haliaeetus leucoryphus*), and one of the Southern Hemisphere's least studied species, Sanford's sea eagle (*Haliaeetus sanfordi*). Finally, the Madagascar fish eagle (*Haliaeetus vociferoides*) is among the world's rarest eagles, being found only in a small area of Madagascar.

The genus *Ichthyophaga* is represented by only two closely related species, the grey-headed (*Ichthyophaga ichthyaetus*) and lesser fishing eagles (*Ichthyophaga humilis*). These two south Asian species have a fairly broad range, but within that area they can be relatively localized. They are characterized by a unique "laughing" vocalization often heard at night.

II. Snake or Serpent Eagles (22 species)

The snake and serpent eagles are a group of species found only in parts of the Old World (Eurasia and Africa), nearly all of which have a specialized diet of reptiles and amphibians. These birds are characterized by heavy scales on the tarsi (legs) and relatively short toes. This group also includes the bateleur (sometimes spelled "bataleur"), an African eagle that eats carrion and small mammals. Some authors have also placed the Philippine eagle (*Pithecophaga jefferyi*) in this group, although we do not do so here.

There are five genera in this group: *Circaetus* (6 species), *Spilornis* (13), *Terathopius* (1), *Dryotriorchis* (1), and *Eutriorchis* (1). The members of the genus *Circaetus* are the true snake eagles. These are large-bodied birds with broad wings and a head similar in shape to that of an owl. Reptiles are the most important part of their diet, sometimes even large venomous snakes. The most widely distributed member of this genus is the short-toed snake eagle (*Circaetus gallicus*), found throughout Eurasia. This species, as well as many of its African brethren, is most commonly found in arid environments, where it breeds primarily in desert trees, often in riparian areas. A few members of this genus are found in more tropical, heavily forested jungles.

The genus *Spilornis* comprises the so-called serpent eagles. Characteristic of most members of this genus is a crest on the back of the head and a reddish breast with distinctive white spots. Some of these species are among the smallest of eagles. The better-known members of this genus, for example, the crested serpent eagle (*Spilornis cheela*), eat many reptiles and live in more heavily forested habitats than the snake eagles. This genus also includes a number of single-island endemics (species found only on one island), including the South Nicobar serpent eagle (*Spilornis klossi*), the Simeulue serpent eagle (*Spilornis abbotti*), and the Nias serpent eagle (*Spilornis asturinus*). These and most of the other species in this genus are incredibly poorly known and ripe for future study.

The genus *Terathopius* is monotypic—composed of only one species—the bateleur (*Terathopius ecaudatus*). The bateleur is an extremely unusual African eagle that fills a niche more similar to that of a vulture than that of a true eagle. Like a vulture it forages by soaring high above the ground, searching for food, most often carrion. Bateleurs are distinctive-looking eagles with a bright red face and long, broad wings and a very short tail (see central color plate). Rick Watson describes his study on this species' foraging behavior in chapter 19.

There are two other species that are often placed in this group, although there is some confusion about their true taxonomic status. The Congo serpent eagle (*Dryotriorchis spectabilis*) is a small and poorly known serpent eagle. Likewise, the Madagascar serpent eagle (*Eutriorchis astur*) is another unusual and very rare species found only in a small part of Madagascar. Lerner and Mindell suggest that this species is actually more closely related to Old World vultures than it is to the other serpent eagles.

III. Booted Eagles (19 species)

This group is composed of the genera *Aquila* (11 species) and *Hieraaetus* (8). Booted eagles are one of the most widespread groups of eagles, and members are regularly found on all of the world's continents, except South America. These are generally big sturdy eagles with large feet; they take correspondingly large prey compared to their body size. Booted eagles are so named because their tarsus (lower leg) is heavily feathered, making them appear to be wearing tall footwear.

The most widespread of all eagles is the golden eagle (*Aquila chrysaetos*), found breeding throughout much of Eurasia, North America, and even into northern Africa. In forest-steppe the niche of the golden eagle is filled by the imperial eagle (*Aquila heliaca*), and in true grasslands it is filled by steppe (*Aquila nipalensis*) and tawny eagles (*Aquila rapax*). In Australia and New Guinea the wedge-tailed (*Aquila audax*) and Gurney's eagle (*Aquila gurneyi*), respectively, fill that niche. This genus also includes one of the world's more rare but well-studied eagle, the Spanish imperial eagle (*Aquila adalberti*; sometimes considered a subspecies of imperial eagles). Miguel Ferrer (chapter 11) shares his intimate knowledge of this species, having studied it for many years.

Members of the genus *Hieraaetus* are smaller than their *Aquila* relatives, but many make up for size with increased aggressiveness. The most well known and widely distributed of these birds are Bonelli's eagle (*Hieraaetus fasciatus*) and the booted eagle (*Hieraaetus pennatus*), both found throughout large sections of Eurasia. These species take large numbers of both small and medium-sized birds and mammals. Other members of this genus are more limited in range, being found in parts of Africa or Asia. One species, Wahlberg's eagle (*Hieraaetus wahlbergi*), is African in distribution and is sometimes placed in the genus *Aquila*.

IV. Hawk-Eagles (13 species)

The hawk-eagles are a diverse group, composed of at least one genus— *Spizaetus* (13 species). Hawk-eagles are relatively large and typically have a long crest on the back of their head that they can erect or lay flat, depending on their mood. Hawk-eagles are primarily a bird of tropical forests, although some species are found on forest edge and other wooded habitats. They take a variety of small and medium-sized prey, often focusing on what is abundant.

There are both Old and New World groups within this genus. Most common of the Old World species is the changeable hawk-eagle (*Spizaetus cirrhatus*), a species whose distribution extends from India across south Asia and into the oceanic islands from Indonesia to the southern Philippines. Among the other Old World species are a number of regional endemics, including the Javan hawk-eagle (*Spizaetus bartelsi*), the Sulawesi hawk-eagle (*Spizaetus lanceolatus*), and the Philippine hawk-eagle (*Spizaetus philippensis*). There are also four New World species usually placed in this genus, the black hawk-eagle (*Spizaetus tyrannus*), the ornate hawk-eagle (*Spizaetus ornatus*), the black-and-white hawk-eagle (*Spizastur melanoleucus*), and the black-and-chestnut (Isador's) eagle (*Spizaetus isidori*).

V. "Harpy" Eagles (4 species)

This is a small but diverse group of species that are morphologically similar but not closely related in evolutionary terms. There are four members of this group—the harpy eagle (*Harpia harpyja*), the crested eagle (*Morphnus guianensis*), the New Guinea harpy eagle (*Harpyopsis novaeguineae*), and the Philippine eagle (*Pithecophaga jefferyi*). All are massive eagles found in tropical forests, all have unfeathered tarsi (lower legs), and all take large prey from trees. The first two species are found in a wider range of Central and South America, the last two only on relatively small islands in the Pacific. Lerner and Mindell suggest that the first three are fairly closely related but that the Philippine eagle may be more closely related to serpent eagles than to the other members of this group.

VI. Other Species (7 species)

There are a number of other species that don't fit well into the above classification system. These include the solitary eagles of the genus *Harpyhaliae-tus* (2 species), the black-chested buzzard-eagle (*Geranoaetus melanoleucus*), the Indian black eagle (*Ictinaetus malayensis*), the long crested eagle (*Lophaetus occipitalis*), the African crowned eagle (*Stephanoaetus coronatus*), and the martial eagle (*Polemaetus bellicosus*). Members of this group are thought to be related to the hawk and booted eagles, although the exact relationships are poorly understood and warrant more careful study.

The sometimes confusing evolutionary relationships between eagles in this group serve to illustrate both the potential and the pitfalls of taxonomy. Historically the field was built on the Linnaean system of nomenclature, with clearly defined relationships defined by morphology and plumage. However, when two species with different evolutionary lineages fill a similar niche (called convergent evolution), they can often evolve very similar morphologies and plumage characteristics. An excellent example of this are the similarly appearing but distantly related Philippine and harpy eagles. Today, effective taxonomy is thought to require a combination of both classical morphometrics and modern genetic analyses. This approach better defines evolutionary relationships and allows scientists to separate convergent evolution from relatedness.

EAGLE ECOLOGY

Some characteristics of eagles are consistent across groups, and others are very specific to individual species. In this section we will try to identify a few broad trends in eagle ecology and behavior, built with examples, and also point out a few of the more unique ecological roles that some eagles play.

In general there are three primary characteristics of all species. For a species to survive, a proportion of individuals must eat, they must live in a habitat that provides food and shelter, and they must reproduce. In addition, many avian species engage in migration and overwintering behavior. Often their dietary and habitat utilization patterns differ during winter and summer.

Diet and Foraging Behavior

Eagles are among the largest of avian predators, and accordingly the prey they take can be larger than those eaten by almost any other species of bird. Among the sea eagles, Steller's probably take the largest prey, regularly consuming salmon of several types. Martial eagles are famed for taking small ungulates, specifically dik-dik and other small African antelope. Harpy eagles also eat large prey, regularly hunting sloths and primates in the trees. Although they can be large, some eagles take exceptionally small prey; steppe eagles are regularly observed catching elate (winged) termites during winter in Africa. Likewise, imperial eagles in Kazakhstan eat locusts.

In addition to taking prey of all sizes, eagles are known to eat prey of all types. Mammals are perhaps the most important resource for many eagles. Several species of eagles are found in conjunction with colonial mammals—Spanish imperial eagles and European rabbits, imperial and steppe eagles with European ground squirrels and marmots, Verreaux's eagles with hyrax. Fish are important primarily to sea eagles, and reptiles and amphibians to serpent and snake eagles.

Few people have the opportunity to observe an eagle killing its prey, and yet it is this aspect of eagle ecology that often attracts the most attention and fear. As such, there are many myths associated with eagles' foraging behavior, often sensationalized by tabloid newspaper headlines, such as "Eagle Snatches Baby." In reality, exaggerations such as this bear little, if any, resemblance to what eagles eat. A few of the authors who have contributed to this book—Todd Katzner (eastern imperial eagle, chapter 9), Janeene Touchton (harpy eagle, chapter 20)—tell stories of watching eagles hunt, but tales of this type are relatively rare. Most of the information we have learned about eagles' diet has been gleaned from the painstaking analysis of regurgitated pellets and discarded prey remains found in and around nests. Jeff Watson (golden eagle, chapter 3) and Rob Davies (Verreaux's eagle, chapter 8) describe these prized findings. Although there are relatively few published observations of eagles' hunting behavior, what is known demonstrates the adaptability and resourcefulness of this group of birds.

Hunting behavior depends entirely on the type of habitat in which the eagle lives, and the type of prey being hunted. For example, eagles that live in open country and feed largely on birds (such as Ayres's hawk-eagle, *Hieraae-*

tus ayresii, in Africa) hunt using soaring flight followed by a swift, steep stoop onto their prey. Other open-country aerial hunting techniques include those utilized by some of the snake eagles, which often hover above the ground like a kestrel, using this position as an aerial "perch" to view their prey below. Similarly, golden eagles in Scotland and other mountainous areas take advantage of upward air currents to maintain an almost stationary position above a mountain ridge from where they can scan the land below for movement. Eagles that inhabit densely forested areas, such as the rainforest harpy eagles, have to employ a different technique, as it is difficult for them to view prey when they are soaring above the canopy, so they most often hunt from a perch within the forest. They have shorter wings and longer tails, which allow them to maneuver skillfully below the forest canopy, enabling them to catch fast-moving prey such as monkeys. Another technique often used by forest-dwelling eagles is to sit on a perch and simply "drop" onto an unsuspecting forest antelope as it passes below. The African crowned eagle is perfectly adapted for this strategy, as its mottled plumage blends with the dappled light of the forest understory, making it difficult to see.

Perch hunting is a very common technique of the sea and fish eagle group. Madagascar fish eagles can often be seen perching on a rock or overhanging tree by a lake, patiently playing the waiting game. When they detect movement in the water, they simply drop down and snatch the fish from the surface, barely getting their feet wet. They have sharp spicules (spines) on the pads of their feet, which help them to grasp and hold slippery wet prey. Sometimes, if the prey is too heavy to lift from the water's surface, the eagle will spread its wings and "float" for a few moments, before flapping its wings forward like a pair of oars to propel itself back to the shore, still holding its prey tightly.

Some sea eagles have a propensity for taking the young chicks of other birds. One of the world's most prolific eagle watchers, the late Leslie Brown, has described watching an African fish eagle hopping from nest to nest in a heron nesting colony, eating chicks in each nest. White-tailed sea eagles in Scotland are known to fly along cliff faces where colonies of breeding seabirds nest, and to land momentarily to grab a chick from its nest. Fulmars (*Fulmarus glacialis*) are a common prey species, and in chapter 23, Justin Grant describes how he used the telltale smell of fulmars to lead him to an otherwise well-hidden sea eagle's nest.

Although most eagle species hunt alone, some hunt in pairs. The Verreaux's eagle in South Africa often hunts cooperatively, one eagle diverting the attention of the hyrax on sentry duty, while the other eagle launches a surprise attack from another direction. Wedge-tailed eagles in Australia employ a similar strategy when hunting kangaroos, as do golden eagles hunting ungulates in deep snow, with both eagles continually swooping at their intended prey until it becomes exhausted. Likewise, pairs of imperial eagles have been observed ganging up to catch more maneuverable avian prey such as rooks.

Some eagles use other species to help locate prey—tawny eagles in Africa are attracted to carcasses by the large groups of vultures circling above. The tawny eagle simply sits and waits its turn to feed, once the larger vultures have ripped open the hide with their powerful bills. Steppe eagles are equally as opportunistic. In Ethiopia, this species stands next to the soil mounds of subterranean mole rats, and when it sees the surface soil moving, the eagle pounces and buries its talons into the soil. In Mongolia, a steppe eagle was recently observed hiding behind a short grass clump next to a ground squirrel's burrow. The eagle lay on its belly for up to half an hour, watching a ground squirrel that was only a matter of inches away. Once the ground squirrel moved away from the burrow entrance, the eagle pounced, but it missed and ended up chasing the squirrel on foot. Other eagle species known to hunt their prey on foot include the lesser (*Aquila pomarina*) and greater spotted (*Aquila clanga*) eagles, which have been observed walking around on marshy ground in eastern Europe hunting frogs and toads. Bald eagles in Alaska simply stand in the shallows, from where they haul dead or dying Pacific salmon to the shore for an easy meal.

Finally, eagles with a bit of cunning can resort to piracy (known as "kleptoparasitism"), whereby they steal the prey that another bird has captured. Usually this involves harassing the unlucky bird until it eventually drops its prize. This method of hunting is particularly common among the sea eagles and tawny and steppe eagles. The usual targets for attack are herons, storks, kingfishers, pelicans, and sometimes other raptors, including ospreys, kites, and even other eagles. In chapter 5, Penny Olsen describes watching a wedge-tailed eagle steal prey from a brown falcon (*Falco berigora*).

Habitat Requirements

Eagles occupy a wide variety of habitats worldwide. Some live in remote areas that are difficult for humans to access; read chapter 2 to learn about the hardships Mark Watson and Martin Gilbert had to endure to find the New Guinea harpy eagle. Others live in closer proximity to humans, often exploiting the opportunity to benefit from human activities; Keisuke Saito (Steller's sea eagle, chapter 10) describes this behavior in detail.

Many groups, especially the booted eagles, regularly breed on cliffs or in forests near open habitats. Martial eagles and some snake and serpent eagles also use open habitats. Alternatively, other species, especially the hawk-eagles and most tropical species, are dense forest specialists. These birds are difficult to find in the forest and are only rarely observed above the canopy. Sarah Karpanty's story in chapter 6 describes the trials of trying to locate the elusive Madagascar serpent eagle. Sea and fish eagles are commonly found near water but in a wide range of habitats ranging from extreme desert riparian habitats to wet boreal forest.

Characteristic of all eagle-breeding habitat is the need for a suitable nest location. Most eagles nest in trees. Clearly, to support a massive eagle nest, a suitable tree must be large. Likewise, because of their large size, eagles are not the most nimble of fliers, and they require trees that are highly accessible. Therefore, when eagles do breed in trees, they most often pick the largest and most exposed trees in a particular area, and tailor their nests to suit that habitat. Some eagles use smaller trees that protrude from cliff faces. Many eagles, especially the sea and fish and booted eagles, also nest on cliff ledges of sufficient size.

In addition to cliffs and trees, eagles make use of two other types of nesting habitats. First, several species nest on the ground. Steppe eagles are known nearly exclusively to build ground nests, on the most exposed hilltop in their territory. However, other species, including golden eagles, Pallas's fish eagles, and white-tailed sea eagles, have also successfully bred on ground nests in large parts of their range. Second, human-built structures have also become important for nesting in some parts of the world. In particular, electrical towers provide an important nesting structure for martial eagles in parts of Africa (read Andrew Jenkins's story in chapter 22) and for golden eagles in Idaho.

Breeding Behavior

The eagle breeding cycle has several distinct phases. Birds occupy and defend territories starting in early spring. Once territories are chosen, nest building and copulation begin; this phase is followed by egg-laying and incubation. Finally, in the nestling phase chicks hatch and then enter a fledgling phase, when they leave the nest but continue to be nurtured by their parents.

Territory Occupancy and Defense

Typically, adult eagles reuse the same breeding home range year after year. Even eagles that migrate for thousands of miles from Europe to southern Africa can return to use the same range repeatedly, as demonstrated by a male lesser spotted eagle in Slovakia that returned to the same site for 11 consecutive years. Such strong site fidelity is probably related to the quality of a particular home range. For example, if a pair of eagles has bred successfully in a given area, and they know that there is a good local prey supply and where to find it, they will likely seek to remain in that home range in subsequent years.

Aerial display flights high above a territory usually signify the onset of the breeding season. Single adults of some species perform breathtaking undulating flight loops to advertise their presence to any un-mated adult who happens to be looking for a partner. Breeding pairs will also display together, as part of the pair-bonding and territory defense ritual. Golden eagles are usually silent as they display, but others such as the African crowned eagle in Kenya and the greater spotted eagle in Poland can be particularly vocal. In addition to being part of the courtship ritual, dramatic aerial display flights are used along boundary lines to indicate territoriality to neighboring eagles. These displays not only tell a neighbor that the territory is occupied (and that the neighbor should keep out), but also allow both parties to avoid harmful combat.

Sometimes, however, an intruding eagle will not be deterred by displays and will try to steal a territory. This invariably leads to fights involving mid-air "talon-grappling" where the two eagles lock their feet together and cartwheel as they plummet toward the ground before releasing their grip and (usually) flying to safety. Another method of territorial advertisement that can help to avoid dangerous fights is vocalizing from a prominent perch within the territory. Members of the sea eagle group frequently use this strategy, and species like the African fish eagle (whose calls are described by Munir Virani in chapter 18) continue to vocalize throughout the breeding season. Traditionally, we think of most eagle species as being highly territorial during the breeding season, excluding all other eagles from their nesting area. However, recent studies indicate that this may not be the case after all. Bernd Meyburg's (see chapter 4) combined satellite telemetry and DNA studies of lesser spotted eagles in Europe have revealed that several breeding females, all with young in their own nests, traveled up to 57 km (35 mi) to visit the active nests of other pairs. Preliminary results from an ongoing DNA study in Scotland have demonstrated the presence of "extra" golden eagles at the nests of some breeding pairs. This behavior clearly challenges our long-held views of how eagles "should" behave.

Nest-Building and Copulation

After the courtship displays, eagles turn their attention to preparing their nests for the forthcoming breeding season. Some eagle species use the same nest year after year, renovating and rebuilding it from previous years. There are reports of an African crowned eagle nest estimated to be 50 years old, and another that had been used for at least 20 years, spanning two generations of the same eagle family. These types of nests can become enormous structures, sometimes as large as a queen-sized bed; the largest bald eagle nest was reported in Florida and measured 6.1 m (20 ft) deep and 2.9 m (9.5 ft) wide, and the nesting material weighed approximately 2722 kg (6000 lb). Other species, like the brown snake eagle in Africa, regularly move nests, although new sites are usually within the original home range. This nest-moving behavior is common among many eagle species, which can alternate between as many as eight nests in one home range. Some eagles may switch nest sites if they have been disturbed during the previous breeding season; other eagles can be successful at a nest during one year and then unaccountably move to another nest the following year.

Nest-building, or nest refurbishment, can be done by both the male and the female of the breeding pair. In some species nest-building activities begin up to a full year before the breeding season. For other species, typically those that migrate long distances, the peak nest-building period is usually just a few weeks prior to egg-laying. Nest structures are usually made from sticks and twigs that the eagles collect either from the ground or from trees. A female harpy eagle in Guyana was once observed hanging upside down in a tree canopy as she tried to snap off a branch with her feet. Depending on the size of the eagle, the sticks used for nest-building can be of considerable size and are sometimes carried for significant distances (several kilometers or miles) back to the nest.

An eagle's nest cup is lined with whatever soft material is available, and can include grass, hair, wool, dung, moss, lichen, heather, seaweed, and feathers. Generally, eagles do not decorate their nests, as do some other raptor species, although rags have been found inside steppe eagles' nests in central Asia. Most eagle species add sprigs of greenery to the nest cup throughout the breeding season. These sprigs are often plucked from trees and are diligently placed into the nest cup lining. It is thought that this constant supply of fresh greenery acts as a natural insect repellant to protect the chicks, as well as a visual signal to passing eagles that the nest is occupied.

Copulation by eagles usually takes place in a highly visible spot, in another display of pair bonding and territory occupancy. Some species engage in talon-grasping as a precursor to mating. During mating (often on a perch or on the nest structure), the male mounts the female, usually with clenched feet to avoid his talons hurting her. However, there are more rare instances where the copulatory position is reversed (i.e., the female mounts the male), as observed in some pairs of Spanish imperial eagles. Copulation often occurs throughout the breeding period, to ensure that no other mates are able to sire the young and also as a way to reinforce the pair bond. Copulation is often proceeded by a calling duet or by intricate flight displays, with the two eagles flying together as a pair throughout their territory. However, it is also common for one of the pair to simply depart for another area of the territory without exhibiting any obvious postcopulatory bonding behavior.

Claims are often made that eagles mate for life. While banding studies have demonstrated high levels of mate fidelity by several eagle species, it is only recently that new research techniques are allowing researchers to investigate this assumption more thoroughly. For example, a recent DNA study of eastern imperial eagles in Kazakhstan revealed that genetic monogamy was indeed very high among this particular population. However, a combined behavioral and DNA study of Madagascar fish eagles showed that some females swapped partners and home ranges between breeding seasons. Some eagles breed in polyandrous trios (one female with two males); this occasional behavior has been reported for some white-tailed sea eagles and Spanish imperial eagles. The Madagascar fish eagle breaks all the rules; as well as breeding in pairs, it is also known to consistently breed in groups, ranging from three to five individuals and comprising either multiple females or multiple males, who adhere to a clearly defined dominance hierarchy. There has even been an instance when two males set up home together, building a nest and defending it vigorously from a visiting female. Ruth Tingay describes her study of this breeding system in chapter 12. To date, this is the only eagle species known to consistently exhibit such unorthodox breeding behavior, and the reasons for its occurrence remain puzzling.

Egg-Laying and Incubation

Egg-laying follows shortly after the nest-building and copulation period. When they breed, most eagles lay between one and four eggs. Some species, for example, imperial eagles, raise all their young. However, other species, such as golden eagles, lay two eggs, and if both hatch, the stronger chick may kill the other. This behavior, called "cainism" or "siblicide," can be facultative (occurs some of the time) or, as for Verreaux's eagles and Madagascar fish eagles, obligate (always occurs). This has consequences, both for the quality of offspring produced and for the capacity of these species to recover if their population size is diminished. Rob Simmons discusses this phenomenon in detail in chapter 15.

If the female eagle is capable of producing a clutch of more than one egg, she usually lays eggs at intervals. The length of that interval depends on the size of the eagle. For larger species, such as the Verreaux's eagle, eggs may be laid seven days apart. Incubation starts immediately after the first egg has been laid and continues until the last egg has hatched. The duration of incubation varies enormously and depends on the size of the eagle, as larger eagles need a longer period for embryo development than smaller eagles. For example, the incubation period of little eagles (*Hieraaetus morphnoides*) in Australia is typically 33 days, whereas the much larger Philippine eagle incubates as long as 64 days. During incubation the eggs need to remain warm to develop properly. Until recently, it was believed that incubation was done exclusively by the adult female, but detailed studies of individually marked birds have since revealed that the adult male also participates, although typically to a lesser extent. Eggs are rarely left unattended during incubation, as chilling would cause the death of the embryo. Often, as one adult is sitting tight on the nest, its partner hunts to bring in food for its mate. This leaves the incubating eagle vulnerable to attack from intruders, so its mate is never far away to respond to the alarm calls of the incubating bird. Some eagles exhibit incredible levels of tenacity during the incubation period; recent video footage from a golden eagle's nest in Scotland showed the adult female incubating her eggs in temperatures reaching −15°C (5°F), her back covered with snow.

Nestling Stage

Once the full incubation term has been completed, the fully developed chick begins to hatch from its egg by repeatedly chipping away at the shell from the inside. If an eagle has laid a clutch of multiple eggs, they hatch asynchronously in the order in which they were laid. Thus, the first-hatched chick could be several days old by the time the last chick hatches. This can be fatal for the youngest chick, as it is often unable to compete for food with its older, larger and stronger siblings. The early stages of the nestling period are when the chicks are most susceptible to predation. They hatch with a covering of soft down on their bodies, but are still totally dependent on their parents for warmth and food as they are helpless and unable to regulate their own body temperature. Adult eagles rarely leave their chicks unattended in these early days, sitting over them continuously to provide warmth and protection. As during incubation, the female takes the lead role at the nest while the male hunts to provide food for both his mate and his chicks, occasionally swapping duties when the female needs a break. When chicks are very young, the adults gently tear off tiny slivers of food and tenderly offer these morsels to their newly hatched offspring. Such delicate behavior is in sharp contrast with the perpetual tabloid image of the "ferocious" and "brutish" eagle (e.g., as recently as December 2008, a government proposal to reintroduce white-tailed sea eagles to England was met with intense opposition by some locals, leading to newspaper headlines such as "Plan to Bring Back Killer of the Skies").

As with the incubation stage, the length of the nestling period varies according to the size of the eagle. For example, little eagle chicks require approximately seven weeks between hatching and fledging, whereas Philippine eagle chicks may need 24 weeks before leaving the nest. After the early stages of the nestling period, the chick develops its own body feathers and regulates its own body temperature. This allows the adult eagles to leave the nest more often, although when the chick is still small the adults remain close by to chase off any predators. With growing chicks to feed, the adult eagles have to catch more prey, and as the chicks get older, adults drop food in the nest and the chicks feed themselves. By the last week of the nestling period, the chick has developed a full set of flight feathers with a distinctive juvenile plumage, different from that of the adults. The young chick spends most of its time on the nest, sometimes flapping its wings and testing their strength, and even getting slightly airborne.

Fledgling Stage

When the eagle chick is ready to leave its nest, this is known as the "fledging stage." "Fledging" is alternatively defined as the time when the eaglet leaves the nest and perches on the nest branch, or the time the eaglet makes its first flight away from the nest tree. Regardless of definitions, fledging is not indicative of the eaglet being self-sufficient. In the first few weeks following fledging, the eaglet is still dependent on its parents for food, which is typically delivered back to the nest. Upon fledging the eaglet spends the first few days close to the nest site, either in surrounding trees or on nearby cliffs. Gradually it gains confidence and undertakes longer periods of flight, often calling loudly to its parents for food. The post-fledging period during which the chick continues to depend on the parents can vary from a few months up to a year. For example, the little eagle becomes independent after two months, but the Philippine eagle may remain dependent and in its parents' territory for up to 12 months. As a consequence, Philippine eagles rarely breed more than once every two years.

Migratory species do not have the luxury of long post-fledging dependence and must be ready to make long-haul migration within months of leaving the nest. Dispersal from the parents' territory is a poorly studied aspect of eagle ecology, mainly because it is more difficult to follow a flying eagle than it is to study an eaglet confined in the nest. Traditionally, the usual method of learning about migration required huge effort with low return on investment. Eagles were banded with a uniquely numbered leg band either as nestlings or when trapped as adults, in the hope that they would be retrapped at a later date in a different location. However, return rates on banded birds were typically low. Al Harmata and Teryl Grubb provide accounts of their bald eagle banding adventures in chapter 7. With the advent of radio and satellite telemetry, more studies are now being undertaken to help understand when and where these young birds go. In chapter 13, Susanne Shultz tells the story of trapping African crowned eagles in West Africa to attach radio transmitters that would enable her to follow the eagles deep into the forest. Ursula Valdez had the same idea for following black-and-chestnut eagles in Peru (chapter 24) but with less success than Susanne! On a broader scale, Carol McIntyre (chapter 3) describes how she has used satellite technology to track young dispersing golden eagles from their nests in Alaska to their wintering grounds in other regions of the United States.

Migration and Winter Behavior

Eagles show four basic types of migratory behavior. Some species, especially those in the tropics and in warmer northern latitudes (e.g., golden and white-tailed sea eagles in Scotland, bald eagles in the central and southern United States) do not migrate. Generally this behavior is controlled by food availability. If there is sufficient food to ensure the eagle can survive the winter, then it will not migrate. This can be advantageous because if the eagle survives, it increases the likelihood that it can either hold on to a breeding territory it possesses, or take a territory from another bird.

Among those that actively migrate, birds can be short-, medium-, or long-distance migrants. Eagles show all of these behaviors, sometimes within a single species. As an example, golden eagles in North America may be resident year-round (in the southwestern United States or Mexico), short-distance migrants (in many parts of the American west), medium-distance migrants (birds from the Gaspe Peninsula in Canada migrate to New York or Pennsylvania), or long-distance migrants (some birds from Alaska migrate to California, birds from northern Quebec can migrate to the southern Appalachian mountains). Other northern-latitude species may show similar patterns. Among the more interesting patterns of movements are those exhibited by white-tailed sea eagles in northern Europe. In winter these birds often migrate east or west, sometimes even north, moving where food resources are more abundant.

Migration has been well studied in several species, including golden eagles and bald eagles in the United States; Steller's sea eagles that migrate from Russia to Japan; and steppe and lesser and greater spotted eagles in Europe, which migrate long distances to Africa. Imperial eagles are generally shorter-distance migrants. Those that have been studied travel from central Europe to the Mediterranean region, from central Asia (northern Kazakhstan) to the Middle East (Iran), and from the Baikal region of Russia to south Asia. The migration of few other eagle species has been so well examined, although as technology develops, we expect to see more studies in this area of research.

On wintering grounds, many eagles appear segregated by age and gender classes. Thus, sites occupied by adult females rarely have males or juvenile females. Likewise, juveniles are usually found in sites with few adults. The significance of this behavior is not understood.

The habitats that eagles use and the food that they eat during winter are often dramatically different from those they use and eat in summer. As noted earlier, steppe eagles, a predator on mammals and birds during the breeding season, can be insect specialists during winter. Likewise, many migratory eagles—golden, bald, Steller's, white-tailed sea—are carrion feeders during winter. In eastern North America and northern Japan, deer carcasses (from roadkill and hunting) are an important food resource sustaining populations of golden and Steller's sea eagles, respectively.

THREATS TO EAGLES

As long-lived birds with low reproductive rates, eagles face a specific set of threats caused by human impacts on the environment. In particular, long-lived species that produce few offspring are highly vulnerable to changes in mortality rates. If an individual fails to breed in any particular year, this has little impact on their lifetime reproductive output. However, a small increase in mortality rates can have dramatic long-term demographic consequences for an entire population. At the same time, massive habitat destruction of the type that humans are currently implementing has severe consequences for eagle reproduction at a grand scale and has population-level impacts. This section focuses on these two different types of conservation concerns that eagles face—direct mortality by human activity and indirect mortality by human activity via habitat and climate change.

Direct Mortality

Direct mortality of eagles by humans results from shooting, trapping, poisoning, and collisions with vehicles and man-made structures. Although relatively simple to identify, it is often difficult to redress the damage. In chapter 23, John Love details the enormous effort involved in trying to reintroduce a population of white-tailed sea eagles to western Scotland, almost 70 years after the species had been persecuted to extinction in the United Kingdom.

The most significant reason why eagles are shot, trapped, or poisoned is that they are perceived as a danger to domestic or commercially reared livestock. As large predators, eagles are often seen as a direct threat to the well-being of sheep, goats, chickens, game birds, and even reindeer. Furthermore, when an animal dies, the carcass attracts many scavengers, among them eagles. Regardless of whether or not an eagle may have killed the animal it is feeding on, an assumption is often made that it did, and thus the eagle is persecuted. In the nineteenth and twentieth centuries in the United States, the shooting of golden eagles was sanctioned by the US government, and many thousands of eagles were shot in response to perceived predation on livestock. Similarly in Australia, the wedge-tailed eagle used to be considered a "pest" species because of its reputation as a "lamb killer," and farmers were encouraged to shoot them; one estimate suggests that 30,000 eagles were destroyed within a single year. In chapter 21, Jason Wiersma describes the intentional shooting of the white-bellied sea eagles he was studying in Tasmania. In the United Kingdom, although the shooting and poisoning of raptors is illegal, it is still regularly practiced by some gamekeepers who consider most raptors (including golden and white-tailed sea eagles) as "vermin" and a major threat to their game bird shooting stock. Since the 1800s, grouse shooting has become one of the major land-uses of upland Britain, where privately owned estates produce large, harvestable surpluses of red grouse (*Lagopus lagopus*) for paying clients to shoot. In addition, many lowland estates rear and release unnaturally high densities of game birds (e.g., pheasants and partridge) onto their land for commercial shooting parties. Eagles and other predators are attracted to these areas by the availability of abundant prey, and conflict often results between the gamekeepers and the eagles. Two factors contribute to the ongoing problem. First, in the interests of maintaining a high profit margin, some estate owners either turn a blind-eye to or encourage the illegal actions of their game-keeping staff. Such owners are unwilling to admit that persecution is prevalent, despite strong scientific evidence to demonstrate otherwise. Compounding this, weak and ineffective legal sanctions against those found guilty of raptor persecution means that there is little deterrent. Despite the best efforts of many, the persecution problem is widespread and relentless, and indeed it is now considered the main threat to stability of the golden eagle population in Scotland.

Eagles are also poisoned or trapped unintentionally, when other predators are targeted. In the western United States, coyote and foxes are targeted with poisoned sheep and other baits. When an eagle feeds on a tainted carcass, it too is poisoned and dies. Such poisonings are also common in other parts of the world, especially Europe, Asia, and Africa.

Eagles are also sometimes caught incidentally in traps intended to supply food or pelts for humans. In much of the developing world, bushmeat hunting is common and provides an important source of protein. As human populations expand, those activities have greater and more consequential impacts on the demography of their prey. Eagles are often incidentally caught in snares and other traps, and when captured, they may be eaten or discarded. Incidental trap mortality is important to the demography of populations of Philippine eagles and of golden eagles in the eastern United States.

Trade in wildlife is another way in which humans directly impact eagle demography. In chapter 17, Vincent Nijman describes how Javan hawk-eagles are taken from the wild and held in captivity by people. Interestingly,

Nijman's recent work documents how the implementation of protected status has actually made the problem worse, by adding perceived value and social status to the possession of this species.

Collisions with human-built structures and electrocution are also important sources of eagle mortality. Although eagles only rarely collide with structures, power lines and poorly sited wind turbines are a relatively recent but potentially dangerous threat to eagles. Collision with power lines kills untold numbers of eagles each year. More significant is mortality due to electrocution. This is a pervasive problem worldwide, and although mitigation is relatively easy (through simple changes in power pole design), it continues to be an ongoing issue. The population of Spanish imperial eagles was likely limited by electrocution in the 1970s and 1980s.

Collision with wind turbines also may kill large numbers of eagles. Two wind energy installations stand out as particularly dangerous. The classic example of a poorly sited wind power facility is at the Altamont Pass Wind Resource Area in the Diablo Mountains in California. The Altamont facility has been in place since 1982, and at present approximately 6500 wind turbines have been built throughout this 160 km^2 (62 mi^2) area. What makes Altamont especially dangerous to birds of prey is that the area supports large populations of California ground squirrels (*Spermophilus beecheyii*). Predatory birds from surrounding areas are drawn to the area in search of food, thereby increasing effective population density and putting far more individuals at risk than just the local breeders. The most recent peer-reviewed literature on Altamont suggests that annual mortality includes approximately 67 golden eagles, 188 red-tailed hawks (*Buteo jamaicensis*), 348 American kestrels (*Falco sparverius*), 440 burrowing owls (*Athene cunicularia*), contributing to a total of about 1127 raptors, and 2710 other birds (S. Smallwood and C. Thelander, 2008, Bird Mortality in the Altamont Pass Wind Resource Area, California; *Journal of Wildlife Management* 72(1):215–223).

Another example of a poorly conceived (from an ornithological perspective) facility is the wind farm on the island of Smøla in Norway. There turbines were erected throughout one of the world's highest-density breeding sites of white-tailed sea eagles. Since the wind farm has been constructed, the density of eagle nesting pairs on Smøla has been reduced substantially, and mortality of eagles has been high. These two case studies are extreme and demonstrate the devastating effect of poorly sited wind turbines. However, mortality rates at most other wind energy facilities are not so dramatic, either because they have not been as well studied or because they kill fewer birds. With proper pre-construction scientific evaluation and post-construction management, wind energy facilities need not be such a danger. A good example is the Beinn an Tuirc wind farm in Argyll, western Scotland, where a combination of pre-construction assessment, habitat modification, and post-construction monitoring has resulted in successful breeding for the resident golden eagles. Fundamental to reducing the risks of wind farms to eagles (and other avian species) is strong environmental protection legislation, a willingness by the government to enforce that legislation, and the availability of expert scientific assessment.

Indirect Effects

There are two key indirect mechanisms by which humans can negatively impact eagle populations and conservation: global and local habitat change and global climate change. Both are pervasive, and both have the potential to be more significant than direct mortality. The impacts of pollution and environmental toxins are less consequential for birds but still significant.

Habitat alteration is an ongoing threat to birds of prey, especially eagles, worldwide. Habitat change can impact birds in two primary ways: through reduction in habitat itself so that there is less preferred space for eagles, or through alteration of habitat so that it supports different eagle prey or different densities of eagle prey. Many of the species most threatened by habitat loss are tropical species with naturally low densities and limited distributions. As an example, one of the world's most threatened eagle species is the Philippine eagle. This remarkable bird historically occupied about 4 of the Philippines' 7000 islands. At present it is only known to exist on 2 islands—Luzon and Mindanao. However, the Philippines has lost about 95% of its lowland dipterocarp forest, the primary habitat for the species. Obviously such destruction has an impact on one of the world's largest eagle species. Hector Miranda Jr. (chapter 25) describes the alarming rate of forest reduction and how he has already seen the effects on the Philippine eagles he studies. Habitat alteration needn't be so close to home to have an adverse impact. In chapter 14, Malcolm Nicoll warns of the potential threats to grey-headed fishing eagles in Cambodia from the construction of upstream hydropower dams in China, which threaten to change the downstream flood regime on which the fishing eagles (and many other species, including humans) depend.

Some eagle species are also impacted by changes in prey densities brought about by habitat change. The Philippine eagle, harpy eagle, and New Guinea harpy eagle, three of the world's largest eagle species, are heavily impacted by depletion of the large mammals on which they depend as prey. What makes this relationship so interesting is that all three of these species are in almost direct competition with humans for prey. Thus, when humans destroy forest or hunt for bushmeat, they not only destroy their own natural heritage but also compete with eagles for a food resource.

Climate change is a significant but poorly understood driver of demographic and ecological change for eagles worldwide. At present the impacts of climate change are just beginning to be understood—glaciers are melting, plants are flowering at different times, and phenology of bird migration is changing. Consequently, the impact of climate change on eagles is not currently well known. However, there are several ways that scientists expect climate change to impact these species. It is expected to have dramatic impacts on local plant communities. These changes will obviously impact the herbivores on which eagles depend as a prey resource. Additionally, climate change will impact the availability of large nesting trees on which eagles depend. Finally, climate change may change nesting phenology, and for those species not able to change their breeding biology quickly enough, it could have dramatic impacts on their reproductive output.

Historically, the largest impact that humans have had on eagles has been through the use of environmental contaminants, especially the organochlorine insecticide dichloro-diphenyl-trichloroethane, otherwise known as "DDT." Widely used with devastating effects following World War II, DDT is stored in tissues of fish and other wildlife. A single prey animal rarely contains enough DDT to cause problems for an eagle. However, each eagle eats several prey items per week. In this way, toxins can amplify such that predators have more and more pesticides in their system. In high doses, DDT can cause eagles to lay thin-shelled eggs, which break prematurely during incubation, resulting in a failed breeding attempt. Populations of bald eagles in the United States and white-tailed sea eagles in Europe have been significantly impacted by DDT, as have other raptor species, such as peregrines (*Falco peregrinus*) and ospreys (*Pandion haliaetus*). In chapter 23, Björn Helander describes his studies on white-tailed sea eagles in Sweden both during and after the DDT era. Although these species have now recovered in the countries where the pesticide was banned, the impact that pesticides and other pollutants have had on them is consequential. Furthermore, there are likely other pesticides in the environment that affect eagles, and it is crucial to watch populations closely to monitor the impact of as-yet-undiscovered threats that could be as dangerous as DDT.

SUMMARY

Although lumped together under the term "eagles," this group of birds is incredibly diverse, and even though many are not closely related, they share some common features. With few exceptions, eagles exhibit most of the characteristics of species vulnerable to rapid extinction: they tend to live at low population density and require vast areas of land for their home ranges. Most have a narrow geographic range and a low rate of population increase. All these factors contribute to a group-wide inability to recover quickly from population decline.

Some eagle species are well studied and are easily recognizable, while others are hardly known at all. The populations of some eagle species are thriving, because humans either have left them alone or have intervened to protect them; other populations have declined and are facing imminent extinction because of direct or indirect human interference. The status and distribution of further populations are uncharted. With the current rate of global environmental change, combined with both direct and indirect persecution, there is an increasing urgency to determine the basic ecological requirements of many eagle species to identify and then protect areas that are critical to their survival.

This challenge may seem daunting, but the fluctuating fortune of the bald eagle serves as both a warning of how we humans can decimate an eagle population and an encouraging example of our ability to repair the damage simply by changing our attitude toward the species. At the end of the nineteenth century, the bald eagle was common in many parts of North America and had enjoyed the reverence associated with being named the national symbol of the United States. At the beginning of the twentieth century and up until the Bald Eagle Protection Act was passed by the US Congress in 1940, the population dramatically declined as the US government encouraged people to kill the birds across the country because they were considered a threat to livestock. Further declines followed after the widespread use of DDT in the 1950s and 1960s. In 1967, with fewer than 500 pairs remaining, the bald eagle was added to the national endangered species list. Over the following decades, government and private citizens initiated scores of protection and reintroduction programs. The population has now recovered to such an extent that in 2007, the bald eagle was removed from the endangered species list. The work to continue protecting this species remains unfinished, as long-term monitoring is required to ensure that new threats do not jeopardize its future. However, the knowledge that in a period of about 100 years, humans managed to almost wipe out and then restore this magnificent species gives us hope for threatened eagle populations everywhere.

2

New Guinea Harpy Eagle

COMMON NAME: New Guinea harpy eagle

SCIENTIFIC NAME: *Harpyopsis novaeguineae*

OTHER NAMES: Kapul eagle, New Guinea eagle, Papuan eagle

IUCN CONSERVATION STATUS: *Vulnerable (population declining)*

DESCRIPTION: A large cream and grayish-brown eagle with short broad wings and a long rounded tail well adapted to hunting in a complex forest environment. This bird has a light-colored underbelly with long bare legs. Like other tropical forest eagles it has a crest, although its crest is smaller than that in most similar species. Flies low, rarely soars above the canopy.

SIZE: Length: 72–90 cm (28–35 in); Wingspan: 121–157 cm (47–62 in); Weight: 1.6–2.4 kg (3.5–5.3 lb)

THREATS: Hunting pressure (hunting for feathers) and habitat loss are primary threats to this species.

DISTRIBUTION: New Guinea (endemic there, found nowhere else)

MOVEMENTS: Nonmigratory; juveniles disperse from breeding areas.

HABITAT: The New Guinea harpy eagle occurs in heavily forested and undisturbed New Guinean tropical rainforest, from sea level to nearly 4000 m (13,123 ft). Because there is so little low-elevation forest remaining, it is now largely a montane species.

DIET: Arboreal and terrestrial mammals (especially nocturnal marsupials of the genus *Phalangeridae*) as well as birds and reptiles. Often hunts by walking along the forest floor.

NOTES: The call of this eagle has been described as, *Bung! Buk-Buk-Buk-Buk-Buk*. Researchers have suggested that when two birds duet, one calls, *Bung*, and the other responds with, *Buk-Buk-Buk-Buk-Buk*.

Author's Biography

MARK WATSON taking
field notes in the Eastern
Highlands of Papua New
Guinea. Photo courtesy
of the author

Mark Watson first became interested in raptors at the age of 13, while living in Sweden, when his mother pointed out a migrant goshawk that had roosted for the night in a pine tree in the garden. He studied medieval history at York University in England before joining the British Army's Parachute Regiment, serving for 10 years. In 1996 he left the army to pursue a career in wildlife conservation, completing his MSc degree at the Durrell Institute of Conservation and Ecology (DICE), University of Kent, on the feeding and breeding ecology of endangered saker falcons in the remote steppe and mountains of northeast Kazakhstan. He then completed a contract for the Game Conservancy Trust on the feasibility of translocating hen harriers as a conservation tool in the United Kingdom. In December 1999, sponsored by The Peregrine Fund and San Diego Zoo, Mark traveled to Papua New Guinea for the first systematic study on the New Guinea harpy eagle, which involved seven months of intensive fieldwork living in cloud forest with Gimi tribesmen. He completed his DPhil degree at Oxford University in 2004, with a thesis investigating the effects of raptor predation on grey partridges on lowland farmland in the United Kingdom. Returning to the steppes of Kazakhstan that summer, he led an international team to conduct a pilot study into the decline of the sociable lapwing for BirdLife International and the University of St Andrews. Mark now works in Norfolk, United Kingdom, as a wildlife manager looking after wild grey partridges on farmland and trout in a lowland chalk stream.

NEW GUINEA HARPY EAGLE, PAPUA NEW GUINEA

Mark Watson

There are a thousand greens in this random cloister of waxy, spiky, shining leaves. Vertical lines of moss-clad trunks of red, orange, black, and white bark. A tangled mesh of branches and vines. Water dripping and glistening. The forest floor of yellow mud is layered with dead leaves, twigs, and rotting trunks. I want to write of the time in the cloud forest when rain starts to fall. Vaporous cloud swirls up the deep ravines carrying moisture-laden air from the Gulf of Papua. There is a hiss of approaching rain sheets that suddenly turns to a loud roar as they arrive overhead and huge cold droplets fall earthwards, battering the leaves in a downward onslaught. Steam rises from the leaf litter to mix with the wraiths of mist and the streams become dangerous torrents in seconds. (Field Log, Tuesday, 5 January 1999)

In 1999 I spent a year in Papua New Guinea studying the least known of the world's large forest eagles—the New Guinea harpy eagle. This eagle lives in the extraordinarily beautiful jungle of this Australasian island, one of the wildest and most diverse places on earth. But first I had to learn how to survive and travel in the remote, wet, cold, and precipitous mountain environment. The rainfall was so great that I remember there were two kinds of day: one when it rained all afternoon and all night; the other when it rained all morning, all afternoon, and all night. Being soaked the whole time was bearable as long as you could collapse into a well-built palm shelter and dry out in front of a roaring fire at the end of each day. For me to be successful in the project it was necessary to find suitable companions among the local people. I settled with the Gimi tribesmen of the Eastern Highlands, a people whose lifestyle and material culture were perfectly adapted to living in such an unforgiving place. I learned to speak Melanesian pidgin, which is a common language for the island's many different cultural groups. On my first journey with them we made an 18-day walk around the flanks of a 3000 m (9843 ft) volcano that had last been active in the Pleistocene (from 1.8 million to 12,000 years ago). Although I had been running and mountain biking hard before leaving the United Kingdom, load-carrying up and down the steep ridges of the volcano was a brutal introduction to the physical demands of getting around in such a place. My guides included village elders, "big men," who were mostly in their forties, but whose assistance was crucial as they were the principal landowners and the most experienced bushmen. Despite their age, these men were superbly fit, with lean, tough bodies honed from a life of subsistence hunting and farming. They combined the role of acting as my guide with their own hunting trips deep into the forest, three and four days' walk away from their villages. They usually traveled armed with bows and arrows and also homemade shotguns, the last of which were often more dangerous to the shooter than to the target.

I studied Gimi behavior closely and tried to copy them as much as I could. For example, on a day of walking they usually roasted sweet potatoes in the campfire before first light and ate several before setting off. They would also carry some cooked ones to eat during the course of the day. These vegetables gave the body carbohydrate energy to sustain it during long marches, and I quickly adopted this habit out of necessity. Sometimes we traveled light, carrying minimum food and equipment, expecting to live by foraging and hunting. On one occasion my hunter companions failed to make a kill and we went three days without eating. Coupled with our long daily marches, this was pure torture for me and I moaned to them about the hunger gnawing in my belly. Being used to an irregular diet, the Gimi men scoffed at my weakness, saying, "You don't know what true hunger is." On other occasions we were able to enjoy the bounties of the forest's rich diversity of plants and animals. There were delicious "Amuli" nuts, a palm shoot called "Wadaba," wild lemons, passion fruits, and various edible starchy roots. Often "dessert" was a plate of the steamed larvae of a wood-boring beetle, lightly dusted with salt and pepper, a dish I eventually came to enjoy very much.

The New Guinea harpy eagle was very difficult to find in such a complex environment. During the 18 days of my first walk in the forest I only heard a single eagle call. It was to be another month of hard work before I actually saw one. This eagle is unusual in that it has a low frequency call, made by expelling a gulp of air from its throat, producing a sound similar to that of a ship's foghorn. Such a vocalization can carry for several kilometers through thick, water-laden vegetation. Because these eagles do not soar above the canopy, tracking calling eagles ended up being the best method of finding them. As part of my studies, I made sound recordings of this and other eagle calls for the Library of Natural Sounds at Cornell University and was able to distinguish between characteristics of calls recorded in different areas of forest to show that they were made by different individuals. In this way I was able to map territories and hence estimate eagle breeding density. None of the other forest eagles has a similar far-carrying, low-frequency call, and it is a mystery as to why this species has evolved such a vocalization. It has been hypothesized that these calls might allow them to claim and defend large areas—important when available prey are at low densities, as they are in these forests.

My closest encounter with an eagle was in May of that year, when I climbed to a nest where a juvenile had fledged four months previously. The nest platform was 36 m (118 ft) above the ground on a lateral branch of a 45 m (148 ft) tall tree. To reach it I used spurs and a steel-cored safety line wrapped around the main trunk. I had to cut a way through clusters of vines and epiphytes that barred the way upward. Pulling on a vine tangle 20 m (66 ft) up is very frightening, as you cannot be sure that it won't give way in your hands! Once at the nest platform I rigged a self-belay over an overhanging branch and could safely walk around on the large compacted mat of epiphytes and moss that formed the nest base. From the nest there was so much foliage in the mid-story that I could only just see my companions, their necks straining up from the darkness of the forest floor below. Looking out through the tree branches, I realized how high the nest tree was on a hilltop, and I could see out for several kilometers over endless jungle-clad ridges. As expected, the nest platform contained some prey remains that gave useful information about the eagle's diet. There were bones of a forest wallaby, a megapode (a type of game bird), and a juvenile cassowary. Since these were large terrestrial species, the eagle would have to have carried them whole or in part up to the nest, giving some indication of how powerful this bird is. As I was scraping in the detritus of the nest, there was a shout from below, and I looked up to see a female eagle advancing rapidly toward me along the nest branch. Because I was tied in to the tree, I could not move and I felt the familiar rush of anxiety that always comes when you are not quite sure what will happen next. The eagle stopped about 5 m (16 ft) away and stared at me with fierce amber eyes, gripping the branch with its powerful feet and standing tall with slightly raised wings and puffed-out feathers. It looked like a giant goshawk, and I could see every detail of the mottled brown and gray upper feathers, the pure white breast, and its heavily barred black-and-white tail, stretched out behind. This was the mysterious raptor that I had heard calling in the chilly mist so often but seldom glimpsed. After a few seconds the eagle turned abruptly and launched into the air on broad wings and fanned tail, diving down through the mid-story canopy and disappearing as quickly as it had arrived. I had to take some deep breaths before retreating in a rather less spectacular fashion, rappelling carefully in two pitches to regain the safety of the forest floor. Here my Gimi friends helped coil the rope and chattered excitedly about the spectacular close encounter they had just witnessed. As we walked back to camp I reflected on how easily the eagle moved around the canopy, only 30 m (98 ft) away from the earth's surface, but a place so alien for us humans.

Although I succeeded in gathering enough data over the course of the year to publish a short paper about the eagle's ecology, the dominant theme of my field journals is of frustration and disappointment. For example, in seven months of continuous wandering in the forest, I spent only 16 hours observing the eagles directly. Likewise, although I visited more than 10 different eagle territories, I never located a nest with a young chick. All my attempts to trap an eagle for radio-tagging were unsuccessful. Sometimes my efforts developing local contacts and logistical support failed even to get me into the forest at all. On one occasion, I went into a village for a prearranged bush trip with my principal Gimi field assistants, who by that time I knew very well. When we met, they told me solemnly that a 4-year-old child in their clan had died suddenly two days previously and that we could not go into the forest until rituals had been performed to identify the cause of death. The next nine days were spent not on fieldwork, but in the village, waiting for the clans to complete their "Sanguma" (black magic). In the traditional spiritual belief system of many New Guinea Highland cultures, unexplained deaths were attributed to poisoning by rival clans. When this occurs, elaborate ceremonies are performed to "exorcise" the evil spirit. Sometimes these ceremonies lead to extreme physical violence, and the resulting blood feuds often continue across generations. In modern times most of these practices have been suppressed by Christian missionary contact, but, as I was to find out, they had not entirely disappeared. Three days after my arrival on this trip, I was walking in the village when 40 warriors of the Hegu clan came running toward me, fully armed with bows and arrows and carrying a "death-stick." The movements of the death stick, which was carried by the close relatives of the deceased, were supposed to reveal the source of the evil. I was disturbed to see that my own field assistants, Asoyama and Iso, were at the head of the group, running in silence, staring intently ahead in a trance-like state. A village elder explained that the stick was to be carried to all the places that the deceased person had visited in the last days of life. For three more days everyone was frozen in fear as the wild-eyed clans charged about. I tried to keep a low profile, but eventually was asked by Asoyama to join the warriors to assist in the ritual. Curiosity drove me forward. The exorcism reached a peak of frenzy when we carried the stick inside the compound of the neighboring Koi clan that was deemed responsible for the death. Their warriors were in formation, fully armed and ready to receive us, as Iso stepped forward with the death-stick carriers, chanting and shouting. There was huge tension, and it seemed as if fighting might break out at any moment. I don't mind admitting I chose not to stand in the front rank! Happily, the conflict was resolved and a peaceful compensation was arranged as an alternative to bloodshed. After three more days, the body was buried, and a huge feast rounded off a strange and unsettling time. The next day, the dreamlike atmosphere evaporated, and with the Hegu clan as porters, we walked off into the forest to begin our much-delayed fieldwork.

Following the training received in the course of that year, Asoyama continues to run a monitoring scheme on the wild eagles. He is now a senior and influential member of the community, and the eagle population in the mountain jungles surrounding his village is protected. His work has helped unravel some of the mysteries of this strange inhabitant of the cloud forest and made a strong contribution to conservation in Papua New Guinea.

Author's Biography

MARTIN GILBERT and friends in Tsomai village in the Eastern Highlands of Papua New Guinea. Photo courtesy of the author

A Scotsman by birth, Martin Gilbert grew up in a veterinary practice in the English Lake District, where he first cut his raptor teeth watching nesting peregrines on the local crags. Within months of qualifying from Glasgow University, with degrees in zoology and veterinary medicine, Martin turned his back on a life of dogs' anal glands and bovine rectums and booked a flight to Madagascar to take up a voluntary post with The Peregrine Fund. A season trapping fish eagles and chasing white-browed owls cemented what had already been a lifelong passion for birds. After brief diversions with penguins in South Africa and marsupials in Western Australia, Martin returned to his veterinary and raptor roots to embark on an investigation into the South Asian vulture crash in Pakistan. Over the course of three years and numerous dead-end leads, this research identified the cause of the greatest contemporary decline in raptor populations as a veterinary drug (diclofenac) used to treat domestic livestock. His pursuit of raptors has seen him marooned on an arctic island in Greenland, being shot at by rebels in Kashmir, and in a near-death encounter with fermented horse milk on the Mongolian steppe. Martin now works for the Wildlife Conservation Society in East Asia, where he is developing surveillance programs for avian influenza and other nasty diseases in migratory species and the wildlife trade.

NEW GUINEA HARPY EAGLE, PAPUA NEW GUINEA

Martin Gilbert

I climbed to my hide in darkness, fighting my way onto the great bough with my heart pounding from the exertion of the last stage of a long journey: the ascent of 27 m (90 ft) of woven climbing rope. Lying against the bark, I tried to catch my breath, clearing mossy dirt from my mouth and feeling the sweat begin to chill against my skin. The first blue hints of daylight drew cautious traces of bird song up through the mists. Dim shapes of trees slowly materialized from the predawn gloom, and beyond them the steep sides of the valley diffused from the sky. The fall of a neighboring tree had torn a great hole in the canopy, allowing me an uninterrupted view of a tangled platform of branches supported by a moss-fringed emergent limb. It was this that had brought me to such a remote corner of the Papuan Eastern Highlands: the nest of a New Guinea harpy eagle.

The New Guinea harpy eagle is as mythical a bird as its name suggests. A powerful forest eagle, it is large enough to subdue a 3 kg (6 lb) forest wallaby and carry it to the canopy. The species is only found in New Guinea, and published accounts of its life history are sparse. What is certain is that it lives at low density in tracts of undisturbed forest. The eagle is hunted in some regions, where its boldly marked feathers are used in tribal ceremonies. The bird's natural history has been loosely pieced together from fragmented accounts, and almost nothing is known of its breeding biology. In an attempt to address these gaps in our knowledge, The Peregrine Fund has been supporting studies within Papua New Guinea since 1998.

As I peered out from my rudimentary hide at the scene unfolding around me, it was hard to believe that barely a week earlier I had been standing on the runway at Boise, Idaho, airport in the grip of the first blizzard of winter. Five planes had carried me through San Francisco, Tokyo, Singapore, and Port Moresby (the capital of Papua New Guinea) to the highland town of Goroka. Yet it was the penultimate stage of the journey from Goroka to the mountain village of Ubaigubi that had been most eventful and proved the old adage that sometimes getting there is half the fun.

Most villages within the Crater Mountain Wildlife Management Area can be reached only by bush plane or by foot. Ubaigubi, I was told, was an exception; it was served by a road. I treated the claims that the journey from Goroka would take us around four hours with some skepticism—I'd heard such claims before but in truth I knew nothing of the distance or road conditions that lay between me and my destination. The sight of my transport, a battered Toyota pickup piled high with cargo, passengers, and livestock, only reinforced my fears. Not a square centimeter of the vehicle's bodywork was free from dents. Its original color was difficult to discern with certainty, but it may have been white. A rough frame of logs bound with creepers held the cargo aboard. Yet despite appearances, the engine started successfully. So off we went, one rickety truck, 11 men, one small dog, four chickens, two squealing piglets, a boy with a pet beetle on a string, four wheels, no treads, and more food and baggage than is surely healthy for one research biologist.

I scoured the packed load space, hunting for a corner that would offer marginally less discomfort than the rest of the shifting cargo. I settled on a can of kerosene that in the very least appeared capable of maintaining my weight and seemed to provide a modest amount of leg room (the word "leg" is given in the singular for a reason). The first stretch of the journey passed uneventfully along a hardtop road spattered with the occasional pothole of only moderate size. We stopped only twice, once for fuel and again for breakfast. Two hours and 3 km (2 mi) later we pulled onto a rough track for a short break while the driver used a hammer to straighten the rear wheel.

It wasn't long before I began to realize the mistake I had made in my seating selection. For a start, the can of kerosene was less well anchored than it had initially appeared, and rocked violently as the swinging truck negotiated the ruts. More disturbingly, there seemed to be a growing aroma of hydrocarbon in the air. I shuffled nervously, trying to ignore it, and smiled at the man to my left for reassurance. He smiled back, sucking heavily on his bush cigarette of rolled newspaper.

We climbed steadily, if slowly, for much of the day, stopping periodically for running repairs. The mood in the truck was friendly, and in the cramped space, humor was a necessity. The road wound along hillsides, thick with forest from which the liquid whistles and cries of birds called unseen. Chuckling streams tumbled down the steep slopes, and fine curtains of mist hugged the ridgelines. As the road took us higher, its condition deteriorated considerably. Rain had turned sections into a slurry of deep ocherous mud. Each passing truck had ploughed deeper into the ruts, digging into the ground until the verges reared over the heads of us passengers like canyons of clay. The source of the dents so far up the bodywork was becoming clearer.

At times the state of the track required us to proceed on foot, providing a welcome opportunity to revive blood-starved limbs and air my trousers, the seat of which by now was soaked in kerosene. Freed from its large load of passengers, the truck was eventually able to summon sufficient traction to negotiate each slippery obstacle and allow us back on board. The vehicle slithered onward from one valley to the next, and the hours ticked by. Already, the trip duration so optimistically estimated that morning had doubled, with no sight of Ubaigubi.

It was late afternoon by the time we encountered the bridge. After we gingerly descended a steep-sided river gorge, our path was blocked by an angry torrent of white water that fought its way past giant boulders and pulled at overhanging vegetation. For all intents and purposes the bridge that spanned this obstacle should have been sufficient for the task intended. Sturdy lengths of iron girder had been laid across the gorge and anchored firmly at both ends. As ever, the shortcoming lay on the surface upon which we were expected to drive. Across the longitudinal beams, a path of branches cut from the forest had been laid, none thicker than my wrist, with nothing holding them in place save gravity. My comrades exchanged dubious glances and we all alighted to inspect the crossbeams, adjusting branches here and there in the futile hope that this might ensure our safe passage.

The driver revved his engine, his eyes set in slits, intent on the other side. We passengers crossed tentatively and retreated to a safe distance. The face of each man, boy, and canine wore a mask of skepticism (the lives of the two piglets and four chickens had been left in the hands of fate back in the truck; the beetle—sadly—had expired en route). The driver released the clutch and the truck jolted forward. Predictably the impact lifted the branches, throwing them violently into the air. On balance, the first couple of meters passed pretty successfully, but in the end disaster was inevitable. The all-too-mobile crossbeams shifted, the wheels lost purchase and then slipped through, wedging the truck to the axles between the iron span of the bridge.

In my previous life, disasters like this simply didn't happen. This is just as well, as people like me are not well wired to deal with them if they did. I will freely admit that at home I am the first to curse at a flat tire, and a broken exhaust will ruin my day. In comparison our situation seemed far more serious, yet my fellow passengers were about to teach me a valuable lesson in humility. By this time, we had been on the road for 10 hours, rain was threatening, it would soon be dark, and our destination was not yet in sight. Our truck was wedged firmly not one-third of the way across a rudimentary bridge as an angry river spat below. As hopeless as our predicament seemed, not a single word was spoken in anger or frustration, and the men surveyed the damage with a practical eye, looking simply to solve the problem at hand, wasting no energy on harsh words. After much experimenting, and a remarkable demonstration of the enduring wonders of the lever, our truck limped free. As we boarded safe on the other side, the man next to me leaned over, his eyes shining beneath a broad brow and tightly curled hair. With a defiant smile and more than a hint of jubilation to his voice he said, "This is how we live!!" . . . everyone smiled, and had I had a glass, I would have raised it to them all.

As the shadows lengthened, the banks of mists coalesced into threatening clouds and we felt our first few drops of rain. Alongside the road we began to encounter small villages with increasing frequency. Little groups of small huts, many on stilts and made of matted sago palm, bordered by curious fences of carved and flattened stakes. The ground (often raised) was hard packed, pounded by the passing of many weathered and leathery feet. Grizzled black pigs ran squealing at our approach, and the sight of a white man among the cargo sparked a good deal of excitement. Children ran shouting and laughing alongside the truck, reaching out their fingers to touch the white man's sleeve, causing great hilarity whenever one achieved the feat.

As the darkness took hold, so did the rain, in heavy drops flung with a force only the tropics can muster. We passengers unrolled a large orange sheet of plastic and huddled beneath in an attempt at shelter. The rain battered hard, pooling above our heads. Beneath us we could feel the truck sliding and slipping, and the men exchanged ominous glances. Sure enough, we came to a hill that seemed to promise inevitable defeat. A slippery wall, more a mudslide than a road, climbed into the blackness. Time and again the engine revved, we raced forward, up and up before skidding, slipping, and losing ground. There was talk of abandoning the truck, continuing on foot to the village and returning the following day with help. Only recently, I was told, a man had been killed on this ascent when the truck he was pushing slipped back and crushed him. The memory was clearly fresh in everyone's minds. But once again the resilience and dogged persistence of these men of the bush won the day, and using ropes they literally pulled the truck up the hill, through the darkness and curtains of rain.

We had now been driving for over 12 hours. My body ached, and looking around, the strain of the day and its disasters was starting to tell. Eyes were tired and a hush fell over the group huddled in moist clouds beneath the polythene. The combination of jolting truck and kerosene-soaked trousers had worn a tender sore on my backside, but in the company of these hardy men, complaint was unthinkable. Then, mounting the crest of the hill, we were there. We had done it. Peering out, I could see people emerging from the darkness. Faces lit by glowing embers of rudimentary torches brought from the fire, spitting showers of orange sparks. We had reached Ubaigubi. Willing hands were held out to us, to help unload the cargo and crew. A line of carriers marched my boxes and equipment up the hill to the head of the village and my destination.

Squelching along behind, I reflected on the day and its string of trials. I had come a long way from Idaho, in distance, culture, and spirit. My goal was still a hike into the forest and 27 m (90 ft) of rope away, but by this stage all I could think of was sleep.

Two days later, as the dawn broke over the canopy, the aches of my journey had passed only to be replaced by a new pain of disappointment. The nest that I had come so far to see was already empty; the young eagle had already fledged. I tried to calm the hollow feeling in my chest and adopt the fatalistic optimism of my fellow travelers from the road, but it wasn't easy. My dreams of unlocking the mysteries of this most elusive of subjects seemed to have slipped away. I resolved to wait for the sun, at least hoping for a glimpse of the birds. I would not be disappointed for long.

Far on the opposite ridge a booming and resonant *Gulp* signaled the arrival of the harpy. Likened to the sound of a hunter's bowstring, the call of a New Guinea harpy eagle is so deep that from a distance it almost seems beyond hearing. Then behind me, a second—or was it an echo?—I couldn't be sure. I strained to get a bearing but could see nothing but trees. First one, then the other, a call and a reply. But I was not alone in noting the arrival of the adults. Across the clearing, not 15 m (49 ft) away, the ghostly white form of the juvenile harpy alighted on a great weathered limb.

My breath caught in my throat. He stood perfectly framed in lichen-blotched branches hanging thick with purple moss, against a backdrop of fresh leaves of soft red and lustrous green. The rising sun cleared the eastern ridgeline, bringing the forest to life and picking the outline of his feathers like a halo. He stretched out his wing and fanned his tail, the backlight catching the delicate barring of his flight feathers. Fingers of mist caressed at the white feathers of his flank and belly, lifting them as if made of air. He seemed completely unaware that I was hidden in my hide, peering across at him.

He was still young, perhaps only a few weeks out of the nest, yet he already held himself with a relaxed air of confidence, hinting at his future dominance in these highland forests. A talon rose to scratch lazily behind his ear, folded into a tight fist, and submerged itself in the luxuriant softness of his white belly feathers. A pair of parrots careened through the mid-story below—a shriek of green and red, slaloming through the clearing at incredible speeds. His tawny eyes were on them in an instant, his head bobbing in pursuit of their course—flashes of color and sound against the gentle backdrop of the waking forest. His great broad head swiveled sharply, catching the flash of an impossibly scarlet honeyeater working the foliage behind him. All the while his parents continued their booming cries across the valley.

Despite his assertive posture, he was still very much a baby and totally dependent on his parents for food. He leaned forward and shook himself, raising the ruff of feathers that rimmed his head, and with an indignant *Cluck!* announced that he was ready for his breakfast. Hardly able to believe my eyes, the youngster unfurled his broad wings like a cloak and flew to a perch on a horizontal branch, not 5 m (16 ft) from my position. He now sat right out in the open, his tactic obvious: "Hear me! See me! Feed me!" Although the young eagle seemed oblivious to my presence, I struggled to remain hidden. My legs were cramping badly, my kerosene-raw behind stung, I was under assault from a squadron of mosquitoes, and an early sweat bee was mining my nostril for moisture and salt. I dared not move; I had come too far to risk alarming this little-known bird now.

The arrival of the adult brought a perceptible change in the air, but there was little else to announce its presence. It remained silent, and I could see nothing, but somewhere close, through the plastic sheeting and fern thatch of my hide, I knew it was there, perched just meters away. The effect on the juvenile was electric. Standing on surprisingly gangly legs, with his long tail bouncing for balance, he ran along the branch calling loudly. He made an unsteady leap, posing for a moment at the edge of the nest tree, his eyes fixed somewhere above me. Then in an instant it was over. The juvenile looked crestfallen, his cries petered to an afterthought—you could almost taste his disappointment—the adult, it seemed, had gone. The youngster stood forlorn and deflated, gazing back down the drainage before taking flight, his calls fading down the valley in pursuit of his parent.

All at once, everything had come together. Each kilometer that had brought me to this magical place was worth it. I had shared a most intimate experience with one of the most enigmatic birds in the world, yet almost fittingly, at the last moment the adult had chosen to withdraw, taking with it the essential jigsaw pieces of its natural history.

3
Golden Eagle

COMMON NAME: Golden eagle

SCIENTIFIC NAME: *Aquila chrysaetos*

OTHER NAMES: Ring-tailed eagle, rock eagle

IUCN CONSERVATION STATUS: *Least Concern (population trend stable)*

DESCRIPTION: A large brown eagle with yellow-gold feathers on the back of the neck. Younger birds have extensive white under the wing and tail; white disappears as individuals age. Long, relatively narrow wings and tail, legs well feathered and feet massive.

SIZE: Length: 66–90 cm (26–35 in); Wingspan: 180–234 cm (71–92 in); Weight: 2.6–6.7 kg (6–15 lb)

THREATS: Persecuted by humans who perceive them as a threat to livestock or game species. Also threatened by habitat loss and human constructions, especially wind turbines.

DISTRIBUTION: Occurs in North America, Europe, Asia, and Africa (6 subspecies). In western North America, golden eagles breed from the Great Plains and Rocky Mountains west and north to northern Alaska and Canada, and as far south as northern Mexico. Northern populations migrate across western North America and as far south as central Mexico. In eastern North America the species breeds in Quebec, Ontario, Labrador, and Newfoundland and winters in mountains from New York to Georgia. May breed in the southern Appalachians. In Eurasia and Asia Minor the species breeds throughout, from the British Isles across to Kamchatka and south to Spain, Israel, China, Iran, and Pakistan. Northern populations are migratory. In Africa, golden eagles breed in the northern parts of West Africa. The southernmost population of golden eagles in the world is in the Bale Mountains of Ethiopia.

MOVEMENTS: Where there is suitable winter forage, golden eagles tend to be nonmigratory (Scotland, western United States, Europe, Africa). Where winter food is limited, golden eagles may be medium- or long-distance migrants (northern Canada and Alaska, Scandinavia).

HABITAT: Golden eagles are habitat generalists. Their "classical" habitat is in mountains, but they are found in the grasslands of central Asia and North America, as well as the deserts of the Middle East and even Arctic tundra of Alaska and Siberia.

DIET: Medium to large mammals, birds, and carrion of all types. Golden eagles are typically associated with hares, ground squirrels, partridge, chukar, grouse (ptarmigan), and other similarly sized animals.

NOTES: Golden eagles are regularly used by falconers in central Asia—Mongolia, Kazakhstan, and Kyrgyzstan. They are so powerful that the largest females are regularly known to fly for prey as large as wolves and deer. There are 6 subspecies of golden eagles; the world's largest is probably the Himalayan subspecies (*A. c. daphanea*).

Author's Biography

CAROL MCINTYRE in a
golden eagle nest in Alaska,
banding the chick and
collecting feather samples
and prey remains. Photo
courtesy of the author

Carol McIntyre's interest in raptors began when she was shown thousands of migrating broad-winged hawks above the Kittatinny Ridge in northwest New Jersey. On that fateful day, Carol gave up her dreams of being a rock-and-roll star and began her career as a professional raptor bum. After earning her BSc degree at East Stroudsburg University, Pennsylvania, Carol "worked" as a hawk watcher on Cape May Point, New Jersey. She soon found out that catching and banding raptors was more interesting than simply counting them as they flew by, so she willingly gave up her membership in the International Brotherhood of Hawk Watchers and became a raptor trapper. After she spent several seasons working on raptor migration projects in New Jersey and Israel, Carol's love of wild places and raptors led her to Alaska. Carol started studying golden eagles in Denali National Park and Preserve, Alaska, in 1987. She returned to university studies in 1989 and earned her MSc degree at the University of Alaska Fairbanks, then her PhD at Oregon State University in 2004 for her studies on golden eagle ecology. Carol currently works for Denali National Park and Preserve, where she continues to study golden eagles, gyrfalcons, and other birds amidst spectacular scenery. She is a coauthor of the golden eagle species account for *The Birds of North America*, Director-at-Large for the Raptor Research Foundation, and board member of the Alaska Bird Observatory, and is active in several bird conservation groups in Alaska. She currently lives in the boreal forest near Fairbanks, Alaska, with her husband, Ray Hander, and their Alaskan sled dogs.

GOLDEN EAGLE, ALASKA

Carol McIntyre

Not much beats the view from a golden eagle's nest. My view from one on Polychrome Mountain on July 21, 1997, was superb. A group of Dall sheep ewes and lambs grazed lazily on the opposite mountainside. The remarkably surefooted lambs bounded across the steep slope but never strayed far from the protection of the ewes. Down the valley a bit, a female grizzly bear grazed in a patch of blueberries, with two spring cubs in tow. The cubs rolled and tumbled over each other as they played. Below me, a Say's phoebe was busily picking off butterflies in a splash of wildflowers and delivering them to her hungry youngsters. As I sat there, I cradled a 63-day-old golden eagle chick in my arms. I had just equipped her and her brother with 90 g (3.2 oz) satellite radio transmitters. The hairs on the back of my neck rose in anticipation as I thought about where these eaglets would travel and what they would see over the next year. Yes, what they would see . . .

I saw my first golden eagle in December 1978 as it soared over a salt marsh in eastern New Jersey. I'll never forget that sighting—the eagle slowly circled overhead, floating on long and broad wings, with golden feathers shining on its neck. I knew that golden eagles rarely nested in the northeastern United States and that this eagle was a migrant from northeastern Canada. But, exactly where did it come from, how did it get to New Jersey, and where was it going? Little did I know that my first encounter with *Aquila chrysaetos* would change my life, foster a lifelong interest in bird migration, and eventually lead me to answer some of those questions.

I went to college near the ancient Appalachian Mountains in eastern Pennsylvania and spent many autumn and spring days gazing at migrating raptors along the Kittatinny Ridge. After college, I "worked" on several raptor and owl migration projects in Cape May, New Jersey, where a sighting of a golden eagle roused everybody's attention. Everybody, including myself, wanted to see a golden eagle. In 1985, I migrated to Alaska and started studying nesting raptors. I finally laid my eyes on a pair of nesting golden eagles in June of that year, and was enthralled with their power and beauty and their wild surroundings. I watched as the female eagle brought a snowshoe hare to the nest, shredded it, and then ever so gently and patiently fed it to her small, down-covered youngsters. I watched the nest for days, and walked away knowing what I wanted to accomplish: I wanted to conduct an ecological study of nesting golden eagles in Alaska. First, though, I needed to decide what aspects of their ecology to study.

After spending much of the next winter scouring the scientific literature, I was disappointed at the lack of information regarding the ecology of golden eagles in the northern reaches of North America. However, this lack of information presented me with a unique opportunity for developing a long-term ecological study of the golden eagle in Alaska. Yes, I wanted to know everything—the size of the golden eagle population in Alaska, their nesting habits and habitats, their food habits, their reproductive ecology, and their migratory behavior. Some people thought that my ideas were too ambitious, but like the eagles I study, I was persistent in pursuing my "prey" and landed an opportunity to start my study in Denali National Park and Preserve (Denali) in 1987.

Denali is a 24,281 km^2 (6 million ac) national park that straddles the crest of the towering Alaska Range. A diverse suite of terrestrial and aerial predators such as wolves, grizzly bears, wolverines, lynx, and more than 12 species of raptors, including golden eagles and gyrfalcons, live in this subarctic sanctuary. Charles Sheldon, a naturalist and big-game hunter, visited this area in the early 1900s and was so awed by his experiences that he led the campaign to designate the area as a national park. Sheldon not only noted the abundance of large mammals in the area but also wrote enthusiastically about the many species of birds, including the golden eagles that were preying on Dall sheep. About 20 years later, George Wright and Joseph Dixon conducted the first biological reconnaissance of the newly designated Mt. McKinley National Park and noted, "The Golden Eagle is an integral component of the fauna of Mt. McKinley National Park." (Mt. McKinley National Park was enlarged and renamed as Denali National Park and Preserve with passage of the Alaska National Interest Lands Conservation Act in 1980.) In the mid-twentieth century, Adolph Murie made the first field studies of golden eagles in Denali and wrote, "The golden eagle, unmolested and free, may frequently be seen soaring in the blue sky over its mountain home. May this magnificent bird survive the many new hazards in the south and continue returning each spring in the future, to contribute beauty and spirit to this northern wilderness." The words of these eagle watchers easily convinced me that Denali was the place to study golden eagles in Alaska.

During the first decade of my field studies, I discovered that about 80 pairs of golden eagles annually inhabited the northeastern region of Denali. This was far more than anyone previously expected, and raised considerable interest in this species in Denali. Further, unlike golden eagles that nest at temperate latitudes in North America, these eagles were migratory and spent nearly 40% of their lives away from Denali during the nonbreeding season. But we could only speculate about where these eagles spent their winters, where they traveled on migration, their migratory behavior, and where the nonbreeding eagles spent their summers.

Until about 1990, scientists had a limited number of tools available to them for studying movements of individual birds. Passive techniques including banding (ringing) or attaching visible markers such as wing-tags required that someone else encounter and report the marked bird. Our banding studies suggested that Denali's eagles traveled over some of the most remote regions of western North America. As such, encounters with eagles banded in Denali were rare (<3% of banded birds were observed elsewhere), and it was apparent that banding was not a good tool for studying movements of these eagles. Active tracking methods such as conventional radio tracking would be useful for studying local movements, but I would need a fleet of small airplanes to track eagles as they migrated thousands of kilometers each year. This just didn't seem feasible or, for someone who gets airsick, very much fun. I needed another tool—one that would allow me to track the movements of many individual eagles at the same time as they moved across western North America. Thankfully, this tool was unveiled in the late 1980s—a lightweight satellite transmitter that could be used on larger-bodied birds such as golden eagles. This amazing technology marked the start of a new generation of bird studies and provided me with an opportunity to fulfill one of my dreams.

I worked diligently to gain funding to study the movements of golden eagles from Denali using satellite telemetry. I hit my "Alaskan gold" in 1996 when the Forest and Rangeland Ecosystem Science Center of the US Geological Survey and the US National Park Service funded my proposal—I was ecstatic!

"Hey, Carol, it's time to get going." Christian's voice startled me and broke my daze. There I was, daydreaming, with my legs dangling over the side of a rather large stick nest placed precariously on a crumbly rock outcrop with a 5.4 kg (12 lb) eaglet in my arms. I turned and smiled at him, and said, "Yes, it is time to get moving." We had been working at the nest for nearly 30 minutes as we attached the radio transmitters to the eaglets using a breakaway backpack-style harness. The harness was constructed from a Teflon-coated nylon ribbon that the eagles couldn't chew through. We wanted to make sure that the harness would eventually fall off, so we sewed it on using cotton thread that would eventually degrade, causing the transmitter to fall off the eagle. While the eaglets seemed quite content with our presence, it was time to leave. Christian and I wished the eaglets a long and productive life, and then we slowly rappelled to the bottom of the cliff. Christian's brother, Paco, who was maintaining a vigil on top of the cliff in the unlikely event that one of the eaglets prematurely fledged, untied our anchor knots and let the ropes slip down the cliff. We packed up everything and high-tailed it across the valley.

I met Christian and Paco Grand, two Swiss eagle watchers, in 1995 at another Alaskan field site where I was studying raptor migration. They had learned about my golden eagle studies from a friend who rescued them when their Volkswagen van caught fire in Fairbanks in 1995. Fate works in mysterious ways. Our friendship grew from our shared passion for golden eagles and wild places, and these amazing brothers returned to Alaska to help me with fieldwork in 1997. Growing up in the vertical terrain of western Switzerland, Paco and Christian were excellent rock climbers. Since the only reason I climbed on crumbly rocks was to get to eagle nests, we made a great team. For the next two days, we watched the nest and the eaglets' behavior from a vantage point on the opposite mountainside. If we observed any signs that the radio-package interfered with their normal behavior, we would return to the nest and remove it. We climbed into our sleeping bags as the sun sank below Polychrome Mountain and watched the snow-covered Alaska Range slowly turn red with alpenglow—we could barely sleep as we thought about our day. In the distance, we heard a hoary marmot's whistling alarm calls. I poked my head out of my tent and looked up to see an adult golden eagle flying overhead. I checked back at the nest one last time; the two eaglets were sleeping.

The adults made several food deliveries to the nest over the next two days. The eaglets grappled for the prey, scrapped with each other, exercised their wings, and slept. They appeared unaware of their radio-packages, and they certainly were unaware of our new partnership.

We visited many eagle nests and radio-tagged 20 more eaglets over the next week. The eaglets fledged in early August, and we made multiple observations of them throughout the month during the post-fledging period. Over time, they improved their flying skills, and we found no evidence that their radio-package was interfering with their normal behavior. Now it was just a matter of time until they embarked on their first migratory journey.

By early September, the snowline was creeping down the mountains and prey was becoming sparse. The days were getting substantially colder and shorter, and arctic ground squirrels and hoary marmots were already hibernating. The recently fledged eagles continued to receive food and protection from their parents, but they moved freely about their natal territories. The big question was, when would they leave?

I was now monitoring the eagles' movements from my office in downtown Fairbanks, Alaska. How ironic that I traded in my view of the mountains for a clear view of "Eagles Hall" across the street. I plotted the coordinates, received via e-mail from two polar orbiting satellites each day, for each eagle into my computerized geographic information system, and I wondered when the eagles would start their first autumn migration. All the waiting and wondering ended on 15 September 1997 when the first radio-tagged eagle left its natal area and headed east. Within 2 weeks, just 6 to 8 weeks after fledging, all the radio-tagged eagles left Denali, and they did so completely independent of their siblings and parents.

The eagles moved slowly at first, staying near the Alaska Range as they migrated toward Canada. They turned south and picked up speed in Yukon, Canada, and migrated across the plains, ridges, and valleys of northwestern British Columbia, Alberta, and Saskatchewan. One of the siblings from the Polychrome Mountain nest migrated across the plains of Saskatchewan, and the other migrated through the valleys of British Columbia. Oh, how I yearned to see through their eyes as they traveled southward!

In late November and early December, I "watched" the radio-tagged eagles as they ended their first migratory journeys and settled on their winter ranges from central Alberta to southern New Mexico. Over the winter, I "watched" as the eagles moved on their winter range, and I "watched" as some eagles died. I recovered many of the dead eagles and found that most died from starvation—not a surprising result given that they were inexperienced hunters trying to survive in unfamiliar areas. Unfortunately, after migrating nearly 2000 km (1243 mi), the male from the Polychrome Mountain nest instantaneously died when it perched on an electric power pole in southern Alberta.

By late April 1998, the radio-tagged eagles were heading back north. The breeding populations had returned to Alaska nearly a month before, and the first-year eagles obviously were not returning to set up a nesting territory. Questions filled my mind—would they return to Alaska by the same route they used in autumn, how many would survive their journey back to Alaska, and would any eagles return to Denali? Much to my surprise, many eagles migrated northward through central Yukon, Canada, and headed to the Brooks Range and the coastal plains of Alaska and northern Yukon. The female eagle from the Polychrome Mountain nest spent her summer nearly 1000 km (621 mi) from her natal nest, on the Lisburne Peninsula in the far northwest corner of Alaska. Who would have guessed that many of the juvenile golden eagles from Denali would spend their first summer so far north of their natal areas? Other radio-tagged eagles spent their summer in the central Alaska Range, but no radio-tagged eagles returned to their natal area and few ventured close to Denali.

Over the next two years, I radio-tagged 28 more eaglets with satellite transmitters in Denali. I watched as they traveled thousands of kilometers across western North America and documented their migratory behavior, migration routes, stopover areas, and winter and summer ranges. I never intended to be a "virtual" eagle watcher, but watching eagles move long distances over some of the most remote places in North America was certainly exciting. Now, when autumn and spring arrive, I think of the thousands of migratory golden eagles flying across western North America.

I've spent countless hours watching golden eagles in Denali, and I often imagine what an adult golden eagle has experienced throughout its life. These migratory birds have adapted not only to changes on their breeding grounds but also to changes along their migratory routes and on their summer and winter ranges. Recently, I've started to wonder how long these magnificent eagles will grace our skies as changes in habitat and climate occur more rapidly than has ever been recorded. I don't know the answer to that question, but I sincerely hope that our research and ensuing conservation efforts allow many future generations of eagle watchers to see golden eagles soaring over western North America.

Author's Biography

JEFF WATSON watching
for golden eagles in the
Highlands of Scotland.
Photo by Vanessa Watson

Jeff Watson was raised in rural Galloway, southwestern Scotland, where his interest in natural history and birds was inspired by his father, the bird artist and ornithologist Donald Watson. In 1974, Jeff received his BSc in zoology from Aberdeen University and then continued studying at Aberdeen for his PhD, writing his thesis on the Seychelles kestrel and graduating in 1977. After returning from the Seychelles, Jeff began his eagle research career by leading a project on golden eagles and land use in the Scottish Highlands for the Nature Conservancy Council. This became a pioneering study of golden eagles in nine ecological regions, which set the highest of standards for understanding the effects of land uses on raptors. In 1997, T. & A.D. Poyser published Jeff's monograph, *The Golden Eagle*, considered by many to be the authoritative text on this species. Subsequently, Jeff was Director of Operations (North) for Scottish Natural Heritage, the government's conservation advisory body, where he had lead responsibility for the designation, conservation, and management of Scotland's special protection and conservation areas. In 2007, Jeff was awarded the rarely bestowed Royal Society for the Protection of Birds (RSPB) Conservation Medal, in recognition of his work. Jeff passed away on 19 September 2007, at age 54. He is survived by his wife, Vanessa, and son, Ronan.

GOLDEN EAGLE, SCOTLAND

Jeff Watson

There have been some powerful, indeed colorful, characters in the lineage of golden eagle watchers in Scotland down the years. The patriarch must surely be Seton Gordon, a sometime-kilted man with a quaint affection for aristocracy and the *pibroch* (traditional Scottish pipe music) played on misty hillsides. He was a husband to Audrey (who was a gifted natural scientist in her own right), a pioneering pre–World War I nature photographer, and a writer whose accounts of the natural history of eagles have inspired and informed generations of eagle watchers in Scotland and beyond.

Sadly I never met him, though I recall a visit to his home on the Isle of Skye in July 1969, the same month that Neil Armstrong landed on the moon. I was a naive teenager with a passion for birds of prey. It was our last collective "family holiday," and as is typical of Skye, it rained almost every day and the midges were fearsome. My father took me to the house of the great man on an off chance he would be home, but instead we were greeted by a housekeeper, who announced that Mr. Gordon was "away from home" for the day, so we retreated to the pleasure of the rain and the midges on the ridge of Trotternish.

Next in the line of eagle duty comes Adam Watson, a protégé of Seton Gordon's and a child of the Deeside glens whose passion for eagles in the Cairngorm mountains began in the 1930s and continues to this day. A brilliant scientist tutored through the Wynne Edwards school of post–World War II avian ecologists at Aberdeen University, Adam combined pioneering work on the population ecology of red grouse with a passion and depth of knowledge about his native Cairngorms that has no contemporary rival. His field notes on the breeding golden eagles in the central Cairngorms, spanning more than 60 years, is surely the longest unbroken sequence for this species anywhere on the planet.

I owe Adam a huge debt on two counts. As an overconfident and probably rather bumptious graduate student in the early 1970s, I presented a seminar on my doctoral research, held in the infamous "green hut" next to the duck pond at Culterty Field Station (a site in northeastern Scotland frequently used by staff and students of Aberdeen University). My attempts to gloss over the shortcomings of some very basic data capture and analysis, and to move on to the exciting and meaty bit of my undoubtedly vital and groundbreaking research, were stopped in their tracks by an acid question from a slight man with a long forehead and shaggy white hair with matching unkempt beard. My response was deeply inadequate, the seminar stalled, and I never did get to the groundbreaking bit, but I was humbled in a way that was educative for life. And then some 10 years later we crossed paths and Adam kindly gave me his support and deep wisdom as I began an intensive period of research into the bird that he knew better than anyone else in Scotland. The naivety of the "green hut" experience seemed to have been forgiven.

A third monumental eagle watcher of Scottish stock was the late and incomparable Leslie Brown. His passion for eagles was probably only matched by his love of whisky and his disdain for researchers who failed to write up and publish their findings. He worked for so much of his life in Africa and yet retained an affection for, and knowledge of, his home country and its special bird. The 1964 paper in the ornithological journal *Ibis* by Brown and Watson remains a seminal publication on the species and its relationship to land use. It may be an apocryphal tale, but I love the story of Leslie Brown's singular campaign against pre-war egg collectors. Incensed by the practice, which was still legal in Scotland until 1954, reputation has it that Leslie would take to the hills in late March, armed only with a fountain pen charged with indelible ink. On locating his precious clutches of eagle eggs, his first act was to scribble profanities in large letters on the shell in the confident expectation that this would deter the thieves.

I was lucky enough to meet Leslie Brown just once. He attended the Fifth Pan-African Ornithological Congress at the sumptuous Mahe Beach Hotel in Seychelles in November 1976. I listened in awe to extravagant tales of times spent in pursuit of exotic eagles in Kenya, Tanzania, and Ethiopia. I remember very clearly how he speculated on the probable occurrence of golden eagles in the rugged highlands of Ethiopia, based on occasional sightings he had made of distant dark brown eagles. This conversation came back to me as I later read the accounts of Michel Clouet, who in 1994 was indeed able to confirm breeding by golden eagles in the Bale Mountains of Ethiopia, the most southerly location for the species on earth. But most of all I recall the fierce stare under exaggerated eyebrows that accompanied the words "You must publish, or else all this research is a complete waste of time."

The mantle of Brown and Watson passed most comfortably to Roy Dennis and Roger Broad in the latter part of the twentieth century. Both were adopted Scots drawn to the country through the famous bird observatory on Fair Isle, but had settled in due course in the Highlands. There can be few more observant or sharper eagle watchers than Roy and Roger. Both have extraordinarily rounded field skills, able to identify on sight, sound, or sometimes even just a feather trace, in combination with field craft skills that embraced an enviable ability to scale any crag or tree, and even to construct an eyrie on it if that was required. I have vivid recollections of a wing-tagging trip with Roy to an eagle site in the central Highlands one magical June day. For some reason we elected to do this nest at 3:00 a.m., and en route to visit a brood of fat merlins. There is a special feeling to be back at the car by 6:00 a.m., with the knowledge that most of the world is still sleeping and you have tagged a couple of eagle chicks and banded the brood of merlins for good measure.

Roger included me in the most illuminating of all my golden eagle nest site visits in the summer of 1982. At a site on the Ardnamurchan peninsula near the western edge of the Scottish mainland we were to band a couple of 6-week-old eaglets. The nest was a midden, with carcasses of grouse and rabbit interspersed with a couple of dozen other items, almost every one of them something different. There was the skin of an adder, wing feathers of a kestrel, a merlin, and a peregrine, spines of a hedgehog, a meadow pipit, a herring gull, the foot of a raven, and a complete nestling hooded crow. Although this was almost the first golden eagle nest I had visited, it remains to this day quite the most diverse collection of material I have ever found at a single site. Some decade and a half later I followed up the diet work that began at this site with a wide-ranging analysis of eagle breeding performance as a function of the diversity of diet. What this analysis showed was that to be successful, eagles were much better off adopting a strategy of concentrated hunting on two or three key species, and, certainly at the population level, where the diet was extremely diverse, the overall breeding performance was markedly poorer than where diet was narrow. I'm tempted to think that the experience of this 1982 nest visit sowed the seeds of an investigation of diet that bore fruit some 15 years later.

With this legacy it is tempting to believe that all would now be well with the golden eagle in Scotland. Certainly some of the historical pressures have eased, and there is little doubt that the size of the population today (about 440 pairs) is substantially larger than at its low point around 1940 (about 150 pairs perhaps). The worst excesses of egg collectors have been curbed, though I can recall even as recently as the late 1980s witnessing a nest robbery in broad daylight. Some of the concerns that we had over the condition of eagle habitat in Scotland in the 1970s and 1980s, such as the rapid and uncontrolled expansion of alien conifer plantations over large swathes of the

Scottish uplands, have diminished as government policy has responded to public criticism. But two major concerns still remain as a challenge to the well-being of this regal bird. In large chunks of eastern Scotland the land is managed for red grouse that are shot as driven game each autumn. It is abundantly clear, as eloquently demonstrated in the recent scientific literature, that the illegal killing of eagles continues in many places where grouse moor management occurs. I find it a depressing indictment of my fellow countrymen that some who work these moors pay such little heed to the laws of the land.

In western Scotland, geography has spared the eagles the pleasure of managed grouse as a near neighbor—the climate is generally too wet to lead to large numbers of this sporting bird. But there remains an insidious threat that is also linked to the management of the land for game. Here the principal game interest is stalking for red deer. In huge areas of these western uplands the numbers of deer are well above anything that could be remotely described as sustainable. The consequence is that other smaller herbivores that are part of the natural fauna of these hills have, in places, been reduced almost to extinction. As a result, eagles throughout much of western Scotland are apparently present in healthy numbers that are sustained by an overabundant supply of deer carrion. Nevertheless, these same birds find little to eat in the summer when they need small herbivores such as grouse and hares to feed their growing young. As a result their breeding performance is remarkably low, and in some years I have found fewer than 10% of breeding attempts successful.

It is thus that there remain two challenges for the successors to Seton Gordon, Leslie Brown, and Adam Watson. First, they must persuade managers of game in the Scottish uplands to squeeze out their compatriots who flout the legal protection of our precious raptors. Second, they must begin to accept and address profoundly and effectively the massive biological degradation that is being caused to these hills by excessive numbers of red deer. Only then will modern threats facing Scottish eagles be addressed, leaving the birds free to persist and be viewed by future generations of eagle watchers.

4

Lesser Spotted Eagle

COMMON NAME: Lesser spotted eagle

SCIENTIFIC NAME: *Aquila (Lophaetus) pomarina*

OTHER NAMES: None

IUCN CONSERVATION STATUS: *Least Concern (population declining)*

DESCRIPTION: A small to medium-sized eagle, nearly entirely brown, although preadult stages are heavily spotted. Head and bill small in comparison to similar species. Long legs are feathered down to the toes. Frequently observed walking on the ground.

SIZE: Length: 55–67 cm (22–27 in); Wingspan: 146–168 cm (57–67 in); Weight: 1.2–2.2 kg (2.2–4.9 lb)

THREATS: Many individuals are shot during migration, and habitat loss is also causing population declines.

DISTRIBUTION: Lesser spotted eagles breed throughout much of central and eastern Europe; some of the highest-density populations are in Latvia, Belarus, Slovakia, and Poland. The species is also found throughout much of Asia Minor and the Caucasus. Lesser spotted eagles are highly migratory; all populations migrate to southern and central Africa. A disjunct Indian population is found in central India; some authors now consider this a separate species (*A. hastata*).

MOVEMENTS: All populations are highly migratory and make long-distance movements to Africa.

HABITAT: Lesser spotted eagles are a bird of moist lowland and mountain forests. During winter they occur in wet woodland areas, often found with other species of eagles.

DIET: Mammals, birds, insects, amphibians, reptiles. During winter, lesser spotted eagles eat elate termites.

NOTES: Recent research has demonstrated that in the Baltic states, Belarus and Poland, this species regularly hybridizes with the greater spotted eagle. This behavior is thought to be unique among wild eagle populations.

Author's Biography

Bernd-U. Meyburg attaching a satellite transmitter to a steppe eagle in Saudi Arabia. Photo by Christiane Meyburg

While playing in woods when he was 14 years old, Bernd Meyburg discovered a black kite's nest and studied the birds intensively, work that culminated in two scientific publications before he left school in 1966. During his studies of medicine and zoology at the Free University Berlin, Bernd spent a great deal of time traveling internationally to study raptors, as his home city of Berlin was surrounded by the Eastern Bloc and cut off from the surrounding countryside. These studies concerned the lesser spotted eagle in Slovakia, the Spanish imperial eagle and the black vulture in Spain, the Madagascar serpent eagle and Madagascar fish eagle, and the Javan hawk-eagle in Indonesia. When the Iron Curtain fell in 1989, Bernd was able to expand his studies, to include work on the lesser and greater spotted eagles, eastern imperial eagle, steppe and short-toed eagles, ospreys, red and black kites, and honey buzzards. To date he has authored over 120 publications on raptors. Since 1982, Bernd has been Chair of the World Working Group on Birds of Prey (WWGBP), which he has developed into a global network of raptor specialists. Together with his colleague Robin Chancellor, Bernd has organized several world raptor conferences in Israel, Spain, Germany, South Africa, and Hungary. He also served a term as an International Director of the Raptor Research Foundation.

LESSER SPOTTED EAGLE, CZECHOSLOVAKIA
AND GERMANY

Bernd-U. Meyburg

I had already become preoccupied with raptors for two of my schoolboy years when, in 1964, I came across a small book about the lesser spotted eagle. Two aspects of the biology of this species immediately fascinated me: the so-called Cain and Abel struggle (also known as "cainism," whereby the eldest chick kills its younger sibling), and the species' lengthy migration routes. The author, Dr. Victor Wendland, who is still the only person to have written a monograph on this species, had already established in the 1930s that the lesser spotted eagle normally lays two eggs, that two chicks usually hatch, but that only one young bird fledges.

I was interested not only in how and why cainism occurred, but also in the question as to whether this phenomenon could be used to protect this endangered species. This was proposed by preventing the death of the younger sibling, thereby doubling the reproductive rate of the breeding pair.

The lesser spotted eagle was once widely distributed in Germany but, over the twentieth century, its local breeding range had shrunk to a small region in the northeast of the then German Democratic Republic (GDR), to the north of Berlin. Although the nearest breeding site was only some 50 km (31 mi) away from my flat, it proved impossible to visit. As a resident of West Berlin, all attempts to arrange observation and studies of these birds were unsuccessful. The Cold War was at its height, and West Berlin, surrounded by a Warsaw Pact country, was seen as a particularly bitter enemy of the Eastern Bloc.

Nevertheless I did not give up, and in 1968 I was able to begin eagle observations and experiments in Czechoslovakia instead. I managed to make contact with local raptor specialists and get the necessary permits to visit. I soon made friends with Jan Švehlik from Kosice, and his room in his parents' flat was quickly converted into a laboratory, which we equipped with an incubator so we could artificially hatch the second-laid eggs and hand-rear the chicks.

During this period I continued my field observations of the events leading up to the death of the second chick in the nest. In June 1968 I sat in a tree hide for the first time only some 14 m (46 ft) away from an eyrie occupied by lesser spotted eagles. I was able to observe and photograph the family life of the eagles at close range, a privilege that only few ornithologists before me had experienced.

Our big day came at the beginning of August that year. Two second-hatched chicks, which had been hand-reared in captivity and ringed by me, were returned to their nests in the wild, and they later fledged with their siblings. I observed them for as long and as well as I could after they flew from the nest, wondering whether both young eagles would continue to be cared for by their parents. This proved quickly and happily to be the case. The next question was whether both would be fit enough to survive the long migration to Africa and back.

The political situation in Czechoslovakia became more and more unstable. Two days after my departure, in August 1968, the armies of the Warsaw Pact invaded the country in a world-shattering act of aggression. I was determined not to let anything interfere with my eagle studies, and even though the country was still occupied by the Soviets, I returned in 1969 and continued my observations for the next five years.

By the mid-1970s, relations between East and West Germany had improved somewhat. Thanks to a new regulation, Berliners were permitted to travel to the GDR for up to 24 hours. I immediately searched for lesser spotted eagles to the north of my home city. The trips were restricted to 30 days a year, which my wife and I exploited to the fullest. On each occasion, on both entry to and exit from the GDR, the border guards checked us thoroughly. We were not permitted to take with us many technical aids, such as maps and Dictaphones for recording our observations, but binoculars and telephoto lenses, although regarded with suspicion, were allowed.

One particular pair of lesser spotted eagles offered exceptionally good opportunities for observation, and my wife and I took full advantage of this. We spent many hundreds of hours observing the pair from a few hundred meters away, and we collected data on the time of the eagles' arrival in spring, display behavior, nest-building, hunting for food, behavior toward other species, and so on. It was particularly helpful that this pair almost always bred in the same eyrie, whereas many other pairs changed their nest annually.

These frequent trips into the GDR raised the suspicion of the East German authorities, even though I had many contacts with GDR ornithologists, including the director of the East Berlin Zoo. What I had always suspected was later confirmed in an alarming way. The Stasi (the GDR secret intelligence service) had been intensively occupied with my case and had put my activities under the microscope. Not only was my telephone tapped, but agents were sent to my place of work in West Berlin and took photographs there.

Many years later I was allowed to see my Stasi file, which was 900 pages long! My trips into the GDR had been recorded in minute detail, and all my movements within the country had been monitored. Agents had followed me in their vehicles for days and had kept me under close observation. Over a dozen ornithologists were asked to report on my activities, including members of my closest circle of friends and acquaintances. The Stasi suspected me of being a military spy and believed that my ornithological interest was just a cover story. Their theory fitted in well with my equipment, which included binoculars, telescope, and telephoto lens.

It took the Stasi 10 years to finally conclude that I was indeed just a harmless ornithologist. I had to grin when I read page-long discussions about why, for example, I no longer traveled into the GDR from mid- to end-September onward. They were at first worried that perhaps the checks at the border were too rigorous and were putting me off. Finally they came to the correct conclusion that the autumn migration of the eagles was the real reason.

The year 1989 signaled political change and the end of the GDR, an important and decisive moment in my life. I found one incident particularly moving. On 3 October 1990, the official date of German reunification, Dr. Vladimir Galushin, a well-known Russian raptor specialist, appeared unannounced on my doorstep. He had been sent from Moscow to East Berlin with an official delegation. However, he saw no point in speaking to representatives of a regime that would no longer exist the next day, so he made his way on foot to my home. He was particularly impressed by the fact that the state border he crossed in the morning would, after midnight, no longer exist. We spent the evening together at the official reunification celebrations in front of the German Reichstag.

During the final months of the GDR regime there were no more political restrictions to research on the lesser spotted eagle. Telemetry studies, unthinkable up until then, were suddenly possible. As early as the summer of 1990 I was able to fit the first young lesser spotted eagle with a transmitter. A large project, with conventional (VHF) telemetry of adult birds began in 1991. In the years that followed I spent countless hours with the receiver antenna in my hand searching for and observing the eagles. The result was the first such study of the size of the eagles' home ranges and use of habitat.

At almost the same time, an old dream of mine, research into the migration of the lesser spotted eagle to southern Africa using satellite telemetry, came closer to being realized. Transmitters had now become more and more miniaturized and finally reached a size and weight that enabled them to be fitted to this medium-sized eagle. In 1992 the great moment came. I fitted the first nestling with a transmitter weighing 50 g (1.8 oz). The eagle sadly lost its way in Greece and did not reach the Bosphorus, the route which we now know the lesser spotted eagle normally uses to reach Asia Minor. The migration of two young eagles with transmitters the following year was also dogged by bad luck, both birds being shot down over Lebanon. One of the transmitters was returned to us with a piece of lead shot lodged in it.

This confirmed our worst fears: that young eagles suffered a high mortality rate during their migration. There was only one solution, namely, the fitting of transmitters to adult birds. In 1994 I was able to fit transmitters to the first four adult eagles in Germany and Slovakia. In one case it was possible to document the eagle's complete migration to Zambia, its overwintering there, and its spring migration back to its breeding territory in Germany. Luck played a big part here as the transmitters were still battery powered. This meant that they had to be programmed to be active only for several hours every few days in order to extend the battery life to almost a year. This complete documentation of the annual route of a European migrant was the first of its kind.

In the following years, transmitters with solar power came on the market. These supplied considerably more data and remained active for up to seven years. This meant that not only could the eagles' migration routes be documented in more detail, but also the routes taken in different years could be compared. This made it possible to identify the eagles' overwintering areas in Africa. According to our telemetry data, many of the eagles were overwintering in Zambia and Southern Africa, and I could not resist the temptation to travel down there to watch the birds up close.

As the population of the lesser spotted eagle continues to decline in Germany and beyond, because of birds being shot and otherwise lost during migration (mainly in the Middle East) and destruction of breeding habitat (e.g., cutting of old forest, agricultural intensification), my previous experience of thwarting cainism came to the fore again. In 2004 two young lesser spotted eagles flew from an eyrie located to the north of Berlin in Brandenburg. One of them had been captive-reared in a conservation station with a common buzzard as its foster parent, before being returned to its eagle nest to fledge.

My old question still remained unanswered though. Were these rescued birds fit enough to migrate to southern Africa and back? In 2005 we got our answer. I had color-ringed the young eaglet in the summer of 2004, and the bird was subsequently observed by another ornithologist in the spring of 2005. This ornithologist recorded the bird's ring details and sent this information to me. The young eagle had returned to the vicinity of its birthplace after only a year. The proverbial needle in the haystack had been found; this eagle, at least, had proved itself fit enough to endure the long migrations and had returned to its natal area.

As a result, another second-born eaglet was also captive-reared in 2005 and was put back in the eyrie with its sibling just before the former flew the nest. It soon became clear that considerably more second-hatched young eagles must be hand-reared every year in order to ensure that the population remains sustainable. In 2004–2008, 26 second-born eaglets fledged from eyries in Germany using this technique. Since 2007, additional Abels were translocated from Latvia (as many as 13 in 2009). Satellite tracking of these individuals demonstrated that, in most cases, they followed the migration route as the German-born birds.

In recent years, new satellite transmitters with an in-built global positioning system (GPS) have transformed our lives. Now my wife and I can check via the Internet not only our eagles' daily movements during their migration period, but also the location of birds that have returned to their breeding territories. Part of our current research is the evaluation of eagle habitat use by means of digital maps and air and satellite photographs. This means spending even more time on the computer and using increasingly complicated technology. Our eagle-watching techniques of the past, armed with binoculars and notebook, dodging the secret police in the GDR, and the techniques we use today are worlds apart. Our eagle watching is no longer restricted by governmental regimes as we can now "watch" our birds from the safety of our home as they migrate over many political boundaries.

5

Wedge-tailed Eagle

COMMON NAME: Wedge-tailed eagle

SCIENTIFIC NAME: *Aquila audax*

OTHER NAMES: Eaglehawk

IUCN CONSERVATION STATUS: *Least Concern (overall population stable; Tasmanian race threatened)*

DESCRIPTION: Large, lean eagle with long, relatively narrow wings; and long, distinctively diamond-shaped tail. Legs fully feathered, with longish feathers on the upper leg that give a "baggy" legged look. Small head and relatively large bill. Plumage dark brown with lighter brown on head and neck; adults, especially males, mostly black.

SIZE: Length: 85–105 cm (33–42 in); Wingspan: 185–230 cm (72–91 in); Weight: 2.0–5.3 kg (4.4–11.6 lb). Females noticeably larger than males.

THREATS: Habitat loss, particularly in Tasmania, is a problem. Sometimes killed by humans who mistakenly view the species as a serious threat to livestock. Vehicle collisions.

DISTRIBUTION: Wedge-tailed eagles breed in Australia, Tasmania, and southern Papua-New Guinea.

MOVEMENTS: Nonmigratory; juveniles may disperse long distances.

HABITAT: Found in a variety of habitats, from mountain forest to almost tree-less plains, except intensively cultivated areas. Hunts mainly in open areas, but also in forest.

DIET: Large and medium-sized mammals (especially introduced European rabbits), birds, and reptiles, as well as carrion.

NOTES: This species is known, on occasion, to attack intruding hang gliders, fixed-wing aircraft, and helicopters that stray too close to the eagle's territory.

Author's Biography

PENNY OLSEN beside
Lake Burley Griffin in her
hometown of Canberra,
Australia. Photo by
Elizabeth Hawkes

Penny Olsen grew up in Melbourne, Washington, DC, and Canberra. After finishing a BSc degree in Canberra, she joined CSIRO (Australia's Commonwealth Scientific and Industrial Research Organization) and spent 12 years working first on the biology of water rats and later on the impact of predation on mouse abundance. Though work on rodents may sound far from scintillating, she found the water rat a most beautiful creature, and a nifty hunter of fish, shellfish, large aquatic insects, and the odd bird. Accumulating evidence of the impacts of organochlorine pesticides on raptors helped to galvanize her interest in that group. What began as a hobby became a vocation. For a blissful but brief dozen years from the late 1980s, when she received a PhD scholarship, followed by two years of postdoctoral work and a three-year fellowship, she was funded to work on raptors. Penny has prepared a number of recovery plans, is a long-time consultant to the Australian Government's (endangered) Norfolk Island owl recovery program, and works as an occasional consultant on other matters of national environmental interest. She serves on the Birds of Australia Research and Conservation Committee, represents that organization on the New South Wales Natural Resources Advisory Council, and is a member of the Australian Capital Territory's Flora and Fauna Committee—the latter two being ministerial committees. Penny has published a number of research papers, books, and popular articles on a diversity of subjects including raptors, the history of bird art, conservation biology, and pest management. Her latest books are *Wedge-tailed Eagle* (CSIRO Publishing, 2005) and *Glimpses of Paradise: The Quest for the Beautiful Parrakeet* (National Library of Australia, 2007). Currently, she is a Visiting Fellow in the School of Botany and Zoology at The Australian National University, where she supervises postgraduate students, none of them, alas, studying raptors.

WEDGE-TAILED EAGLE, AUSTRALIA

Penny Olsen

Near Canberra, Australia's capital, wedge-tailed eagles nest on the gentle hillsides and hunt in the valleys below. They also build in large gum trees along the rivers, where there is rarely a scarcity of prey in this otherwise drought-prone country. Over the years the species has quietly found its way into the outer suburbs, nesting in bushland within several hundred meters of houses. When I first started studying raptors, some 30 years ago, this would have been unthinkable. We all believed that after so many years of persecution the survivors had been selected to be wary of humans. For, until the 1970s, the wedge-tailed eagle was arguably the most persecuted of all raptors. Australia grew on the sheep's back, and the eagles were perceived to threaten that industry. Between 1958 and 1967, bounties were paid on an average of 13,000 eagles a year, and that was in just two of the seven states, Queensland and Western Australia. In 1969 alone, the estimated toll was 30,000 nationally. Even their smaller cousin, the little eagle, and the whistling kite, known (incorrectly) to some as the whistling eagle, suffered in the slaughter, though neither have any hope of killing a healthy lamb.

By the late 1970s the heartbreaking sight of 20 or so eagle bodies strung along a fence-line was becoming rare. Such displays were claimed to deter other eagles, but were more likely the macho posturings of landowners. The conservation era had begun, and eagles were given the full protection of the law. Research in the preceding decade had confirmed that eagles took a tiny minority of viable lambs, instead feeding on the dead or dying, a fact that their defenders had been repeating all along. They had been the scapegoat for poor husbandry, normal losses, or other farmer frustrations. So, in the late 1980s, when we first noticed eagles infiltrating the bushland suburbs, we were delighted. It was a sign of increasing tolerance, by both eagles and humans.

Still, it was surprising how few people noticed the eagles' bulky nests, here overlooking a freeway, or there in an open woodland fringing homes. The huge structures—a drayload of branches strong enough to hold a person—are often the product of many years of labor. The old, sheltered nests can become massive constructions, some reaching 2 m (6.6 ft) across and 3 m (9.8 ft) deep with over 400 kg (882 lb) of wood. Even a brand new nest—an unruly stack on the robust, forked branch of a sturdy tree—is hardly a modest structure.

For the experienced researcher-climber, scaling such a tree to reach an eagle's nest is the easy part, provided care is taken with the notoriously brittle eucalypt branches. The hard part is getting up and around the nest to access it—rather like conquering an overhang when ascending a cliff. The adult eagles usually disappear at the first sign of intrusion, and the nestlings tend to lie flattened in the nest, hoping to go unnoticed. Larger eaglets occasionally put up some pretense of a fight—mouth open in warning, they lean back and present their impressive, oversized feet. But they are clumsy and uncertain, so, despite their size and weaponry, when handled efficiently, with feet secured, they are quite easily scooped into a bag. It was usually my job to receive the hessian bag—lowered by rope—measure and band the bird, and send it aloft again. Often, as the sack descended, I could see several scimitar-like black talons piercing the fabric, a warning that the contents were to be respected.

At the base of the nest trees, we often contemplated the scattering of castings—the great wads of regurgitated fur that bind fragments of rabbits, skinks, and birds and speak of struggles lost to eagles. I have never been present when an eagle made a kill, nor have I seen a pair or group hunting cooperatively. Others, though, have told me of how the great birds take turns swooping at or striking the victim, a large kangaroo or dingo, until it is exhausted and easily overcome. Nor have I watched these versatile hunters snatch a possum from its dray in a large forest tree. Alas, I have only seen eagles with "prey" as many other Australians have, feeding on roadside carrion. However, I was fortunate enough to witness an exciting theft from a noisily protesting brown falcon frantically clutching a young rabbit. The eagle coolly tailed the smaller raptor until it was so panicked that it dropped the bunny. The exchange was over within seconds.

On one memorable occasion, my colleague Tony Ross and I were standing beside our boat, a few paces from a flock of wood ducks resting prone along the riverbank, seemingly unfazed by our recent arrival. The sound of wind rushing over taut wings reached us seconds before a huge dark form sped over from behind, its draught ruffling the hair on our heads. The backs of our necks bristled. Almost in sequence, the line of ducks tipped their bodies and fell the half meter or so into the water—*plop, plop, plop, plop*. Looking up we saw a large black eagle sweep on between the trees and up through the canopy, empty-footed. Of course, we had been in no danger—the eagle had simply used us as a diversion—but we had a brief intimation of what it might be like to be targeted as prey.

Once, I was there when an adult female took advantage of a lapse in concentration by her handler and drove her talons through the first body part she could grab. As so often happens, this was a hand. Her hind talon slipped over the thumbnail and into the quick. We failed to pry open her feet and pull her off—that only made her grip tighten automatically—so, instead we encouraged her to relax. By the time she released him, the handler was faint from the shock. Such is the impact of these mighty birds even on experienced researchers. It was a sharp reminder that nature must be respected, especially when it takes the form of an eagle with a vice-like grip.

The eagle's foot also features in a number of Australian Aboriginal morality tales. Some were recorded by Daisy Bates, a tiny Irishwoman who, in the early 1900s, took it upon herself to study the disappearing customs, dialects, and legends of several western and southern indigenous groups. One story relates how Warragunna the eaglehawk betrayed his hunting companions. The penalty was death, and as a cautionary sign to all, his foot became the four-pointed star cluster known as the Southern Cross. To other Aboriginal tribes the Southern Cross is the eagle itself flung up into the heavens. That great austral constellation has guided humans for eons as they navigated the southern half of the globe, and it is fitting that local mythology portrays it as having eagle origins.

Anyone who has worked with eagles has the same deep awe and respect for these birds of earth and ether. Australia's wedge-tailed eagle might struggle, full-cropped from a fly-encrusted roadkill, lolloping along in a most ungainly manner to become airborne, but within minutes it transforms into a majestic creature that spirals effortlessly heavenward to soar watchfully over its domain. Long may eagles live beside us unmolested, long may they adapt to our altered landscapes, long may they hold a place in this increasingly humanized world.

6

Madagascar Serpent Eagle

COMMON NAME: Madagascar serpent eagle

SCIENTIFIC NAME: *Eutriorchis astur*

OTHER NAMES: Madagascar forest eagle, long-tailed serpent eagle

IUCN CONSERVATION STATUS: *Endangered (once thought Extinct; population may be currently declining)*

DESCRIPTION: A small "accipiter-like" snake eagle with broad short wings and a long, rounded tail. Back is dark brown and breast is white, heavily streaked with brown, sometimes appearing brown with white flecks. Has a small crest on the back of its head and a short bill.

SIZE: Length: 57–66 cm (22–26 in); Wingspan: 98–110 cm (36–44 in); Weight: 700–1000 g (1.5–2.2 lb)

THREATS: Habitat loss from slash-and-burn agriculture and sometimes persecution by humans

DISTRIBUTION: Madagascar (northeastern and central-east; endemic)

MOVEMENTS: Nonmigratory, apparently does not disperse far (limited to Madagascar).

HABITAT: Broadleaf evergreen forests, most frequently primary rainforest, although sometimes seen in secondary forest. Occurs from sea level to 1200 m (3937 ft).

DIET: Reptiles, especially lizards (chameleons and geckos), and frogs of a variety of types

NOTES: This species was, for about 60 years, thought to be extinct. It is severely threatened by habitat loss and persecution. It is often confused with species that threaten domestic fowl and is killed by people who think they are protecting their flocks.

Author's Biography

SARAH KARPANTY taking a break while surveying migrating raptors in West Virginia, United States. Photo courtesy of the author

Sarah Karpanty was born and raised in Toledo, Ohio, and has been chasing eagles and other elusive birds since her high school biology teacher took her on a birding field trip, just over 14 years ago. After completing her undergraduate degree at Miami University, Sarah moved directly to State University of New York, Stony Brook, to study for her PhD on raptors and lemurs in Madagascar, under the supervision of Patricia Wright and Charles Janson. Sarah is currently an assistant professor at Virginia Tech in Blacksburg, Virginia, where she spends her free time hiking and biking in the Appalachian Mountains. She continues to study Malagasy raptors and their lemur prey.

Loret Rasabo, mentioned in this story, is still an active tourist and research guide in the region of Ranomafana National Park in eastern Madagascar. Tongavelona Justin, the village president mentioned here, has passed away. However, his desire to reforest abandoned farmland with native trees is being carried on by his wife, son, and many other village residents.

MADAGASCAR SERPENT EAGLE, MADAGASCAR

Sarah Karpanty

I landed in Madagascar in August 1997, a young, green college senior on a mission to study the predator-prey relationship between the raptors and lemurs of southeast Madagascar. For many years, primatologists had documented strong antipredator reactions of lemurs to several species of raptors, including the Madagascar buzzard, Madagascar harrier-hawk, and Henst's goshawk. Yet, despite vigorous alarm calls and avoidance behaviors by many lemur species at the sight of a large raptor, there had been no observed instances of predation on the larger, diurnal lemurs. Some scientists had hypothesized that today's day-living lemurs experienced no predation by raptors, but that their vigorous antipredator responses were "evolutionary remnants," or behaviors left over from the not so distant past (500 to 1000 years ago) when two large eagle species roamed Madagascar. Those two eagles are now extinct and are known only from their subfossil remains.

If any primatologist had seen a Madagascar serpent eagle recently, they might have also observed lemurs giving loud aerial alarm barks, dropping low in the canopy, and high-tailing it away as fast as they were able, as they do when encountering the other large raptors. However, I imagined then that few lemurs, and even fewer scientists, had seen this elusive eagle. The Madagascar serpent eagle is one of the most rarely seen raptors in the world. This secretive, primarily sub-canopy eagle was believed to be extinct until a series of papers in the mid-1990s presented conclusive evidence of its continued existence in the northeastern rainforests of Madagascar. A Malagasy/American research team from The Peregrine Fund provided the irrefutable evidence of the eagle's presence by discovering a nest of the serpent eagle in the Masoala Peninsula and by capturing, photographing, and radio-tracking an adult serpent eagle in the mid-1990s.

When I began my studies of predation on lemurs by raptors, I didn't plan on considering the possible impact of the Madagascar serpent eagle on lemur populations. After all, the Masoala Peninsula, in the northernmost part of Madagascar, was the only location holding this rare raptor, certainly a species that, although no longer "extinct," was not abundant. Or was it more common than we thought?

During my first six months in Madagascar, I experienced many things in common with other tropical eagle biologists—giardia, heat exhaustion, homesickness, to name a few. I also fell in love with the beauty and intrigue of Madagascar as well as the kindhearted and generous Malagasy people. Somehow, I managed to have some extra time to witness something that no other raptor biologist or primatologist had been lucky enough to observe. I saw Henst's goshawks and Madagascar harrier-hawks feeding lemurs of all sizes to their young chicks, ranging from the tiny 32 g (1.1 oz) mouse lemur to the nearly 3500 g (7.7 lb) Verreaux's sifaka. Those lemurs knew what they were barking about and running from after all, and they just needed a biologist to sit and watch a raptor's nest to prove it!

After this initial confirmation that lemurs had something to fear from the large raptors of Madagascar, as well as a fairly deep hypnosis with the magical nature of the island, I decided to visit several parks in the eastern rainforests to pick out the best site for a long-term project, one with lots of raptors and a diversity of lemur species. I left for an austral summer expedition with one of Madagascar's most famous local bird guides, Loret Rasabo, with a pack on my back, a rented four-wheel-drive truck, a tape-player, and a suite of cassette tapes with raptor vocalizations that had been recorded by other raptor researchers in Madagascar. The plan was to conduct systematic surveys of the raptor communities at several rainforest sites in central and southeastern Madagascar by walking 5 km (3 mi) long straight-line transects through pristine and disturbed forest while broadcasting the calls of different raptor species every 800 me (.5 mi). Many raptors are territorial, and if they hear the calls of other raptors of the same or different species, they will come closer to check out the intruder. My goal was to use the tapes to lure the raptors to defend their territories and make their presence known so that I could estimate population densities of the birds in different potential study sites.

I was skeptical about using a recording of the serpent eagle as this rare bird was confined to the northern regions of Madagascar, and I was about to survey areas nearly 1287 km (800 mi) to the south. Then, one evening while sitting around a blazing campfire on a freezing cold July night, I played the serpent eagle cassette to Loret to help pass the quiet night hours. That is when the hunt began.

I didn't tell Loret what vocalizations I was about to play. It was the night before we were going to begin our first acoustic-based survey, and I thought that I would "quiz" him. I say "quiz" because Loret really was, and always will be, my professor of Malagasy ornithology. I was normally the one being tested. Loret spent his childhood, and is now raising his own family, in Ranomafana, a small rainforest village in the southeastern part of the island. His childhood fascination with wildlife, especially birds, positioned him to excel in his current role as expert guide and ornithologist. As we hugged the fire that evening, Loret quickly recognized and identified the vocalizations of the Madagascar buzzard, harrier-hawk, and Henst's goshawk. As soon as I played the vocalization of the serpent eagle, a froglike *koua, koua, koua* followed by *wah, wah, wah,* he froze and asked to what species that call belonged. When I told him the Madagascar serpent eagle, he was in excited disbelief. Several years before, he had seen a large "goshawk-like" bird dive in a predation attempt (unsuccessfully) into a group of Milne-Edward's sifaka lemurs in Ranomafana National Park, but there was something about that bird that did not mesh with a Henst's goshawk identification. He also had previously heard the strange vocalization that I had just played, but had never observed the creature making it and so could not put the visual and auditory sightings together. Playing this cassette had just solved a mystery for Loret, and opened one for me. We crawled into our tents that night determined to start incorporating the serpent eagle vocalizations into our survey routes the next morning in case Loret's suspicions, and my hopes, were correct. We were determined to find a serpent eagle in central and southeastern Madagascar if one existed, or exhaust ourselves trying.

What ensued from that casual "quiz" over the fire was a seven-year-and-counting search for signs, and potentially nests, of the Madagascar serpent eagle south of its previously known range in the northern region of the island. In our first three months of survey work, we focused our efforts in both pristine and secondary rainforest in two national parks in central and southeastern Madagascar. The long-term search was fueled, and continues to be sustained, by our early success. During those first three months, our search could be described in general as follows:

Week 1–3: Wow, I didn't know that the rainforest could be so quiet! Are there any raptors out there? We have walked over 300 km [186 mi] in transects and seen very few raptors!

Week 4: Loret and my students are sick with malaria. The winter time is the worst for recurrent malaria, which becomes as common as the common cold during this cool, rainy time of the year. I try to do my best without them, and do find some buzzards, an occasional goshawk and harrier-hawk.

Week 5: Woken up one morning this week at 04:15 to a "koua, koua" call. I think that it is the eagle, but I am so tired and cold that I can't even be sure where the door to my tent is located. I thrash around wildly, finally get it open, stumble out in into the muddy camp centre and collide with my pajama-wearing guides as we stumble into the clearing, bleary-eyed to see a large raptor fly away. Together, we were awoken by the same call, saw the same large bird fly away, but to all of us it seems like an apparition. Loret chased the "ghost-like" bird, but could not catch up to get a positive identification.

Week 6–10: The ghost-bird is still on our mind. We doubt that it is real since we have seen no sign of a serpent eagle since then. We are happy with our findings of the nests of the other raptor species, but we remain vigilant and hopeful.

Week 11: It is 6 pm on a Wednesday. I think about how back home, Wednesday is "hump day," a fictitious weekly holiday celebrating the approach of the weekend. Out here in the middle of Ranomafana National Park, it is just another day to celebrate the sunrise and sunset. Weekdays and weekends are meaningless. I am bathing by a remote river site. There is a simple rule: everyone else stays in camp until I come back fully clothed and give the all-is-clear sign. Remote field camps are self-policed and almost always are the most orderly, cleanest, and best managed social systems around. When you are in the wilderness, survival depends on mutual trust and respect, which is too valuable to betray by sloppiness or rudeness. I look up. Yes, I am staring at a serpent eagle perched down river approximately 100 m [328 ft] away. There is no doubt. This is an area that we had been hearing the vocalization on previous days, but had not confirmed it with a visual sighting. I threw a towel around myself and went tearing back into camp, grabbed my camera, confused (but luckily didn't expose myself to) my guides, and went running back down to the river. I got a short video clip of a serpent eagle rump as it flew away. Unfortunately the film was not enough to confirm the identity of the bird. The search continues.

In Toledo, Ohio, where I was raised, some people may call our search for the serpent eagle a "wild goose chase." During that wild summer eagle chase, however, we managed to make multiple positive visual and auditory identifications of the bird. These sightings, though few and far between, expanded the known range of this eagle from 17° to 21° latitude, as well as documented the serpent eagle not only in pristine rainforest but also in secondary rainforest that had been previously logged by humans. In short, it taught us that there was a lot still to be learned about these eagles and encouraged us to keep looking for them in previously undocumented areas.

In the course of our surveys that summer, we decided to focus our research efforts in Ranomafana National Park because it was home to a large number and high density of raptor and lemur species. We focused the last month of our efforts on finding nests of the raptors that I could study for the long term. We found 10 nests of the same three species of birds that I had studied in southern Madagascar. For one species, the Madagascar harrier-hawk, we found only one nest, located outside of the park boundaries on the edge of a small, subsistence farming village. In fact, 5 of 10 nests were outside of the formal park boundaries, a result most likely of local knowledge being closest to home, not in the difficult, trail-less park terrain. Before returning to the United States for graduate school responsibilities, I spoke with the villagers who lived around the harrier-hawk nest about the plans for the project. I asked them that if possible, would they not cut down the harrier-hawk nest-tree if they needed to convert more land to agriculture using slash-and-burn techniques. They agreed.

I returned to Madagascar just over two months later after completing some required coursework. My team and I reunited and set off to check the status of the nests that we had discovered earlier. The picture that developed was disheartening at best. Within a week, we found that 4 of the 10 nest-trees had been cut down in the process of clearing forest for subsistence-level agriculture. I don't blame the farmers for cutting down the nest-trees to make farmland; by no means do they have excess of anything, let alone food! We were not hopeful as we walked the 10 km (6.2 mi) from the road to check the final nest, the only nest of the harrier-hawk that we had discovered. As we crested the final hill, I sighed when I saw a field of black charcoal. My worst fears had been confirmed. Every single nest-tree that we had discovered outside of the national park boundary had been cut and burned in just a two-month period.

Then, something in the middle of the charcoal field caught my eye. There was a bare tree still standing, and in it was the harrier-hawk nest, now with three chicks. The villagers had taken me literally, they had invested a tremendous amount of effort in creating a fire-break around that single tree, and it had not been cut down. Sadly, the chicks did not survive that season. Without the cooling effect of surrounding forest, they literally baked in the hot subtropical sun. As a trained scientist, I am normally very good at separating facts from emotions. But that night I cried because my emotions could not separate themselves from the cold, hard facts that I had just observed.

When I awoke the next morning, I allowed myself no more time for raw emotions, it was time to act. I set out with my team to talk to the president of the harrier-hawk village about what had happened. In my head, I couldn't help but wonder what it meant for the health of the larger ecosystem when 50% of a known predator population is lost in just two months. Yes, I allowed the environmental doomsday scenarios to resonate throughout my head during the hot hike to the village. I had a plan though. If the local villagers need to cut down some trees to make farmland, then we would just plant native trees on fallow land to make up the difference. Fight deforestation with reforestation.

When we arrived at the village, I didn't even have a chance to pitch my grand scheme to the village president, Tonga. He told me that he was angry about the incident too, and that he wanted to talk to me about his idea to reforest areas of old farmland with trees having multiple uses to his villagers, including providing fruits, construction materials, and medicines. He recognized that there was very little forest left outside of the national park, and he was worried about the future of his farming community. He also mentioned that in his belief system, the ancestral spirits reside in the forest and that this was an equally important reason to plant new trees, so that they would not be destroying the spiritual resting grounds.

It was a meeting of like minds. That day we sealed our partnership by offering the local rum, *tokagasy*, and a leaf-full of honey to the ancestral spirits. Now, seven years later, I have worked with the villagers to plant over 20,000 trees on fallow farmland around their village bordering the national park. We continue to hunt for the elusive serpent eagle and to study the other birds of prey in the area, always hopeful that someday we will find that eagle nest and watch its chicks take flight over a forested boundary between park and village that even an eagle eye cannot detect.

7
Bald Eagle

COMMON NAME: Bald eagle

SCIENTIFIC NAME: *Haliaeetus leucocephalus*

OTHER NAMES: White-headed eagle, white-headed sea eagle, American eagle

IUCN CONSERVATION STATUS: *Least Concern (population increasing)*

DESCRIPTION: A large brown fish eagle with long, broad wings and a short, rounded tail. In adult plumage bald eagles have a striking white head and tail; juveniles are dark throughout, often with light spotting.

SIZE: Length: 70–90 cm (28–36 in); Wingspan: 180–230 cm (71–91 in); Weight: 2.5–6.3 kg (5.5–14 lb)

THREATS: Historically threatened by DDT poisoning. At present most populations are increasing. Habitat loss, mercury, and lead poisoning may be the greatest current threats.

DISTRIBUTION: North America—United States and Canada, throughout; parts of northern Mexico

MOVEMENTS: Most populations in interior northern latitudes (>46°N) are migratory; mid-latitude populations are generally nonmigratory. In winter, large groups often gather near large bodies of open water and abundant food sources.

HABITAT: Breeds and forages primarily near water, although especially in winter is often found far from water. Nests are often placed in large trees overlooking water.

DIET: Takes a wide variety of prey, especially fish, but also birds and mammals of many types as well as carrion.

NOTES: Bald eagles were once essentially extirpated in the eastern United States and were rare in the western United States. The species has rebounded remarkably through eradication of DDT and by reintroduction programs. The bald eagle is the national symbol of the United States.

Author's Biography

AL HARMATA prepares to release an adult male bald eagle, captured for contaminant monitoring, along the Gallatin River floodplain in southwestern Montana, United States. Photo courtesy of the author

Al Harmata was born to lower-middle-class parents in suburban New Jersey. Al's academic performance in elementary and secondary schools was somewhat less than stellar, but being a better-than-average fullback in soccer paved his way to college, where he studied forestry in his freshman year but was politely asked not to return for his sophomore year— something about disciplinary and academic problems after the soccer season. He was drafted into the US Army in 1966, trained in radio-teletype communications, and promptly sent to Vietnam as an Air Cavalry infantryman. While there, his interest in biology was kindled by a book his mother had sent him. In the midst of artillery, small arms, and mortar fire, air assaults, mosquitoes, monsoons, and mud, Rachael Carson's *Silent Spring* ignited a rage at what humans were doing to the planet that transcended the war and its inherent travesties. After being severely wounded in action and permanently disabled, he returned to New Jersey, married, again entered college, and produced two children. US Senate hearings investigating widespread eagle killings in the American South-west focused his wartime goal of contributing to the welfare of the natural world, and he resolved to pursue raptor research and management. He received a BSc in biology from the University of Illinois, an MSc in wildlife biology from Colorado State University, and a PhD in fish and wildlife management from Montana State University. During this period he was employed as a raptor biologist/warden for the National Audubon Society, eagle-capture technician for the US Fish and Wildlife Service, and a wildlife consultant; and his wife dumped him. He is a founding member of two regional Bald Eagle Working Groups, a member of the Western Peregrine Falcon Recovery Team, an active bird bander, and an affiliate research professor at Montana State University; and he is remarried.

BALD EAGLE, UNITED STATES

Alan R. Harmata

In August 1967, after 10 months in Vietnam serving as an infantry radio-man, a cacophony of mortars, AK-47s, and light artillery fire again filled the air. A 75 mm recoilless rifle (3' cannon) round delivered by a North Vietnamese army gun crew hit me in the left foot, neatly relieving me of my left arm 7.6 cm (3 in) below the shoulder and my left leg at mid-calf. After receiving the last rites and having my evacuation from Vietnam delayed due to my anticipated demise, gangrene and army surgeons took more of my leg, to above the knee. I submit the former not to evoke pity, sympathy, or whine; I mention it only to provide context and perspective for some of the following incidents.

The first healthy, wild bald eagles I handled were in the San Luis Valley (SLV) of southern Colorado in the winter of 1975–76. In those days, the origins and movements of wintering bald eagles in most areas of the country were virtually unknown, and one of the most common questions asked by wildlife managers was, "Where do they come from?" To try and answer this question, Dale Stahlecker, a native of the valley whom I met while in graduate school, and I had initiated a banding and color-marking study of bald eagles in the SLV. Both recent graduates with an MSc in wildlife, we were familiar with the capture of most raptors, but not specifically bald eagles. Wintering bald eagles congregate around ungulate carcasses to feed, so we decided to try a cannon net during our initial trapping attempts in the SLV.

Our cannon net, borrowed from the waterfowl guys of the US Fish and Wildlife Service in Denver, consisted of three steel tube cannons about 46 to 61 cm (18 to 24 in) long with a muzzle diameter of about 75 mm (3 in) (ironic, eh?). The 3.0×4.5 m (10×15 ft) rope mesh net expanded when the cannons fired three 2.3 kg (5 lb) projectiles tied to the net. The projectiles were fired by 12-gauge shotgun shells with the shot removed and reloaded with 4f black powder positioned in each breach and ignited by an electronic detonator. Our ignorance of cannon nets required a couple of test fires prior to deployment. Because the SLV was snow-covered that winter, we found one of the few snow-free areas in the valley large enough to test our trap—the parking lot of the Sangre De Cristo High School in Mosca. It never occurred to us that there was a flaw in our test strategy until the split second we fired. We watched in perverse amusement as one projectile broke free from the center position of the net and zipped straight at the thin corrugated steel wall of the occupied high school gym about 27 m (30 yd) away. Our laughter was of relief as we watched it, almost in slow motion, sail over the roof, narrowly miss the ridge, and disappear out of sight behind the building. We realized with a simultaneous, "Oh ——!" (expletive deleted), that there might be a problem on the other side of the building. We stealthily tiptoed around the corner of the gym and peaked at the running track and football field on the other side, half expecting to see a prostrate, bleeding athlete. Dale says he doesn't remember this, but I clearly recall seeing kids running around the track and on the football field, totally oblivious to their danger. After walking around the field whistling with our hands in our pockets, as if we were birding, we found the projectile mostly buried in the snow. If things had gone differently, I can imagine the tabloid headlines: "Innocent Athlete Hit by Errant Eagle Trap" or "High School Hit by Mortar Round/Asteroid, Terror Reigns." It wasn't until after the event that we realized we should have pointed the trap toward the empty barley field in the other direction.

Not to be deterred and learning virtually nothing from that experience, we continued to use the cannon net. Our last deployment of the cannon net was late in the season. It failed to attract any eagles and thus wasn't fired. Breaking down the net for shipment home required removing the projectiles from the cannon for transport safety reasons. Unfortunately, as we tried to pull one projectile out of the cannon with the net rope, it broke at the base. The dilemma was how to get the projectile out: either force it out with a drift pin through the breach (it was really stuck), or retie the net rope to the projectile and pull it out. We had no drift pin of the right diameter handy and the latter was utterly impossible. So, having watched the spreading net on previous fires and being somewhat familiar with the trajectory characteristics and range of 60 mm and 81 mm mortars in the military, I suggested shooting it out. Dale foolishly agreed, and I foolishly proceeded to position the muzzle—not at a ditch bank, but straight up. How far could it go? Figuring the projectile would just *bloop* out (the sound we attributed to the report of a 40 mm grenade launcher in the Vietnam War), I hooked up the wires to the "hell box" (the Hollywood movie–style dynamite detonator plunger) and fired. To our horror, it went out of sight, straight up, with the velocity of a rifle bullet. I never felt so naked (or stupid) in my life. We had no idea how high it had gone or, of more importance, where it would land. So there we were, two guys standing in an open potato field, trying to present the absolute minimum profile to a falling object, exclaiming over and over, "Oh ——!" (expletive deleted), "Oh ——!" (expletive deleted), "Oh ——!" (expletive deleted). After what seemed like 15 minutes, we heard the distinctive thud of the projectile about 9 m (30 ft) away. We just stood there for a bit, and I for one checked my underpants. Had it hit one of us, I could just see the tabloid headlines: "Eagle Researcher Killed by Own Trap."

One thing I thought might help to increase our capture success was a live "lure" bird to draw free-flying eagles to our baits and traps. A good friend, Mike Lockhart, had developed the technique a few years earlier, specifically for catching golden eagles, but as far as I knew, the technique had not been used for bald eagles. Mike shared the details with me and the Colorado Division of Wildlife provided a rehabilitated 9- or 10-month-old female bald eagle as a lure. We used the lure bird and managed to catch three bald eagles that first winter—two immatures and an adult. As agreed, at the end of the season, I banded and released the lure bird north of Ft. Collins, Colorado, in late February 1976.

Recently, the Bird Banding Laboratory called and asked if I minded if they gave my telephone number to someone who had recovered one of my bands. Within minutes I received a call from Marge Gibson, a raptor rehabilitator. She gave me a band number that I insisted wasn't mine, but I told her I'd look at my records and call her back. After some initial confusion, I determined it was the one I had placed on the lure bird in Colorado so long ago. I assumed somebody had found just the band (or at most, found it on just a leg bone) at the bottom of a lake, stream, or some other long-lost, obscure location. It turns out it was found on a live, healthy adult bald eagle that Marge had recently rehabilitated for lead poisoning and released back at the eagle's breeding site . . . in Wisconsin . . . at 30 years old!

In the summer of 1980, I had turned my attention to banding nestling bald eagles in the Montana portion of the Greater Yellowstone Ecosystem (GYE) with Kurt Alt, who was finishing his master's degree on bald eagles and osprey in the GYE. We were with my daughter, Caryn (then 10 years old), on the Cliff Lake Bench, a seldom-visited (at that time) area of southwestern Montana. After observing a nest in a dead tree and judging the tree to be unclimbable, Kurt decided to search the vicinity around the nest tree and go down a steep incline back to the boat on the lake. He wanted to look for bald eagle food remains, molted feathers, and potential eagle carcasses. I decided not to abuse my only knee anymore on steep slopes and found a gentle game trail to follow to a place on the lake shore where we arranged for Kurt to pick us up. The trail ran through an open meadow, about 2 ha (5 ac) in area, surrounded by thick forest, mostly Douglas fir and Lodgepole pine.

With Caryn behind me by about 15 m (45 ft), I took the lead toward the meadow. As I approached, I noticed a large brown mass near the close edge of the meadow about 46 m (50 yd) away. Thinking it was merely a bull elk, I proceeded obliviously to within 27 m (30 yd) of it when it caught our scent and stood on both hind legs. Now, when I finally computed that ungulates don't normally stand erect on their hind legs, it immediately morphed into a large boar grizzly. It was the last thing I expected to see because, among other reasons, in the early 1980s grizzlies were exceedingly rare outside of Yellowstone Park, which was about 121 km (75 mi) to the east. I froze and exclaimed, "That's a bear!" while turning to see where my daughter was. Caryn was already 274 m (300 yd) back from whence we'd come. She always was a good sprinter. The bear stayed erect for about 30 seconds, turned, and bounded back into the forest. Good bear. Although he looked right at me, he never saw us—just smelled us. He wanted to put as much real estate between him and us as quickly as possible. In retrospect, we were never in much danger because back then, bears near humans were often shot at outside the national park. The bears knew it and avoided humans at all costs.

That was the first of several encounters with bears I had during bald eagle banding, but it was the only one outside of Yellowstone. As the 1980s and 1990s progressed, grizzly bear populations increased in the GYE. I began to see more evidence of bear visits around bald eagle nest trees, presumably attracted by the eagle droppings and food remains, especially fish and waterfowl that fell out of the nest. The number of human encounters with bears also increased, some being fatal, and the evening bar talk during the eagle banding season often turned to details of the latest mauling. One plausible theory was that because the Park had closed the garbage dumps and feeding stations in the 1970s, the only bears that survived and bred were the very aggressive ones that could kill bull elk and bison.

Around this time, my good friend, colleague, and climber George Montopoli began to be more insistent that I accompany him on backcountry nestling banding trips in Yellowstone. George has been a climbing ranger in Grand Teton National Park for nearly three decades, in addition to being a mathematics and statistics professor at Arizona Western College. He hangs from ropes from helicopters at 4572 m (15,000 ft), free-climbs the scariest cliff faces in the Tetons during rescues and body recoveries, and has recently received the US Department of Interior's Award for Heroism. He's no wimp. That's why I didn't connect his insistence to concerns about his safety, but the reason gradually became clear to me, beginning with a trip to band nestling bald eagles at Eagle Bay on Yellowstone Lake in about 1986. At that time virtually no one visited the backcountry of Yellowstone Lake. Kurt, George, and I had been dropped off by a Park Service boat and we walked less than a kilometer (about a half mile) to the active eagle nest. The large Lodgepole nest-tree was located about 137 m (150 yd) from the shoreline of a small inlet that held abundant cutthroat trout. The tree was surrounded by thick willow that was nearly as tall as me, and by chest-high shrubs and grass, almost like that pernicious elephant grass in Vietnam that had knife-edge blades, held leeches, and concealed booby traps and ambushes. I immediately became uneasy. George and Kurt climbed to band the nestlings and I belayed them (controlled the rope so that a falling climber would not fall far). They had been up there for about three minutes when I smelled it— the unmistakable odor of a grizzly bear. As every pore on my body slammed shut, I yelled to them to inspect the area for a bear. They nonchalantly responded that they couldn't see anything, but said I shouldn't move because I was belaying them, and they continued their work. Of course, they couldn't have seen an armored tank in that tall, thick understory. The odor became intense. I detected movement in the brush. I sensed a presence. The implications of being a mobility-impaired lower-extremity amputee were never clearer to me. I told Kurt and George to start throwing large sticks down, to try and frighten away anything that might have been lurking in the grass. I heard them mumbling up the tree and then I heard the characteristic sound of a carabineer unclipping, then another. They were unhooking themselves from the rope in case I got dragged away! But they still insisted they saw nothing. Perhaps the falling branches deterred the bear, perhaps my yelling, or perhaps it was a sow that caught our scent and left to protect her cubs, but I never saw it. To this day, neither George nor Kurt admits to seeing it either.

Since those early years, I've banded nearly 700 eagles, one of which was a wintering bald eagle captured and radio-tagged in 1992 at Big Bear Lake, California, 145 km (90 mi) east of Los Angeles. It was about nine months old when it was captured for a study funded by the US Forest Service to identify and protect roost sites around the lake. In August 1994, I was contacted by a guy who told me that while hiking with his dog off-trail in a remote area of the forest, he had found a large eagle that had been dead for about a month, with a silver ring on its leg. I asked if he had inspected the ring for a number. He said no but he'd go back and look. A few days later, he told me the band number, and it belonged to the Big Bear Lake eagle. The curious thing was that the guy was my next-door neighbor and he had found the bird in Montana about 80 km (50 mi) from our houses! Now what are the chances of a bald eagle (or any bird for that matter), banded by me 1609 km (1000 mi) away from my home, being found two years later, 80 km (50 mi) from my home, by my next-door neighbor? Perhaps I'll start buying lottery tickets.

Author's Biography

TERYL G. GRUBB prepares
to climb to a bald eagle
nest in Arizona, United
States. Photo courtesy of
the author

Teryl Grubb graduated from Colorado State University in 1968 with a
BSc in wildlife management. During his summers on the Kodiak National Wildlife Refuge, Alaska, he became interested in bald eagles and
soon landed a fellowship for graduate research at the University of Florida.
These eagle studies were interrupted when Teryl served as a lieutenant in
the Navy's Underwater Demolition/SEAL teams at the end of the war in
Vietnam. Afterward, in 1976, he attended the University of Washington,
where his MSc in wildlife ecology focused on analyzing bald eagle nesting
habitat. When funding fell through, he had to learn to fly an aircraft
so he could do his own aerial surveys along the entire marine coast of
Washington. Following initial employment working on bald eagle
management plans in the then Washington Department of Game, in 1977
he joined the US Forest Service Rocky Mountain Research Station in
Arizona as a scientist in wildlife research to study the population and
habitat requirements of the bald eagle (and peregrine falcon). In Arizona,
Teryl was responsible for conducting early pioneering surveys of nesting
and wintering bald eagles and for determining the habits and habitats
critical to both distinct populations. He and the local Tonto National
Forest biologist conceived, designed, and implemented the volunteer
Arizona Bald Eagle Nest Watch Program, which is still used today to
monitor and protect active nest sites. Teryl was part of a rescue team for
bald eagles in Alaska's Prince William Sound following the *Exxon Valdez*
oil spill. He helped relocate eagle chicks from Washington, Alaska, and
British Columbia for successful reintroduction efforts into California. He
continues to work extensively in Michigan and Minnesota, still climbing
eagle nests for banding and blood sampling as part of a Great Lakes'
bio-sentinel program.

BALD EAGLE, UNITED STATES

Teryl G. Grubb

"One of you boys will continue radio-tracking bears, and the other will start climbing trees to band bald eagle nestlings . . ." That's how it all began for me back in the summer of 1967, on the Kodiak National Wildlife Refuge in Alaska, my first summer job in the wildlife field. And as it turned out, that inauspicious beginning has led to a fascinating, sometimes adventuresome, 43-year odyssey of watching, studying, and enjoying bald eagles throughout much of their North American range. There have been numerous exquisite, priceless moments along the way, like . . . lying quietly on a snow-covered, frozen lake in the still of a −29°C (−20°F) predawn morning and hearing the quiet whish of the wind through the feathers of an adult eagle gliding into a perch above me . . . or encountering an exceptionally precocial, uncharacteristically defiant, still gray young eaglet who charged me at the edge of the nest and remained there, unabashed with little chest out and stubby wings spread, with his head almost in my armpit as I removed his sibling for processing below . . . or coming upon an adult female bald eagle trading lunges with a full-grown coyote at an elk carcass one snowy winter day, with neither one giving quarter. But there have also been the inevitable embarrassing, occasionally hair-raising, and always humbling misadventures that none of us like to talk about much. Still they are part of the fabric of our experience, and while often good for a chuckle after the fact, they can usually help guide us to improve our efficiency for future efforts. What I'm about to share is one of those misadventures. I do so with the guarded hope that age, seniority, and experience might insulate me from whatever chastisement this tale elicits from fellow eagle biologists and experienced climbers.

Bald eagles are an incredible species. Their opportunistic adaptability is truly amazing. Think about it: their nesting habitat ranges from 6 m (20 ft) mangroves in the tidal swamps of south Florida, to 61 m (200 ft)-plus, giant Douglas firs and Sitka spruce in the Pacific Northwest. They are fish eagles to be sure, but they also successfully prey on birds, particularly waterfowl, and small mammals, even taking an occasional reptile or amphibian. If sufficient live prey is unavailable, they will switch to carrion, relying on whatever type of food is most abundant and easiest to obtain. Their habits and habitats can vary seasonally and geographically, as environmental and climatic conditions dictate. All of this notwithstanding, as a budding young wildlife biologist in 1977, when I was offered a research position with the US

Forest Service to study bald eagle distribution and habitat requirements in the desert Southwest, I was totally unprepared to find bald eagles nesting on cliffs among cactus. And, as I was soon to discover the hard way, I was woefully unprepared for climbing into those cliff nests to band young eaglets.

I had learned to climb bald eagle nest-trees on Kodiak Island during my two summers of banding there. Plus, in the time between my experience in Alaska and this new job in Arizona, I had learned to rappel and use ropes during my Naval Special Warfare training. So, I reasoned confidently, how big a deal could it be to take my specialized military training and adapt it to getting down a cliff to an eagle nest? To facilitate this first rappel, as well as be sure I could impress my colleagues and attending graduate student with my prowess, I purchased a new mountaineering harness to replace the rudimentary rope tie-off I had used in the Navy. However, I neglected to try the new system in advance. If I had, I would have discovered the new harness dramatically changed the way a carabineer handled the rope in a military rappel setup. An ex-Marine friend tended my rope from atop the 76 m (250 ft) nest cliff, while the others in our small banding party waited at the base of the cliff for me to lower the nestlings down to them for processing.

Excited to be making my way into an eagle nest once again, down I went. During the first 4.5 m (15 ft), as I worked down the vertical cliff face, I noticed my old military attachment was not giving me enough friction to control my descent effectively once my feet lost contact with the overhung face, extending the next 18 to 21 m (60 to 70 ft) below. Too late . . . *Snap! Zing!* Down I went, pretty much out of control, but *really* impressing my unsuspecting colleagues on the ground below. Fortunately, I landed on my feet on a broad ledge where I could regroup out of sight. With blistered hands, even within my heavy leather gloves, I cleaned out tangles in the rope and reset my attachment, doubling the wraps of rope around the carabineer this time for more friction.

My revised setup seemed to work better, permitting me to move down the remaining face under control to about 3 m (10 ft) above the nest, which was actually near the bottom of the cliff on a vertical rock protrusion. Okay, I thought, all is good again, no harm done. Onto the business at hand, but first I'll just check everything before lowering on down to the nest. Then my eyes fell on my single carabineer attachment. OH MY GOD!! My rope was pinched in the open gate of the carabineer and that was THE ONLY THING HOLDING ME on the side of the cliff!! To make matters worse, the pinched rope was jammed so tightly I could not free it to go up or down. I quickly reattached myself to the climbing line, but was still left with the dilemma of to how extricate myself. Talk about humiliating! An ex-Navy SEAL stuck on the side of a cliff above an eagle nest. So much for impressing my colleagues. As for the two chicks below (well off to the side of my fall line, in case you were wondering), they just seemed to be watching passively, appearing to be totally fascinated, probably thinking to themselves, "Wow, what a jerk! Mama never told us there'd be days like this with so much comedic entertainment!"

The eaglets' amusement notwithstanding, I had to somehow get out of my rope jam. I tried inching up far enough on the broken irregular surface of the lower cliff face to release the tension on the jammed carabineer, only to have the strength drain from my fingers and have to fall back on the rope, with a very unsettling bounce. By the third attempt, however, there was enough stretch in the rope from the previous bounces to release the jam before my fingers gave out. Hurrah! Life is good again! But alas . . . no . . . that cliff wasn't done with me yet. *Snap!* The carabineer released again, and *Zing!* down I went past the nest outcrop, past the grad student, who had scrambled up to the base of the nest outcrop, all in a blur, this time with fleeting but full expectations of imminent pain! Yet, just that quickly I came to an abrupt stop, feet just touching the talus slope 4.6 m (15 ft) below the nest. My glove and shirt had got caught up in a kink in the rope, and all three (glove, shirt, and rope) got sucked into my carabineer to arrest my latest wild descent (any experienced climbers reading this will be cringing at this point). *Whewee,* I cannot believe it! Maybe not all of the spirits of this cliff are against me after all! Undaunted, I went ahead and climbed back up into the nest to retrieve the young eagles for processing. Since the climb from below was only 4.6 m (15 ft), you might be wondering why the plan was to rappel down to it in the first place, right? The original answer was to be fast and efficient, but sadly that ship had sailed much earlier! After we banded and attached radio tags to the chicks, I descended part of the way down off the nest outcrop, but again undaunted and still not realizing the underlying cause of my difficulties, I thought, just as one should get back in the saddle after being thrown from a horse, I'd rappel down the last 3 m (10 ft) or so. Unwise . . . as by now I'm sure you are expecting, once again came that horrifyingly familiar *Snap!* followed by the *Zing!* of the screaming rope as, once more, I fell uncontrolled to the ground, tearing all the remaining unbroken blisters on my hands and adding the last possible measure of humiliation to my disastrous first cliff nest climb/rappel in Arizona. Ahhhh! I was so relieved to be down and on terra firma once and for all, having cheated death three if not four times, I didn't even care anymore. The grad student and I gathered our gear and happily set off slip-sliding down the lengthy talus slopes below the nest cliff, both of us enjoying the easy descent. The adult eagles came back to the nest site quickly, and once more all seemed good. That is, till we slid to a stop above a hidden 4.6 m (15 ft), near-vertical incline above the dirt roadway. We were able to get just enough of a short-lived foothold for one of us to make it off to the side, but given the day I was having, would it surprise you that I'm the one who slid straight on down to the road . . . and broke my wrist on impact? Really nice, here I survive the cliff, only to get injured walking back to the truck!

What a perfect ending to a perfect day, right? But oh no, there's still an epilogue. When my ex-Marine buddy came down from above, he first asked what the heck had happened on the cliff rappel, as we did not have radios back then to keep him updated. Next, looking rather pale, he pulled me aside and said, "You've got to see this," and showed me the climbing rope. Apparently each of the bounces I had taken had seesawed the rope over a sharp rock at the cliff edge, unbeknownst to either of us at the time. Two of the rope's three twisted strands were entirely severed, and the third did not look like it could have withstood another bounce. We looked at each other silently a moment, then he said, "I think we had better get some formal climbing training before we try this again." We did soon thereafter, plus we purchased and learned to use state-of-the-art equipment. Not long after, several of us from cooperating resource agencies in Arizona adopted an informal policy to not climb or rappel into any new cliff nests for the first time when chicks were present. Better to discover the site's idiosyncrasies and hazards when there were no youngsters in the nest to harm (or amuse, as the case may be).

Youth, false bravado, naive confidence in inappropriate, mismatched, and untested equipment, and a lack of proper technical training all contributed to this wild episode that makes a great story now, but that easily could have ended this enthusiast's eagle watching on a much more serious note long ago. Also, all evidence from this episode to the contrary, I have since made it a personal policy over the years to climb as fast and efficiently and as safely as possible, using proven techniques and equipment, and making every effort to minimize the time and impact on the pair of eagles whose privacy and home space we are intruding upon for our research endeavors.

Even so, I still remember the exhilarating emotional mix of excitement, honor, and humility I felt in the very first bald eagle nest I climbed into on

Kodiak so many years ago. That feeling has never diminished, even after more than 40 years. Yet I must admit occasionally now, when age, diet, and conditioning all conspire each succeeding year to make climbing into eagle nests a little more challenging . . . when sometimes on the way in to the nest site, especially if the hike is difficult through fallen timber or swampy wetlands, or if the tree itself is a tough climb . . . I start thinking, "Naw, maybe it's just not worth it any more." But then, when I get up to the nest . . . smell those "sweet" distinctive odors from decaying nest vegetation, rotting prey remains, and drying fecal material . . . come eye to eye with those captivating young eagle chicks, no matter what their age—big, brown, and defiant, or gray, gangly, and docile . . . scan around to take in the lofty, spectacular panorama of surrounding waters, coastline, or countryside . . . and look up to see those majestic white-headed, attending adults soaring overhead or perched at nest level in a nearby treetop . . . Then, as fast as *Snap! Zing!* all those second thoughts and doubts disappear like a rope whipping through an open carabineer of a naive, young climber. It still *is* worthwhile . . . much more so even. It still is one of the greatest privileges and pleasures any eagle watcher could ever hope to experience.

8

Verreaux's Eagle

COMMON NAME: Verreaux's eagle

SCIENTIFIC NAME: *Aquila verreauxii*

OTHER NAMES: African black eagle, black eagle

IUCN CONSERVATION STATUS: *Least Concern (population stable)*

DESCRIPTION: Large, very dark, almost jet black with a white "Y" shape on back and rump, with long paddle-shaped wings. Large head and bill, legs fully feathered. Unlike most eagles, males and females are very close in size. Feet are massive even for an eagle, as big or bigger than a golden eagle's.

SIZE: Length: 78–90 cm (31–36 in); Wingspan: 181–219 cm (71–86 in); Weight: 3.0–5.8 kg (6.6–13 lb)

THREATS: Depletion of prey resources (hyrax) has been shown to impact populations of this species. Also susceptible to poisoning and shooting in some areas. Other threats include electrocution and drowning in steep-walled farm reservoirs.

DISTRIBUTION: Afromontane belt, extending into the Sahara and some parts of the Middle East.

MOVEMENTS: Verreaux's eagle is nonmigratory; juveniles appear to be short-distance dispersers.

HABITAT: Montane, rocky foothills, gorges, primarily dry areas populated by hyrax. Occurs in elevational ranges from sea level to over 5000 m (16,404 ft).

DIET: Verreaux's eagle is a specialist on rock hyrax. In addition, it is known to take other birds and mammals of similar size.

NOTES: Verreaux's eagles are one of the few eagle species to practice obligate siblicide (when two chicks hatch, the eldest will always kill the youngest).

Author's Biography

Rob Davies with
Samburu, a juvenile
Verreaux's eagle that
eventually became
independent in the
Drakensberg Mountains
of South Africa. Photo
by Annelise Crean

Rob Davies grew up in Wales and developed his love of birds of prey watching kestrels and peregrines along the Pembrokeshire coastline. After studying zoology at the University of Exeter, Rob moved to South Africa in 1982, initially to do a study on springbok and merino sheep on a game farm in the Karoo. This involved spending 80 days sitting on a windmill watching sheep graze, something he could probably have done back home in Wales, but it was a chance to learn about the fascinating wildlife of the Karoo, including a young martial eagle that was learning how to hunt in the area. This young martial attacked and killed all manner of large prey except for the merino lambs bedded down under his roost tree, so Rob could not understand why so many farmers in the Karoo continued to kill every eagle they saw in the belief that they were all lamb killers. During the drought of 1984, Rob witnessed an irruption of rock hyrax on such a farm where nearly all of the predators had been killed; the hyrax eventually consumed all the forage on the farm and the farmer was forced to move his sheep elsewhere. This experience persuaded Rob to do a study of Verreaux's eagles in the Karoo National Park for his PhD through Pretoria University, which he completed in 1994. Rob did the pencil sketches for Val Gargett's wonderful monograph on the Verreaux's eagle and at the time of this writing was completing the plates for a field guide on African birds of prey with author Bill Clark. Rob's own book on the natural history of the Karoo should be out soon in Cape Town after the longest gestation period for any book. Rob directed the African Raptor Information Centre in Johannesburg for a couple of years, and he worked as a consultant for the Peace Parks Foundation and Conservation International in Cape Town. In 2001 he returned to Wales to help the Hawk and Owl Trust and later the West Wales Biodiversity Information Centre. He is now a freelance ecological consultant.

VERREAUX'S EAGLE, SOUTH AFRICA

Rob Davies

At the end of each nesting season I tried to collect as many bones, skulls, or tortoise scutes that I could find left over by the black eagles beneath their lofty nest cliffs. This was quite an arduous part of the study because it involved scrambling up and down steep rocky screes and wrestling with thorn bushes for the skeletal remains held in their tight embrace. One type of bush released clouds of irritant powder every time it was touched. Others lacerated unprotected skin. Consequently, I could be seen on occasion in the heat of a Karoo summer (40°C [104°F]) dressed in the densest canvas clothing and gloves, wearing a gas mask or handkerchief, cursing but, at the same time, enjoying this biological lucky dip. Hyrax and hare bones were those I found most often, and I became so familiar with their shapes and sizes that when something out of the ordinary cropped up, like bones of birds or carnivores, I eagerly anticipated my next trip to see Graham Avery, the archaeologist at the Cape Town Museum who painstakingly matched my offerings against the vast collection of animal remains held in the museum archives. Our most precious find was the bones of Cape vultures from a time when they roosted on the same cliffs, but they are now extinct in this part of the Karoo.

On this great continental escarpment of the African plateau, Verreaux's eagles can be found nesting at one of the highest densities known for any large eagle along a linear mountain range. In the Karoo National Park, near Beaufort West, where I worked for five years, only 2 km (1.2 mi) separated each pair. Sounds manageable? In fact, I could hike for nine hours continuously from the closest access road and still not reach some of their nest sites. In these remote places it was best not to argue with the towering columns of loose ironstone, the noisy troupes of baboons, or the silent Cape cobras that sunned themselves on the scree slopes. There was always adventure on these forays.

Early one morning, after an unusual spate of cold and rain, I found myself driving through the dark drizzle up the Molteno Pass, wondering why on earth I hadn't listened to my colleagues at the university and studied seabirds instead—they bragged how they could check hundreds of nests and measure all the chicks in one day and come home with files crammed full with data. If I worked really hard I could get to about three or four nest cliffs in a day and that still left a dizzying gap of 50 m (55 yd) between me and any chicks on the nest. Why on earth study eagles?

I was getting fit, I supposed, as I traipsed up through the mist to the top escarpment carrying the heavy rucksack of telescope, tripod, and other eagle-watching equipment. At least it was cold this morning. There was even a spattering of white snow atop each rocky outcrop that I passed, left by the cold front from Antarctica that had swirled unexpectedly across the mountains of the southern cape. I stopped near the top to make myself a cup of coffee and take it all in, hoping that the cloud would lift. But it was brighter farther up so I carried on upward, rewarded by the occasional glimpse of blue sky. At an altitude near 1830 m (6000 ft) I stepped, quite suddenly, out of the top of the fluffy white clouds and onto a sunlit island of rock. The spectacle, looking south to the Swartberg Mountains 200 km (124 mi) away, took the last of my breath away. A few hundred meters on, another red rocky island rose from the cotton-wool sea of cloud, and I recognized the promontories of the main escarpment as they arced away into the distance like skipping stones bouncing across a white pond. A jet black shape appeared suddenly beneath me and crossed the gap in the clouds below, the first time I had ever seen a Verreaux's eagle flying against snow. My worries about statistics evaporated into the thin air. I knew why I was studying eagles.

I got to work—descending into the cloud again to follow the base of the cliffs. Soon I had two large plastic bags filled with the annual rotting or rotten leftovers of one pair of eagles and their chick. Fortunately the heat and dry of the Karoo had bleached most of these bones white and baked them into desiccation. I wondered what the grazing hyrax or "dassies" thought as they clipped the green leaves of the *Grewia* branches among which the skulls of their unlucky relatives were intertwined. Verreaux's eagles use these flat bushes for their butcher blocks. Most of the space in the plastic bags was filled with the solid little hyrax skulls. Was it because these last so long on the screes and shine so white? Or was it because the Verreaux's eagle really is unusual among raptors by preying so heavily on one species? Something to think about, but here were lots and lots of beautiful data—well, beautiful to an eagle biologist at least. Many of the skulls were smallish with pointy incisors and the second molar emerging. These were the young males expelled from the safety of their natal colonies at the age of 18 months by the dominant males when the youth started to threaten their monopoly. Old females made up most of the remainder. Very old females often sit up on the rocks on duty to watch out for the group, but, like the young males, they don't have anybody on guard duty looking out for them, and I had seen how skillfully the eagles targeted them when they scampered solo down the slopes to catch up with the rest of their clan.

By lunchtime I had collected from another site and most of the cloud had burnt off, but it was still cold and the day was perfect. There were crystal clear views to distant blue mountains in all directions across the vast space of the Karoo. I walked along the cliff tops toward the third nesting pair of eagles, hoping to see the peregrines that were nesting close by. Everything was squeaky clean from the rain and sparkling with icings of snow. Concentrating on the round rocks at my feet, which could readily sprain an ankle, it wasn't until I arrived at the top of the nest cliff that I looked up ahead and to my amazement saw an eagle perched right in front of me. She was sitting on a snowy lookout and giving me a stare that quite clearly meant, "I'm not budging." Obliged, I sat down quietly, and although this was the closest that I think I had ever been to a wild Verreaux's eagle (except on their nests), I brought her into sharp focus in my binoculars. This was a very different eagle indeed. Across her back and chest, which ought to be black mantle, were pure white teardrop-shape feathers. She was a partial albino. But the other thing that made her look special was that she just looked old, very old. This is not the sort of statement that scientists like, but there were no annular rings to measure her age. I think it was her feet, all gray and battle-scarred, and, dare I say it, the look in her eyes. I felt they had seen many seasons pass. I think she was resting and enjoying the day as I was.

Perhaps she was over 40 years old, and I wondered to myself how long she had lived here and "owned" this territory. It was certainly my first chance to gain her acquaintance. Some of the eagle nests I had seen were enormous. I measured one that was 3.6 m (12 ft) high from top to base. Radio-carbon dating of sticks from this base indicated the birds had started to build it in 1972. In trying to understand the close relationship between this predator and its prey, I was struck by how significant the rocky habitats were both to predator and to prey. Unlike most other mammals eagles prey on, rock hyrax cannot create their own refuges or burrows. Their sanctuary is determined by the nature of the rock crevices, and these are set in stone. Perhaps this is why, even in the changeable Karoo, rock hyrax numbers do not vary as dramatically as those of, say, rabbits or prairie dogs. Consequently, with all eagle territories occupied and stable in rocky mountainous terrain and adult eagles living to a grand old age, it must be very difficult for young Verreaux's eagles to mature and find an opportunity to breed. Changing of the guard for Verreaux's eagles probably doesn't occur very often, and I think this is why each time two chicks hatch out in a Verreaux's eagle nest, one will kill the other. These eagles need to grow up very strong indeed.

Beyond the mottled eagle on the rock was a huge empty space; the ground had dropped 914 m (3000 ft) by the time I saw it again, and by then it was blue and 20 km (12 mi) away. Like the eagle, I peered down over the edge across the wonderful Karoo National Park and remembered how daunting it had been when I first arrived, looking up from below at the massive mountains and wondering how I was ever going to come to grips with these elusive birds and their even more elusive life stories. But now I knew that there was a pair on the other side of the Lion's Head, that each of three adjacent pairs defended exactly 52 km (32 mi) of linear rock outcrops, that the pair below had had their nest trashed by the baboons, and that two years in a row a small grey mongoose had visited the Doringhoek nest to plunder it of young eaglets and hyrax prey. As I sat there on the mountain edge looking down, I realized that I would probably never get to know a piece of land as well as I did now, and I realized how lucky I was to have been able to focus my life entirely on this captivating subject for a few years. Apprentice eagle watchers should not be easily put off by the apparent challenges of studying elusive species; the hard-won results eventually pay great dividends.

Suddenly "White Lady's" mate flew into view out over the slopes below. Male Verreaux's eagles hang under very outstretched wings. Val Gargett, a prominent Verreaux's eagle watcher, had noticed that they often fly with their tails tucked in. This one pulled in his wings, thundered down the scree, and shot up into the sky like a black bolt, spreading his wings as his momentum expired, revealing the white patch on his back as he stalled and tumbled down into another dive. The display flight of a Verreaux's eagle is very eye-catching. Without me noticing, "White Lady" had slipped away off her snowy perch and sailed out to join him, and they drifted out of sight to the west, their first chance to hunt together after two days of rain and snow. I spent the rest of the day recovering the remains of their successful hunts and returned home with rucksack and soul fulfilled.

Two seasons later, "White Lady" disappeared from her post on the top escarpment, and I had to conclude, sadly, that maybe she had just come to the end of a long life.

I was more familiar with the lower escarpment pairs who were more accessible, in particular one pair that conveniently nested on top of a knife edge of a ridge. If I sat on that ridge with big binoculars on a tripod, I could watch this pair hunt and follow them almost anywhere they went in their huge range. They taught me more about how Verreaux's eagles hunt than any of the others. The male was a real show-off and frequently performed double and even triple backward somersaults with wings outstretched at the top of his undulation display.

From 600 m (1968 ft) up, the eagles would spy their prey and to my amazement would often fly off in another direction until they apparently knew they were out of sight from their intended victim. They would then close their wings and dive to the ground, thundering into the valley where the hyrax were feeding, at speeds of up to 180 km (112 mi) per hour, a few meters off the ground using all the cover available to them, and only 10 or 20 m (33 or 66 ft) apart. I was amazed that any hyrax survived such terrifying attacks but quite often they did—they stayed very close to the rocks and made good use of their early warning system. The only way the eagles could get a second strike or flush the hyrax from bushes was by hunting together. This was my biological explanation for the exceptionally strong pair bond of Verreaux's eagles.

Unraveling the biological and behavioral relationships between this predator and its prey kept me enthralled throughout my PhD thesis, but it was the spiritual experience of watching these eagles that stays with me now. The very last evening as I watched my favorite pair on the ridge, they came and stilled into the wind so close to me that I could see the glint of the setting sun in their eyes. For me this was a gift and a sign of acceptance. Anybody who has won the trust of a wild creature will understand the thrill it gave me.

Eagles face so many difficulties surviving in the modern world, and Verreaux's eagles are no exception. We feel responsible for their survival now, but the study also taught me that they have to face as many natural difficulties as they do man-made ones. They deal with both in a manner of resilience and defiance that is truly an inspiration for us. On my last trip around the nests before I left the Karoo, I visited the Doringhoek site where the mongoose had killed the chicks. Both adults flew out over their koppie and I watched them through my binoculars. I was shocked to see that the left wing of the female was badly misshapen, but she was still managing to fly. Presumably she must have broken or sprained it in an accident or a fight. She landed for a moment, and when I trained the telescope onto her I was astonished to see a familiar pattern of white feathers all over her breast and back—"White Lady"! Lowered in the elevation of her status, perhaps from the grand upper escarpment to a humble koppie, she had survived and found another mate. I was so happy to see her again. As she flew out to join her mate, she gamely drew in her one good wing and her one broken wing to swing down and then up in a magnificent, albeit slightly wonky display flight. In spirit, she was all eagle, and my heart went out to her.

An African fish eagle in Kenya. Courtesy of Munir Virani

The African crowned eagle's cryptic plumage helps it to remain camouflaged when perch-hunting in the forest understory. Courtesy of Munir Virani

The colorful bateleur of Africa has a distinctive short tail. Courtesy of Mark Warrillow-Thomson (www. raptorphotography.com)

Resident on four continents, the cosmopolitan golden eagle is one of the most well-studied eagle species. Courtesy of Todd Katzner

The harpy eagle of South America is one of the largest eagle species in the world. Courtesy of Ryan Phillips, Belize Raptor Research Institute

A juvenile eastern imperial eagle in Kazakhstan. Courtesy of Todd Katzner

This female Madagascar fish eagle was part of a breeding trio (with two males) for many years. Courtesy of Ruth Tingay

The martial eagle is blamed for killing livestock and suffers from extensive persecution in parts of Africa. Courtesy of Mark D. Anderson

A juvenile New Guinea harpy eagle; this species is heard more often than it is seen. Courtesy of Martin Gilbert

Very little is known about the solitary eagle of South America. Courtesy of Bill Clark

Steller's sea eagles have enormous and distinctive yellow bills for tearing open fish flesh. Courtesy of Pete Morris

The stunning Verreaux's eagle is most often found in high mountainous regions in Africa. Courtesy of Mark Warrillow-Thomson (www.raptorphotography.com)

A pair of Wahlberg's eagles in Kruger National Park, South Africa. Courtesy of Neil Gray (www. graybirds.net)

A young white-tailed sea eagle on its nest in Lappland. Courtesy of Björn Helander

9

Eastern Imperial Eagle

COMMON NAME: Eastern imperial eagle

SCIENTIFIC NAME: *Aquila heliaca*

OTHER NAMES: Imperial eagle

IUCN CONSERVATION STATUS: *Vulnerable (population declining)*

DESCRIPTION: A large dark eagle with relatively long, narrow wings. Back of the head and neck are very brightly yellow-gold, tail is shorter than the similar-looking golden eagle. Imperial eagles often (but not always) have highly visible white patches at their shoulders. Preadult forms are light, sometimes almost white with darker streaking.

SIZE: Length: 68–84 cm (37–33 in); Wingspan: 176–216 cm (70–85 in); Weight: 2.5–4.5 kg (5.5–12 lb)

THREATS: Electrocution, persecution by humans (especially during migration and in winter), sometimes habitat loss, poisoning, and nest robbing

DISTRIBUTION: Eastern imperial eagles are distributed throughout forest-steppe of Eurasia. In the east their range extends into Hungary, west through Ukraine, Kazakhstan, and Russia. Although the species occurs primarily at the interface between southern steppe and northern forest, it is also found in the Balkans and Asia Minor.

MOVEMENTS: Most populations are migratory, and the species winters in Africa, the Middle East, the Indian subcontinent, and even Southeast Asia. Western populations (Hungary, Balkans) are either nonmigratory or short-distance migrants.

HABITAT: Forest, steppe, desert; nests in trees, forages in grasslands.

DIET: Imperial eagles are often found near ground squirrel or marmot colonies; they also take many corvids and other similarly sized birds and mammals.

NOTES: Imperial eagles are a bird of the forest edge, a species that generally occurs between the ranges of golden eagles (to the north) and steppe eagles (to the south). Some authors consider the Spanish imperial eagle to be a subspecies of imperial eagle, rather than a separate species.

Author's Biography

TODD KATZNER at an imperial eagle nest at the Naurzum National Nature Reserve, Kazakhstan. Photo courtesy of the author

Todd Katzner developed an appreciation for wildlife and for being outside primarily through time spent indoors, watching nature shows on television. Todd received a BA in biology from Oberlin College in 1991. He then took a year off from schooling and followed field research opportunities in Minnesota and Hawaii. Resuming school, he attended the University of Wyoming, eventually receiving an MS in zoology and physiology in 1994 for his studies of the endangered pygmy rabbit in southwestern Wyoming. He then took another year and a half off from schooling, working on field jobs in Idaho, Wyoming, and Alaska before returning to academia at Arizona State University. His dissertation research there focused on the community ecology of the four species of eagles that coexist at the Naurzum National Nature Reserve in north-central Kazakhstan (the site described in his contribution to this book). Subsequent to completion of his dissertation, Todd accepted a fellowship from the US National Science Foundation to study the demographics of eagles and vultures at Imperial College, London. In his present position he is Director of Conservation and Field Research at the National Aviary in Pittsburgh. He has retained his research program in the former Soviet Union, taking new approaches to his eagle and vulture projects in Kazakhstan and adding field sites in other parts of Asia. Todd is a research associate at Hawk Mountain Sanctuary and at the Wildlife Conservation Society, and is on the editorial board of the journal *Animal Conservation*.

EASTERN IMPERIAL EAGLE, KAZAKHSTAN

Todd E. Katzner

It wasn't until I'd been in Kazakhstan for six summers that I even started to understand eagle behavior. As is the case with so much research, especially biological field research, the years and years of hard work were only the backdrop for an epiphany, a shining moment that, in an instant, swept away years of haze. For me, that moment of clarity came on a cool June morning when I was watching eagles in north-central Kazakhstan.

My colleagues and I had come to the southern end of the Naurzum National Nature Reserve to observe foraging eagles. Beyond us to the south was a colony of sousliks (European ground squirrels, similar in almost all regards to North American prairie dogs). These colonies were massive, stretching for at least 20 km (12 mi) across the steppe. From our earlier research, we knew that sousliks made up the greatest part of the eagle diet and almost certainly supported the many local eagle pairs. It is because of these colonial rodents that Naurzum is the best place in the world for eastern imperial eagles—there are about 40 of their territories spread throughout the reserve. In addition, there are territories of white-tailed sea eagles (about 20), steppe eagles (5 to 15), and golden eagles (about 4).

We were perched on a small hilltop: an overgrown sand dune sparsely populated with bunch grasses. The flat expanse of the souslik colony stretched out before us, broken only by a streambed cut deep because of overgrazing by domestic livestock and vegetated with the occasional tamarisk and salt-brush. Between us and the stream, the colony was covered in a sea of grass, mown short around the burrows of the chisel-toothed sousliks but longer and undulating in uninhabited patches. Our sand dune, only a meter or so (a few feet) above the souslik plane, was on a habitat edge, and to our backs was the Naurzum forest, a multispecies mix of pine, birch, and aspen trees where the eagles nest.

Our goal this day was relatively simple—to watch eagles to learn how they moved from their nests to their hunting grounds and back. Ultimately we intended to use these observations as the basis for trapping, figuring that if we knew where the birds forage, we'd know where to set our traps. Once an eagle was trapped, we intended to outfit it with a radio-telemetry device so that we could follow it in greater detail and with more accuracy than would be otherwise possible. This particular bump in the land was one of the highest points around, and it was also located between several eagle nests. In fact, from that spot we could see directly into two nests—one of an eastern imperial eagle pair, the other belonging to a pair of sea eagles—and we were within sight of two other imperial eagle territories.

I had expected to see something important this day, but the significance of what we did see was so much greater than I ever could have predicted. We arrived on our hilltop at about 7:30 a.m.—later than I'd wanted, but still early enough, as it turned out. The weather was typical for summer in north Kazakhstan—clear azure skies interrupted by ribbons of clouds moving slowly in the morning breeze. That day I was working with Dr. Evgeny Bragin, my partner in crime for the past 10 years of eagle research in Kazakhstan. Evgeny had studied imperial eagles at Naurzum for over 25 years and knew more about the species than anyone else I'd met. In spite of our long collective experience, neither of us had ever sat and simply watched birds flying to and from their hunting grounds (most of our previous studies having been focused on nesting biology). That morning as we set up a tripod with a telescope and began to watch, we were hoping to see something new. It wasn't long before our efforts were rewarded.

At 8:15 a white-tailed sea eagle appeared to our right, flying south out of the forest until we lost track of it on the horizon. Fifteen minutes later an eagle, apparently the same one as before, suddenly appeared, backtracking into the forest and this time carrying ground squirrel–sized prey within its strong talons. As we watched, the massive predator flew past us and then turned right, flying directly to the closest sea eagle nest behind us. These observations gave us, for the first time in all these years, a glimmer of insight into the relationship between eagle nests and eagle foraging sites.

The flight of the sea eagle was, however, simply a prelude to what was to come. A few minutes later, at 8:39, an imperial eagle took off from the nest closest to us. As it glided down from its perch, it gained speed and, locking its wings, began to circle leisurely, as if it was riding a high thermal. After gaining about 100 m (328 ft) in elevation, the bird dropped down quickly toward the souslik colony that stretched out from its nest on the forest edge. Approaching the ground, it pulled out of its dive, leveling off at about 3 m (10 ft) above the ground. Still carrying speed from its stoop, the eagle moved over the souslik colony. Although it flapped strongly, its velocity was not great and its flight was meandering, almost aimless, while simultaneously taking it farther and farther from the nest.

As it flew, the great bird picked up accompaniment. Like mosquitoes to a warm body, small birds swarmed around the eagle, determined tormenters bent on perturbing and pestering their larger kin. Mobbing like this is common, but the reasons for the behavior are not clear—defense and display have been proposed as explanations. Regardless, mobbing an eagle is a dangerous game that smaller birds sometimes lose, paying with their lives. Among the worst of the tormenters were the jackdaws, black and gray masters of the air. Fast, intelligent fliers, they swerved among their slower crow and magpie cousins to target the eagle. Also present were falcons—lithe kestrels and the lightning-fast red-footed falcons—whose high-pitched calls and sharp talons made them even fiercer than the corvids.

Through it all, the eagle gradually moved away from us, appearing nonplussed and focused, responding to the harassment far less intensely than I'd seen before. Dodging back and forth, moving farther and farther away from the nest, the eagle flew on, covering wide swaths of the souslik colony. Suddenly it banked left, hard, and with a flurry of outstretched wings and talons, dropped to the ground. Just like that it was over. From our hilltop perch 3 km (1.9 mi) away, it was an undramatic end to a chase, and neither Evgeny nor I was sure what had happened. However, we realized the result when, after a moment of mantling, the eagle began to eat something at his feet. What we had just witnessed—a successful hunting flight, from start to finish— was a rarity for any large raptor, seldom observed or noted in literature. Furthermore, when we checked our watches, our jaws almost hit the ground. It was 8:42—three minutes had passed since the eagle left its nest. Harassed by nearly 20 birds, within easy sight of its nest and mate, this eagle had given us a spectacular demonstration of hunting skill and made foraging for food look easy.

The big bird sat for another six minutes, eating and glaring at the rooks and jackdaws now encircling it on the ground, waiting for leftover scraps of meat. Then it took off again, this time in a direct and powerful flight, and at 8:50 arrived back at the same perch from whence it departed. Eleven minutes had passed between the time the eagle left its perch and the time it returned. Eleven minutes was all it took for this bird to go out, kill an animal, eat it, and return home. Eleven minutes—seeming like an eternity to Evgeny and me—in which our years of research had suddenly crystallized around a new understanding of what it is to be an eagle at Naurzum.

Our day was not quite done and about 45 minutes later the sea eagle flew out again, this time hunting within our field of view. As we watched, it tried for and apparently missed a ground squirrel, and then started off again on a nearly identical flight as the imperial eagle. Low and fast, meandering but apparently purposeful, it too suddenly banked hard and, like the imperial before it, landed on a ground squirrel. This time the whole process took about 15 minutes.

As a field biologist, I am motivated in part by a desire to be outside and by the opportunity to see animals doing remarkable things. Patterns, though, are the foundation of science, and recognizing patterns in natural systems is central to understanding ecological processes. Although the successful hunt by the imperial eagle was one of the most spectacular sights I'd seen, the consequence of the moment was even greater when I realized the similarity of the successful hunting technique that both eagles used. This style of hunting flight—low, fast, with a sudden drop on a surprised souslik—was new to us and is clearly an extremely effective technique for high-density mammalian prey such as sousliks.

Most important, I was shocked at the speed and ease with which these eagles caught and killed prey. Suddenly I was asking myself questions about the local eagle community in a completely different light than I did before. If you can catch and kill a ground squirrel in less than 15 minutes, then you probably have all the food you need, all the time. Before that fateful morning on the sand dune, I used to ask myself why there were so many eagles in this area. Now my thinking had come full circle, and I had started to wonder why there are so few eagles here!

I had often wondered why eagles can afford to sit for hours on a perch, surveying their territory. When I began my work at Naurzum, I usually assumed that a perched eagle was a hunting eagle—a classic "sit and wait" predator. To this day, an eagle perched above the souslik colony still triggers these thoughts. However, after that remarkable day on the dune, the nature of a perched eagle had a new meaning to me. It was a sign of complete mastery of the environment. As humans, we revel in the technology and tools that allow us to dominate everything else on the planet. Even with all our technology, however, it is a rare human who can leave home and, within three minutes, obtain a full meal, as did the imperial eagle. These eagles are, in fact, superbly crafted creatures, adapted to excel in their environment, and well worth the watching.

10
Steller's Sea Eagle

COMMON NAME: Steller's sea eagle

SCIENTIFIC NAME: *Haliaeetus pelagicus*

OTHER NAMES: Pacific sea eagle, Steller's eagle, white-shouldered sea eagle

IUCN CONSERVATION STATUS: *Vulnerable (population declining)*

DESCRIPTION: A massive dark eagle with a great deal of white on its shoulders and the leading edge of the wing and the wedge-shaped tail. Has a massive and often bright yellow bill. Legs are well feathered, down to its enormous feet.

SIZE: Length: 85–105 cm (33–42 in); Wingspan: 195–230 cm (77–91 in); Weight: 4.9–9.0 kg (11–20 lb)

THREATS: Coastal development for fossil fuel extraction; logging and pollution; persecution. Lead poisoning from bullets in hunter-killed deer scavenged in the winter.

DISTRIBUTION: Steller's sea eagles breed in extreme western Siberia and the Kamchatka Peninsula, possibly in North Korea. They winter directly south of these areas, in China, Japan, and Korea.

MOVEMENTS: These birds are either nonmigratory (where water stays open year-round) or short-distance migrants (from frozen to unfrozen areas).

HABITAT: Coastal areas, breeds in trees or on cliffs. May winter farther inland (especially in northern Japan).

DIET: Steller's sea eagles eat primarily fish, especially salmon and trout, during breeding season and fish and carrion during winter. Other birds and mammals are occasionally taken as well.

NOTES: Steller's sea eagles are massive birds that often congregate in winter gatherings with white-tailed sea eagles, especially close to fishing vessels.

Author's Biography

KEISUKE SAITO preparing to release a Steller's sea eagle after treatment at the eagle veterinary hospital in Japan. Photo by Gilles Martin

Keisuke Saito is a Japanese wildlife veterinarian who has been studying Steller's sea eagles for more than 10 years. He is based in Hokkaido, the northernmost island of Japan, where he is involved with field and veterinary studies on this and other endangered raptors. Keisuke's field research has concerned the wintering ecology and breeding behavior of Steller's sea eagle, and his veterinary studies have included rehabilitation techniques. Keisuke is committed to understanding the numerous threats to the survival of Steller's sea eagles and to working toward effective conservation management plans for this special bird.

STELLER'S SEA EAGLE, JAPAN

Keisuke Saito

I am a Japanese wildlife veterinarian and I have worked with Steller's sea eagles for more than 10 years, mostly on Hokkaido, the northernmost island of Japan. My work includes not only ecological investigations but also conservation and rehabilitation of eagles. For the past seven years, in addition to my study of eagles on their wintering grounds, I have worked on the breeding grounds on Sakhalin Island, where some of the eagles seen in Hokkaido spend their summer. So, essentially my annual movements mirror those of Steller's sea eagles, and this, I feel, gives me some insight, especially in relation to conflicts with humans. While undertaking such "normal" studies of the eagles, however, I do sometimes get to see some unusual things.

In Japan, more than 130 eagles are known to have been killed by lead poisoning from rifle bullet and shotgun slug fragments they ingest in the deer carcasses they scavenge. On Sakhalin, large areas used by eagles for breeding and feeding are threatened by extensive oil and gas developments. Because I want to determine the general health of eagles and take blood samples to determine levels of lead in their bodies, I try to capture free-flying individuals using either a bow or rocket net to trap them. Typically, Steller's sea eagles are very wary of humans, and it is always difficult to attract eagles, much less capture them. On one occasion I aimed to net eagles using a deer carcass as bait. However, after a month of waiting and watching the eagles, as they waited and watched the bait but never came near enough to trap, I decided to change tactics and use a decoy eagle. If the eagles could be tricked into believing that the carcass must be "safe" because another eagle was already feeding on it, they may be more willing to approach the bait. A proper taxidermically prepared mount is expensive to obtain, and a permit for the use of a live eagle as a lure is also difficult to obtain, so my colleagues and I decided to use a frozen eagle carcass instead. We defrosted an eagle carcass we had at our institute (the Institute for Raptor Biomedicine, in Hokkaido, Japan), set it in a feeding position over our deer carcass, and refroze it. At the time, the temperature in the mountains of Hokkaido where we were trapping was often −30°C (−22°F) so we thought that our decoy would not melt and would stay nicely in position. After we had carefully arranged the frozen eagle decoy, it looked, to our eyes at least, just like a scavenging eagle.

Unfortunately, it was not important that we thought it looked realistic, but that the free-flying eagles did. Apparently they did not trust our bird because although they would sit in trees nearby (and perhaps laugh), no eagles would come near "Frosty." In the course of a month and as spring approached, the decoy itself seemed to lose enthusiasm as the temperature warmed. From its active feeding position, it slowly drooped its head, sat down, and then eventually lay on its stomach in melted despair at its inability to attract anyone.

Somewhat paradoxically, although Steller's sea eagles can be incredibly wary, sometimes they are easily approached by humans. In eastern Hokkaido, where there are many lakes, nets are set under the ice in a traditional form of wintertime fishing. Fishermen often throw fish parts onto the ice, and these are an important source of food for the gulls, crows, and black kites. Steller's sea eagles and white-tailed sea eagles also congregate in these areas to take advantage of the abandoned fish.

In the early morning, when the fishermen start making their rounds of the nets by snowmobile, eagles take flight from the trees in unison and follow on behind the fishermen. As the nets are hauled in, the eagles settle on the ice, sometimes only a dozen meters away, to watch the proceedings. When the fishermen start to throw the fish on to the ice, the eagles are unable to hold back and slowly approach. Once an eagle actually gets a fish, a feeding frenzy erupts. Eagles rush under the feet of the fishermen and battle fiercely for the fish. As the frenzy proceeds, the eagles become oblivious to the fishermen and large numbers of eagles surround them. At times the fishermen threaten the eagles by their voice and body language, but when the eagle scramble heats up, the angry fishermen must physically pull the eagles off their catch. Despite this rough treatment, the eagles return day after day to scavenge at the nets.

Having seen this behavior, we asked a fisherman for help to allow us close observations of eagles and perhaps an opportunity to trap them, by accompanying him on his rounds the next day. However, having a sense that something was a little out of the ordinary, the eagles did not approach within 50 m (164 ft). On the next day, we tried again, this time disguising ourselves in the jackets and rubber boots of the fishermen. This had the effect of shortening the distance the eagles would approach, but they never came really close. Evidently, Steller's sea eagles recognize us individually and by things more subtle than clothing!

Every year, many raptors are brought to our veterinary hospital at the Institute in northern Japan. Steller's sea eagle is one of the most exciting and nerve-wracking species for us to receive. Over 10 years ago, when I was an inexperienced veterinarian, I had a brush with the extraordinary power of this species. A female adult eagle had been hit by a car and was brought to our hospital. She had a fracture of her left thighbone but was still very aggressive and hissed at us. After undergoing surgery, she was put under postoperative recovery management. The following day I decided to change her bandage alone, using a pair of leather gloves traditionally used for Japanese falconry. Everything was going well and I concentrated on the wound I was dressing. Suddenly, I felt a severe, sharp pain in my left wrist, and I looked down in disbelief at the two claws that had passed clear through the glove and my wrist, in one side and out through the other. In abject pain, and bleeding like a stuck pig, I tried to use my other hand to release my wrist from her grasp. Amazingly, within a split second, my right hand was grasped by her left foot (the foot at the end of the injured leg we had repaired), and another talon was buried 3 cm (1.2 in) into my flesh! So, there I was, both arms incapacitated by the eagle, losing blood and starting to feel light-headed. I tried to stay cool, hold still, and come up with a plan to get myself out of this bad situation. Quickly, I grabbed a nearby towel with my teeth and flung it at the eagle's face. The eagle, caught by surprise, released my wrists and quickly grabbed the towel. In this way, I was freed from the strong power of the Steller's sea eagle and was allowed to turn my medical expertise toward the more injured of the two parties . . . me.

Steller's sea eagle is known as the "God of Eagles" for the Ainu, the aborigines of Hokkaido. For my part I have committed what remains of my life to understanding and protecting this most godly of eagles.

11
Spanish Imperial Eagle

COMMON NAME: Spanish imperial eagle

SCIENTIFIC NAME: *Aquila adalberti*

OTHER NAMES: Adalbert's eagle

IUCN CONSERVATION STATUS: *Vulnerable (population stable)*

DESCRIPTION: A large dark eagle with relatively long, narrow wings. Back of the head and neck are very brightly yellow-gold, tail is shorter than the similar-looking golden eagle. Spanish imperial eagles have highly visible white patches at their shoulders, more so than eastern imperial eagles. Preadult forms are more rusty orange than similarly aged eastern imperial eagles.

SIZE: Length: 68–84 cm (37–33 in); Wingspan: 176–216 cm (70–85 in); Weight: 2.5–3.5 kg (5.5–7.7 lb)

THREATS: Persecution, electrocution, poisoning. Loss of preferred prey (rabbits) may be resulting in population declines. Also threatened because of small population size.

DISTRIBUTION: Endemic to the Iberian Peninsula—exclusively found in Portugal, Spain. Was found breeding in northern Africa at one time. It is thought that populations once were linked to eastern imperial eagle populations.

MOVEMENTS: Generally nonmigratory. Juveniles disperse, although not extremely long distances (but some appear to have recently crossed the Strait of Gibraltar into northern Africa). Adults usually hold territories year-round.

HABITAT: Woodlands (especially cork oak), plains, and marshes of southern Spain (where the species has been most intensively studied). Also occurs in higher elevations outside of protected areas in central Spain.

DIET: Medium-sized mammals, especially European wild rabbits, as well as other mammals and birds of a similar size

NOTES: Spanish imperial eagles are among the most rare of birds of prey, primarily because of their highly limited distribution. In parts of their range where they were once common, their population is now declining. However, in other parts of their range they are becoming more numerous.

Author's Biography

MIGUEL FERRER on a visit
to Hawk Mountain
Sanctuary, United States.
Photo courtesy of Hawk
Mountain Sanctuary
Archives

    Miguel Ferrer started his relationship with Doñana National Park
(Spain) and raptors when he was 15 years old, and his research interest has
since focused on the dynamics of small populations and the conservation
biology of endangered birds of prey, particularly the Spanish imperial
eagle. In addition to conducting research and publishing widely on a
variety of other raptor species, especially booted and Bonelli's eagles, and
other bird species such as gulls and penguins, Miguel has investigated a
diverse array of issues facing raptor conservation. These range from the
impact of wind power, power lines, and electrocution on raptors, to the
development of plasma biochemistry to aid understanding of raptor
ecology. His PhD dissertation was awarded in 1990 and investigated the
juvenile dispersal behavior of Spanish imperial eagles. To date he has
authored more than 100 papers in scientific journals and several books, as
well as presented his results at over 50 conferences in different universities.
Since 1993, he has worked for the High Council of Scientific Research of
the Spanish Administration. Miguel is a professor of research with the
Doñana Biological Station and was Director of this scientific institute
from 1996 to 2000. He was a Director-at-Large for the Raptor Research
Foundation during 1998–2000. From 1986 to date he has carried out
more than 40 research projects, with the support of the Environmental
Administration of Andalusia and different power companies, among other
organizations. Miguel is also a research associate at Hawk Mountain
Sanctuary and President of the MIGRES Foundation. He has won awards
from the Andalusia Environmental Administration (1999), the IRF
Global Road Achievement Award [Environmental Section] (2003), Special
Distinction of the Andalusia Government (2004), and the Raptor
Research Foundation's Fran and Frederick Hamerstrom Award (2005).

SPANISH IMPERIAL EAGLE, SPAIN

Miguel Ferrer

September 22, 1988, 7:00 a.m. and more than 25°C (77°F) in Doñana National Park's dry marshes. It was another hot day in southern Spain. I was watching an eagle family with two adults and two young near the end of the breeding cycle. I was trying to study juvenile dispersal and my mind was full of questions. When do the juveniles leave their natal territory? Where do they go afterward? How do they spend the nearly five years that occur before they begin breeding? Not too much was known about these topics in the 1980s and these questions were the main objective for the PhD research I had started in 1986.

My personal experiences with the Spanish imperial eagle began eight years before when I undertook my first study on the effects of power lines on Doñana's bird population. During one year I found more than 400 raptor carcasses under electrical poles. Among them were a dozen specimens of an incredible eagle species that especially impressed me and forever conditioned me for my professional career. These were Spanish imperial eagles. Ten years later, after a lot of effort and several scientific publications, news shows, and TV programs, pylon designs dangerous to raptors were forbidden by law, first in the region of Andalusia and subsequently throughout all Spain. It was the first but not the last battle I have fought for the Spanish imperial eagle.

Now, I'm at the border of the marshes following the last days that this eagle family will spend together before the young start to disperse. Eleven o'clock in the morning and I haven't seen one of the young in the last two hours. The signal from the long-lived solar-powered radio transmitter that I had fixed to its back two months ago was clear and steady, indicating that the young female was close to the nest, probably perched quietly. I could not see the bird but she was almost certainly not more than 500 m (547 yd) from the rest of the family, who were all still at the top of the nest tree. One hour more and nothing had changed. I developed a bad feeling about this situation and decided to try to locate the young female eagle. My previous experiences have shown that mortality during the first months of a young eagle's life is a regular occurrence and that sometimes a timely intervention would save a young bird with problems. Carefully, avoiding making any noise, I walked slowly under the trees surrounding the nest site, looking for the location of the radio transmitter, trying to see the eagle before she could see me.

After 30 minutes of walking very slowly, I arrived to a place where the transmitter's signal intensity increased, indicating that the eagle (or at least the transmitter) was nearby. I began to search for the transmitter, which I supposed had fallen from the eagle as I was sure that the bird was not there. I was on my knees moving the vegetation with my hands when a small sound made me turn my head. She was there, only a half meter from my face, perching in a low arm of a small tree and watching with curiosity this strange mammal carrying all these antennas, receiver, and binoculars that she never had seen before and so close. Slowly I started to walk back, unable to part my eyes from her face. She followed me with her eyes until I disappeared again in the forest. I was exultant because she was well and because we had been face-to-face—face-to-face with one of the most beautiful animals in the world. Would you ever in your life forget something like that?

Cadiz, La Janda area, 150 km (93 mi) from Doñana National Park, first days of December 1991. The female with whom I'd been face-to-face was three years old. She had changed her plumage, and now the first black, small feathers typical of adult birds were appearing. I saw her flying by the same oak savannah that she had used during the previous years as one of her dispersal areas. She was together with 12 juvenile Bonelli's eagles that also used the same area and roosted in the same small forest. In spite of the cold of the morning, the female managed to find a thermal and started to fly in circles, following the rising air. Within a few minutes she had reached about 300 m (984 ft) in elevation. Suddenly, as if following an order, she initiated a long, high-speed flight with a clear direction. I started the car and using a nondirectional antenna began to follow her. With the eagle disappearing quickly from my view in a northwest direction, I drove the car to the nearest road and accelerated, trying not to lose the signal. One hour later it was clear that she was moving back to Doñana, as she had several times before during the three years that I had been following her movements. I closed the windows of the car and accelerated down the highway to Seville. At three o'clock in the afternoon I saw her flying very low against the wind, crossing the more western marshes of Doñana. She seemed to know very well where she wanted to go. Two hours later I was in Doñana, at the border of the marshes, an incredible area full of life. The signal from the transmitter took me to a tall old oak tree, in front of a beautiful lagoon. In the evening, with the sun going down, I saw two eagles roosting together at the top of the tree—"my" female and a three-year-old male! Finally, she was looking for a partner, and by all appearances, she'd found one. The next few days, I watched as they shared the geese they hunted and how they selected the same tree in which to roost every night. One week later, I was watching my favorite pair early in the morning. Suddenly, a very strong and repetitive eagle call coming from behind made me look at the sky. Two adults from the neighboring territory finally had realized that these two young eagles were there, and they decided that it was time to be violent. My pair was looking with anxiety to the sky. The young female was the first to leave the tree, flying low and quickly to the marsh in the opposite direction of the adults. For some reason the young male decided that he must stay to fight—fighting for the territory, for his female, or for his eagle honor. Whatever the reason was, there is no doubt that this was a bad decision. First, the adult female and afterward the adult male made strong attacks. The young male tried to flee to the marshes but the adult male was not completely satisfied. Two more attacks and the young male fell from 50 m (164 ft) into the water of the marsh. Still two more attacks by the adult male seemed finally to be enough for him, and he returned with his adult female to their territory. Completely soaked, without honor but full of dignity, the young male was able to jump to a small wooden pole over the water and opened his wings to get dry as quickly as possible.

July 1992, Doñana. My female and her partner had decided to move to another area after the encounter with the adult pair. I found the place, centered on a solitary eucalyptus tree in the middle of the marshes. The eagles had made a big new nest and the female was brooding. During the preceding months I had had the opportunity to see how the birds fell in love, how they made a new nest, how the male fed her when she was incubating, and how carefully she fed small pieces of meat to her first offspring. Today was the day I was going to ring and tag the nestlings.

I arrived at the nest at eleven in the morning. I take all these actions with the highest level of security and efficiency when I am disturbing an endangered species such as the Spanish imperial eagle. It is, for me, a huge responsibility. First, I had to ensure the safety of the eagles and then to get all the scientific data I could in the least amount of time possible. The pair had three chicks, all about 45 days old; two were males and one was female. Taking measurements, blood samples, rings, transmitters, etc., left no time for thinking about anything else. When I had finished, I replaced the chicks in the nest, and then I saw her, the proud mother, flying over me, not more than 10 m (33 ft) above, defending her offspring bravely. A long time ago we had met very close and now I am not a stranger to her. I've been following her all her life, from when she was a chick to now, as a mother, and I felt in that moment that, in some way, I was like a part of the family to this eagle, and in some way she was a part of mine. As I was leaving the nest area, I was thinking how fortunate I was, how many brilliant moments the eagles had shared with me, and I surprised myself wishing all the best to "my grandchildren."

12
Madagascar Fish Eagle

COMMON NAME: Madagascar fish eagle

SCIENTIFIC NAME: *Haliaeetus vociferoides*

OTHER NAMES: Madagascar sea eagle, Ankoay (Malagasy)

IUCN CONSERVATION STATUS: *Critically Endangered (population trend disputed, either stable or declining)*

DESCRIPTION: A striking medium-sized eagle with long rounded wings and a short tail. Has a dark brown body, with a white tail and facial cheeks and long legs. Slightly smaller with relatively shorter wings and longer legs and tail than the closely related African fish eagle.

SIZE: Length: 60–66 cm (24–26 in); Wingspan: 165–180 cm (65–71 in); Weight: 2.2–3.5 kg (4.8–7.7 lb)

THREATS: Small population size (approximately 222 individuals) makes this species vulnerable to a wide variety of threats. Individuals are persecuted by humans and vulnerable to habitat loss and competition with people for food and trees.

DISTRIBUTION: Endemic to Madagascar, where it occurs only on the western seaboard.

MOVEMENTS: Nonmigratory; juveniles may disperse long distances.

HABITAT: Occurs primarily in coastal areas and large inland lakes and rivers. Roosts and nests in large trees near rivers or on coastal cliffs.

DIET: Primarily fish, which they catch themselves or are pirated from other species such as yellow-billed kites and herons.

NOTES: This is the only eagle species known to consistently breed in cooperative groups of between 3 and 5 individuals. Some groups comprise one female with multiple males (polyandry); one male with multiple females (polygyny); or multiple females with multiple males (polygynandry). The reasons for this unusual breeding behavior remain unclear.

Author's Biography

RUTH TINGAY in western
Madagascar with Cut Off,
the one-footed fish eagle.
Photo courtesy of the
author

Ruth Tingay left school in Derbyshire, England, at the age of 16, with an abysmal academic record and no interests other than a fondness for dogs and an encyclopedic knowledge of Led Zeppelin albums. Working as a kennel maid for both Battersea Dog's Home and on the QE2 cruise-liner, it took a further eight years before her interest in raptors developed after a chance encounter with a sparrowhawk while walking her dog in Windsor Great Park. This interest led her to work on various raptor conservation projects over a period of years, in Africa, North America, Central America, Europe, and the Middle East, but she harbored an underlying desire to work with raptors in Madagascar. Rick Watson of The Peregrine Fund eventually offered her the opportunity to study the critically endangered Madagascar fish eagle, but on condition that she enroll in a degree program. With no undergraduate degree and no academic aspirations whatsoever, she reluctantly agreed and talked her way into an MSc program at the University of Nottingham, where the first semester was spent learning that you didn't need to use a ruler to center text on a computer screen. Six happy months doing fieldwork, camping on a remote lakeshore in western Madagascar and following the daily lives of a dozen noisy and comical fish eagles, made it all worth-while. After completing her MSc, she was offered a PhD scholarship at Nottingham and returned to Madagascar over the following years to expand her fish eagle research. Having graduated in 2005, Ruth is currently studying eagles in Scotland, Cambodia, and Mongolia. She is a research associate at Hawk Mountain Sanctuary, a member of the Scottish Raptor Study Group, a member of the review board of the European Science Foundation and has served two terms as an International Director of the Raptor Research Foundation (RRF). At the time of writing, she is embarking on her first term as President of the RRF. She still rates Led Zeppelin, especially if accompanied by a cold gin and tonic and a large dog or two.

MADAGASCAR FISH EAGLE, MADAGASCAR

Ruth E. Tingay

Today was the day I was going to catch my favorite eagle. I knew I wasn't supposed to have a favorite. As a scientific eagle watcher, my role was to retain a dispassionate objectivity about my study species and to observe and record their daily behavior in a methodical and impartial manner. That had all changed when I met a special eagle called Cut Off.

Cut Off had only one foot. He was one of 40 Madagascar fish eagles whose behavior I had been studying. These eagles were unusual because they lived in polyandrous breeding groups comprising two to four males and one female, rather than the normal monogamous pairings. Cut Off first came to our attention in 1996 when my colleagues from The Peregrine Fund were trapping eagles to fit them with colored leg bands for individual identification. I didn't know how he had come to lose his foot. However, judging from the healed-over stump at the bottom of his right leg, it appeared that his foot had been sliced away—hence, the name we had given to him. (Cut Off was the only eagle with a proper name; I referred to all the others by the color of their leg band.) There were several possible explanations to account for his predicament. He could have become entangled in a fisherman's net and had his foot amputated to release him. Or he could have been the victim of local witch doctors who were known to covet the foot of an eagle for adding strength to their virility (pre-Viagra) potions. His foot may have been removed by locals to steal the aluminum leg band that they mistakenly believed was made of silver. Alternatively, he could have been caught by one of the large Nile crocodiles that lurked in the lake as he bathed or drank on the lakeshore. Whatever had happened to him, Cut Off was a remarkable eagle because not only had he survived in the wild with one foot for several years but also he held a dominant social position within his breeding trio (comprising Cut Off, Blue female, and Red male), successfully chasing away Red male from the nest at every opportunity. Ever supportive of the underdog, Cut Off had sealed his position in my affections.

My research involved finding out how each individual eagle behaved within its group, its genetic relationship to other group members, and, most interestingly, which of the males (dominant, subordinate, or both) sired the eaglets that hatched in each nest. To do this I had to trap each eagle to collect a small blood sample so I could compare its DNA and work out all the family relationships. I had already spent endless weeks and months paddling around the lakes in my canoe, watching the daily activities of each eagle, and eagles being creatures of habit, I knew exactly where Cut Off would be loafing this morning. I had seen him only yesterday as I had been in his territory to catch Red male; my efforts were nearly thwarted because Cut Off, being dominant, had tried to interfere when Red male was swooping down toward my floating fish trap, but luckily, Cut Off aborted his attack at the last moment and Red male was caught. Today I was after Cut Off.

I crawled out of my tent in the predawn darkness and made my way over to the fire pit for breakfast. The primitive field camp was in a remote area of the Tsimembo Forest at the edge of one of the three fish eagle lakes, and I shared it with eight local Malagasy men who had been hired to work as technicians on the fish eagle project. We had no electricity or running water, no telephone or e-mail, and no vehicle. If one of us injured ourselves, we faced a three-day walk across roadless terrain to reach the nearest airstrip, some 80 km (50 mi) to the north. Our nearest neighbors were a troupe of white, furry lemurs that danced through our camp every morning like demented ballerinas. Farther along the lakeshore there were small clusters of mud and straw huts, inhabited by fishermen from the regional Sakalava tribe who came to the lakes to take advantage of the fishing opportunities. The nearest village, Masoarivo (translated as "The Place of a Thousand Crocodile Eyes"), was a good four-hour walk away through the forest.

Our chief technician was a Malagasy called Loukman, and he had already stoked up the fire by the time I arrived in the camp's "kitchen." Loukman was my main eagle-trapping partner, and we carefully checked over our traps while waiting for the pot of rice to boil. As dawn broke over the mist-covered lake, and with bellies full of warm fish and rice, we slipped into our canoe and set off on the 50-minute journey toward Cut Off's side of the lake. We wanted to get there early before he started to hunt for his breakfast; if he hadn't eaten he would be more likely to come for the bait in our trap.

Midway across the lake we saw a local fisherman's boat and stopped to buy some fresh fish, both for Cut Off and for our supper. The elderly fisherman's eyes never left my face as Loukman leaned over to select the fattest fish from his slimy haul at the bottom of his boat. Being the only white woman for hundreds of kilometers around, I had become used to the inevitable stares that seemed to follow my every move, so I just smiled at him and pretended it was normal to see a man dressed only in yellow underpants sitting in a hollowed-out-tree-trunk canoe in the middle of a lake at six o'clock in the morning. As he stared, he had a brief conversation with Loukman, of which

I didn't understand a word. Loukman turned to me and translated—there was to be a circumcision ceremony that evening, the highlight of the social calendar, and I was invited to be the guest of honor. I really didn't want to go but I also didn't want to offend anyone. So I found myself feigning enthusiasm and nodding my acceptance to his surreal invitation; and he broke into a yellow, rotten-toothed smile as we paddled away.

I didn't have time to contemplate the evening's events because I had spotted Cut Off in his favorite hunting tree and my thoughts were focused back to the job in hand. With some fish eagles we had to approach in stealth mode when setting the trap, for fear of frightening them away, but Cut Off was an extraordinarily nosey eagle, so I knew he'd be curious about our activities this morning. There was no sign of Blue female or Red male, and I noticed that Cut Off's crop (a food storage pouch in the throat) was empty so it looked like he hadn't eaten yet; all the signs were good, and we started to set up the trap.

Our trap was simple—a floating fish covered in nooses. Fish eagles hunt by using their feet to snatch fish from the water's surface, and the nooses on this fish were designed to ensnare the eagle. After the eagle grabs the fish and then flies upward, one or more nooses should tighten around its foot. Since the trap is attached to a long rope and a bungee cord (to lessen the shock on the bird's legs) and anchored at the bottom of the lake, the eagle is then held by the noose and rope until we can grab it.

The responsibility of setting the trap properly was huge. I had to ensure, first and foremost, the safety of the eagle and, second, the safety of Loukman and me. We had the potential to cause serious injury to the eagle, and likewise, an eagle's powerful talons could rip open our flesh in a second. My greatest fear, though, had always been that once we had "downed" an eagle and it was floating on the water's surface, a crocodile might lunge from below and snap up the eagle in its massive jaws before we could get there to pick it up. For this reason, whenever we were setting a trap, one person would be on "crocodile look-out," scanning the water for that telltale snout, while the other person set the trap. Once it was laid, we would retreat a short distance but never, ever take our eyes off the trap, so when the eagle came for it, we could instantly dash over and lift it into the safety of our boat.

We didn't have long to wait this morning. Cut Off had watched me lay the trap over the side of the canoe, and even as we paddled away, I saw his head bobbing as he tried to view the fish from all angles. He waited until he considered we were at a safe distance, then opened his broad wings and silently glided down toward the floating fish. Loukman and I held our collective breath as we watched him skillfully grab the fish and fly in an upward thrust away from the water. The rope reached its full extension and there was a short jerk as the bungee cord became taut. This was the moment of truth. If he had managed to avoid a noose he would drop the fish and fly free. If his foot had become caught, he would be brought down to the water's surface. We were in luck. We watched him fall back toward the water, and before he'd even landed we were paddling toward him in an adrenaline-fueled frenzy. He was remarkably calm as we approached, his enormous wings outstretched to keep him afloat, and he didn't attempt to struggle even as I lifted him by his legs and gathered him from the water. Cradling Cut Off in my arms, Loukman collected the rest of the trap and rowed us over to the shore.

Once on land I disentangled Cut Off's foot from the noose and passed him to Loukman. We had to work quickly because I was feeling the guilt as Cut Off eyed me with his fearful brown eyes. I felt I'd betrayed his trust (so much for my scientific detachment), and I wanted to show him that we meant him no harm. His ordeal was over within a matter of minutes as I carefully cleaned the needle's puncture wound in his wing vein and labeled the precious vial of blood. Loukman carried Cut Off back to the edge of the lake, and after apologizing and saying our good-byes, we released him gently. He flew directly to his favorite perch tree, shook the spray from his ruffled feathers, and glared at us as we packed our gear back into the boat. As a peace offering, I untied the fish from the trap and threw it toward Cut Off, who watched it land with a splash underneath his tree. He defiantly ignored it until he thought we had paddled out of view, but I smiled to myself when, from a distance, I watched him through my binoculars and saw him pick it up.

As we paddled back to camp for a celebratory mug of boiled lake water (an acquired taste), I asked Loukman about the evening's impending social engagement. What did one wear to a circumcision ceremony? (Hopefully, filthy old field clothes.) What was the etiquette? Would I be required to watch? Make a speech? Offer a gift? Who would brandish the knife? What about hygiene or painkillers? What would happen to the foreskin after it was cut?

All was revealed later that night as I found myself ushered into the village elder's hut to sit cross-legged on the floor and partake in a bottle of overpowering moonshine. The doorway was filled with the faces of inebriated young fishermen, egging me on to say something in English and then collapsing in a heap of laughter every time I spoke. Outside the hut a large bonfire blazed and I watched the shadows of dancing women as they whooped and sang around the fire. Underneath a tall baobab tree slouched a handful of men too drunk to stand. Loukman pointed toward one of them and whispered that he would be the one to perform the ritual at dawn. According to Loukman, he had a razor blade in his pocket and he had "great experience of doing this," allegedly. Two young boys no more than 10 years old were presented to me in the hut; these were the sacrificial lambs and I didn't fancy their chances much. Loukman translated my wishes of luck to them and they looked bemused: a case of blissful ignorance, perhaps.

I was beginning to feel uncomfortable with all the attention I was receiving, and I had a nagging fear that, as guest of honor, I might be invited to eat the severed foreskin (I had read about this happening somewhere else). I asked Loukman for some reassurance and he laughed. His explanation of what would happen went like this:

> Only the strange tribes in the central highlands of Madagascar eat the foreskin, and it has to be the boy's grandparents, who leave the foreskin on the roof all day and eat it at sunset. Here in the west, the Sakalava tribe are not so strange. We put the foreskin onto a fizzy [a firework] and send it off into the sky.

As I listened to the boys' painful cries at sunrise, I mused on Loukman's interpretation of the word "strange." I concluded that strangeness, like most things in life, was all relative. I had become immersed in the lost world of Madagascar, my days filled with the sex lives of deviant fish eagles and my nights interrupted by biting fleas and persistent mosquitoes. I speculated that my friends at home in England would probably deem my life strange, but to me, being an eagle watcher was what I liked best.

13

African Crowned Eagle

COMMON NAME: African crowned eagle

SCIENTIFIC NAME: *Stephanoaetus coronatus*

OTHER NAMES: Crowned eagle, crowned hawk eagle

IUCN CONSERVATION STATUS: *Least Concern (population declining)*

DESCRIPTION: A large, very dark eagle with mottled rufous breast, a distinctively barred under-belly and a crest it can erect or lay flat. This species has a large bill and fully feathered legs with powerful feet. Like many other large tropical forest raptors, its wings are short and broad, and it has a long tail. Preadults are noticeably paler than adults.

SIZE: Length: 80–95 cm (31–38 in); Wingspan: 151–181 cm (60–72 in); Weight: 2.7–4.7 kg (6–11 lb)

THREATS: Habitat loss is probably the greatest threat this species faces, as well as pressures from hunting and competition with humans for food resources.

DISTRIBUTION: Sub-Saharan Africa, primarily forested areas in equatorial Africa and the eastern parts of southern Africa

MOVEMENTS: Nonmigratory but juveniles do disperse.

HABITAT: Usually heavily forested areas, but also riparian areas and even open savanna. Has also been observed breeding in eucalypt plantations. Forages in a wider variety of habitats.

DIET: Primarily forages on mammals, especially small antelope, hyraxes, and monkeys. Also takes birds and even large reptiles (e.g., monitor lizards).

NOTES: A small piece of a skull from a human child was once found in the nest of an African crowned eagle. Some people have suggested that the eagle killed the child, but it is more likely that the eagle scavenged the skull from the child's corpse.

Author's Biography

SUSANNE SHULTZ feeding
a recently trapped African
crowned eagle in the Taï
National Park, Ivory
Coast. Photo courtesy
of the author

Susanne Shultz originally became interested in raptors as predators of
social mammals when, during her studies for an MSc in ecology and
evolution at the State University of New York, Stony Brook, she realized
how underappreciated raptors are as major predators of mammals in
tropical forests. This focused her research interests on predator behavior,
and she decided it was her ambition to study one of the large "monkey
eagles" found in tropical forests. Her first field experience with raptors
came from helping the New York Department of Environmental Conservation with monitoring and tracking ospreys and bald eagles on Long
Island and on the Hudson River. Around the same time, a primatologist,
Ronald Noë, was looking for someone to study African crowned eagles as
part of the Taï Monkey Project in the Taï National Park, Ivory Coast.
Fortunately, the two were put in touch and Susanne was given the
opportunity to study the eagles as part of a comprehensive research
project, which collected data on the abundance of most of the prey species
of African crowned eagles as well as the other main predators in the forest.
Susanne completed her PhD on the ecology and behavior of the African
crowned eagle with Robin Dunbar at the University of Liverpool. Following her PhD, Susanne held a position as the project manager for the Asian
vulture declines project with the Royal Society for the Protection of Birds
(RSPB). During her time there, the project confirmed Diclofenac, a
veterinary drug used on cattle, as the cause of the catastrophic population
decline of vultures in India. Susanne currently holds a Royal Society
Dorothy Hodgkin Fellowship in the Institute for Cognitive and Evolutionary Anthropology at the University of Oxford.

AFRICAN CROWNED EAGLE, IVORY COAST

Susanne Shultz

In 1998, through sheer good fortune, I found myself involved with the Taï Monkey Project in Taï National Park, Ivory Coast. People find primates fascinating because they are social, intelligent, and easy to empathize with. One of the most likely explanations for primates' sociality is that living in a group helps individuals evade predators. Although many people had looked at how monkeys behave around predators, very few had looked at how predators behave around monkeys. African crowned eagles are one of the three large forest eagles in the world that are capable of grappling with wily monkeys, the other two being the harpy eagle found in South America and the Philippine eagle.

I found myself in the towering Taï forest looking for eagles as part of my PhD research. Crowned eagles have a split personality; when they want to be seen, they are extraordinarily noisy and obvious. Nearly every day around midday a pair flies above its territory in an elaborate display, choreographing their whistling call with whirls and swoops. However, apart from this display, these huge birds have the ability to vanish in the forest. Occasionally, a massive and silent shadow is cast overhead by passing eagles, and it provokes terror and alarm cries from monkey groups. Unless there is a young eagle giving a telltale call from nearby, even their huge nests can be strangely difficult to find. Two local research assistants—Sio, who was nearly as wily as the monkeys and as difficult to pin down as the eagles, and Roger, who was as dependable as Sio wasn't—helped me to locate 26 eagle nests. All of these nests provided valuable information on eagle density, diet, and breeding behavior, but what I really wanted to know was where the eagles were going and how they managed to catch monkeys. To do this, I needed to attach radio tags to the eagles. I made a few initial attempts at catching the eagles, but I was no match for them. I would set traps near their nests and sit and wait and wait and wait and wait. I had previously helped trap ospreys and bald eagles. No matter how lovely those two species are, they are not the intellectual challenge that crowned eagles are. You don't learn to outsmart monkeys without being on the ball, crafty, and perceptive.

It was recommended that I should get in touch with a Mr. Simon Thomsett. Simon is somewhat of an African raptor guru and has been called in by research groups to trap bearded vultures in Ethiopia, kites in Cape Verde, and just about every raptor in East Africa. Simon has kept "problem" crowned eagles in his collection for several decades. He has a breeding pair and has released their young back into the wild. After my dismal failures to trap a crowned eagle, I thought, what the heck, I'll send this guy a letter and see what happens. At that time Simon didn't use e-mail, didn't have a phone line connected to his house, didn't have an office where he could be contacted during the day, but could pick up letters at the post office and faxes sent to a travel agent's office somewhere in Kenya. I had little hope of receiving a reply, but I sent off a letter explaining that I knew where a lot of crowned eagles were but I could not catch any of them. Could he, please, offer some advice. Not only did Simon answer my letter, but he offered to help.

Over the following months we arranged that Simon would come to the Ivory Coast for several weeks. We settled on an approximate day that Simon would come over, but between this and the actual day he arrived, communication totally broke down. We had no telephone in the forest, so I had to make all arrangements from the capital, Abidjan, which was a nine-hour drive from the research station. Telephone service to the research center where I stayed died two days before Simon was due to arrive. I went to phone kiosks in the city and contacted Simon's travel agent (remember, there was no direct phone line to Simon), who thought he had already left for the Ivory Coast. Amy, another student, and I went to the airport to try to meet the next possible flight on which Simon could be arriving, but with no success. I phoned the travel agent again, but Simon hadn't been heard from. The research center was a good 20 km (12.4 mi) out of the city; most taxi drivers didn't know it by name, but they knew the nearest settlement on the highway. We still had no phone service, so Simon couldn't contact us. Oh, and Simon didn't speak French, and most Ivorians don't speak English. We were sitting on the terrace outside the research center trying to figure out what we should do when a spluttering and smoking taxi pulled up to the office and a very beleaguered and tired man stepped out. Simon had arrived the previous day and was nonplussed that he had spent the night in a fleabag hotel/brothel.

Fortunately, logistics improved from this low point. We set off to Taï and I tried to make amends to Simon for the mix-up. Once in Taï, Simon was eager to go and see some nests, so we walked to the nearest one, and then he wanted to see another, then another. I started to realize that part of his enthusiasm for the trip was to see whether the nests were actually at the density I had estimated. Once satisfied, Simon set about organizing his trapping strategy. As we needed supplies, we went to the nearby town of Taï (a few dusty roads, two or three shops, and a market). We visited all the shops; Simon poked at various hardware items in the market, puzzled over them, and tried to explain to me how he could use things like a door hinge, a bracket, or a shoelace to catch an eagle.

Simon's arrival generated somewhat of a circus atmosphere. I accept some responsibility for making him a sensation as I had built up the arrival of the eagle trapper. Most of the people who worked in the forest had respect for the eagles and agreed that it was impossible to catch these clever and dangerous birds. Simon helped build his own personality cult by refusing to wear the standard green and gray forest uniform and rubber boots, preferring to walk through the sodden forest barefoot and in khaki shorts and choosing to sleep in a tent under the eagles' nests when trapping rather than in a room at the research camp.

While Simon camped in the forest, I spent my time ferrying food and drink and bits of string to him. One morning when I arrived on the rock outcropping that overlooked one of the nests, a very large white-breasted juvenile eagle was sitting calmly tethered to a log. Jeffrey, as I called him, was a recently fledged male who, like all very young crowned eagles, spent his days impatiently waiting for his parents to bring him tasty treats. Therefore, when Simon offered him a baited morsel, he leapt at it. Being so close to a crowned eagle, even if it was an overgrown, awkward, and fussy adolescent, was awe inspiring. These eagles are not only big, they are solid. They have massive legs and talons, wide chests, and large forward-facing eyes that look straight into yours. They are absolutely lovely.

Simon decided that if we held onto Jeffrey we just might distract his mother enough that she would make a mistake and fall for one of his traps. Jeffrey didn't seem too bothered with this decision; he started to take food from us almost immediately, and after about a day he didn't have his "crown" raised the whole time we were holding him.

Two days later we caught Jeffrey's mother, and boy, was she angry. Knowing just how dangerous an unhappy crowned eagle can be, Simon and I had discussed how we would handle her before we lowered her from the trap set on a high branch. I would lower her until she was about shoulder height and hold her there. Simon would approach her, grab her loose foot first (as the other foot was held by a noose), and then slowly reach around and grab her noosed foot. We would then lower her to the ground, cover her, and put a hood over her head and jesses around her legs so we could handle her safely. Unfortunately, she didn't cooperate. As I lowered her down, Simon quietly walked up to her and caught her free leg. She was so strong that she surprised him by instantly lifting herself up, twisting round, and sinking the talons from her noosed leg into Simon's arm. Simon very calmly asked me to come over and help him. I stepped over and saw that her long rear talon entered one side of his forearm and exited on the far side. As I gaped at the gory scene, Simon urged me to be calm as he would quickly lose the ability to flex his forearm. I had to pry her talon out using both hands; we then covered her, radio-tagged her, and released her as quickly as we could. We then released Jeffrey, who flew straight back to his nest and mother. She was still angry, he was confused, but both were unharmed and we could now follow them through the forest.

We then had to deal with Simon's wounds. As mentioned previously, the field station was a nine-hour drive from the capital and the nearest decent hospital was not much closer. Shortly before we trapped Jeffrey's mother, she had brought in the leg of a red colobus monkey for a meal. All I could think of was that her talon had just infected Simon's arm with all sorts of nasty things that fester in dead monkeys. Simon was more composed. We took him back to camp, used syringes to clean inside his wounds, gave him a course of strong antibiotics, and put his arm in a sling as he had very little movement in his hand. Over the following days we were relieved that the wounds healed, and he slowly regained movement in his hands. His personality cult grew; not only was he an eagle trapper, he actually caught two in Taï, had scars to prove it, and was shortly back in the forest for more.

Although this story has been about the drama of Simon's first visit, what I enjoyed the most was hearing his stories about flying his birds, how they behaved, and watching how he outwitted the very birds that flummoxed me. I learned more about the eagles in the two weeks he spent with us than in the previous year I had spent sitting under their nests and collecting their prey remains. Crowned eagles are formidable birds. By radio-tagging them I was able to see just how clever they are when they hunt monkeys: they anticipate their movements, spend patient hours waiting for just the right opportunity to attack, and then ambush them. Without having Simon there as my interpreter, I don't think I would have ever been allowed into their world. Oh, and about Jeffrey and his mother. We kept track of Jeffrey for another year, and eventually we heard his signals less and less frequently; he must have dispersed to find his own territory somewhere else in the forest. His mother allowed us to follow her around for about four months, then one day I found her transmitter bleeping on the forest floor. I still saw her at her nest, but I think she must have had enough of cooperating.

Crowned eagles, because they are quite adaptable, live in a variety of habitats, including open woodland, and montane and primary forests. However, the Upper Guinea forests where Taï is are endangered, as are the many species that are restricted to these forest habitats. Very little is known about some raptors that are found in these forests because they are difficult to find and to study. I feel very fortunate that I was able to spend time studying eagles in such an amazing place, and I hope that the remaining forest in West Africa will be preserved for the future to protect the fantastic biodiversity it contains.

14

Grey-headed Fishing Eagle

COMMON NAME: Grey-headed fishing eagle

SCIENTIFIC NAME: *Ichthyophaga ichthyaetus*

OTHER NAMES: Ceylon grey-headed fishing eagle, greater fishing eagle, tank eagle

IUCN CONSERVATION STATUS: *Near Threatened (population declining)*

DESCRIPTION: A medium-sized fish eagle, generally dark brown with a gray head and neck. Pale to white below, tail white with a thick nearly terminal dark band. Breast brown. Juveniles similar to adult but streaked brown.

SIZE: Length: 66–77 cm (26–31 in); Wingspan: 140–175 cm (55–69 in); Weight: 1.6–2.7 kg (3.5–6.0 lb)

THREATS: Habitat loss, competition with humans for food (overfishing), human disturbance, and pesticide contamination. This species has not been well studied, and the threats it faces are not well understood.

DISTRIBUTION: Indo-Malaysia

MOVEMENTS: Nonmigratory; juvenile movements unknown

HABITAT: Freshwater lakes and rivers, coastal lagoons and estuaries, forested woodlands and lowlands near slow-moving or still water

DIET: Mostly fish and water snakes, but also birds and mammals. Diet of this species is poorly known.

NOTES: In parts of Cambodia, it is considered taboo to kill a fish eagle, as by doing so, the locals believe their gods will punish them by reducing their annual fish harvest.

Author's Biography

MALCOLM NICOLL looking
for desert elephants in
Damaraland, Namibia.
Photo courtesy of the
author

Malcolm Nicoll was raised on a farm in Dorset, England, and when he was not at school or working on the farm, his time was spent shooting, fishing, and observing wildlife, particularly birds of prey. His fascination with raptors began at an early age. He started training as a falconer at the age of 10 and managed to continue this passion throughout his school years by convincing school officials that a falconry club was needed. Two kestrels, three buzzards, and some ferrets provided more than enough of a distraction from schoolwork. However, despite this he still managed to gain a place at Edinburgh University, where he studied for his BSc in wildlife and fisheries management. He graduated from Edinburgh and headed to the western Indian Ocean, where he worked for seven years on a range of endangered species recovery programs and island ecosystem restoration projects. In 1999 he swapped the tropical island life for England, to develop a PhD study on a reintroduced population of the endangered Mauritius kestrel. The study took longer to develop than anticipated, so he moved to Perthshire in Scotland to work as the senior falconer for the British School of Falconry at Gleneagles. There the "working" days were spent training and flying a range of eagles, hawks, and falcons. His PhD study commenced in 2000, and his time, for the next three and a half years, was divided between Mauritius and the University of Reading. Since 2004 Malcolm has been employed as a postdoctoral research fellow at the Centre for Agri-Environmental Research at the University of Reading, where kestrels in Mauritius and fish eagles in Cambodia provide a welcome respite from the office environment.

GREY-HEADED FISHING EAGLE, CAMBODIA

Malcolm Nicoll

In 2005, I was fortunate enough to join a field trip to Cambodia to study the grey-headed fishing eagle, a species that lives in the extraordinary flooded forest surrounding Asia's largest freshwater lake, the Tonle Sap. This may seem relatively unremarkable but for two reasons. First, as a result of the political instability associated with the Khmer Rouge regime, until the mid-1990s few western scientists had been allowed into Cambodia to study the wildlife. Second, very little is known about the grey-headed fishing eagle anywhere across its range. In fact, we were to be the first wildlife biologists to go to Tonle Sap Lake to study this particular species. As neither of us had even seen this eagle or visited Cambodia before, it was a venture into the unknown.

The area of flooded forest we planned to visit was part of the Prek Toal protected area, at the northwest end of Tonle Sap Lake. To reach the site required a full day's travel from Cambodia's bustling capital, Phnom Penh, first by road then by boat. The taxi ride north proved to be a test of endurance and nerve, as the road frequently changed from "smooth" to "spine jarring." Likewise, traffic appeared to be in a perpetual state of chaos, resembling a computer game with every conceivable form of transport and hazard occurring at once. Transport varied from ox-drawn carts to luxury air-conditioned coaches, but mopeds were by far the most common, frequently carrying up to five people. Mopeds were also used to move anything and everything around, including livestock such as poultry, ducks, and pigs. A common site was an adult pig strapped upside down to a plank on the back of the moped, while piglets traveled en masse in wicker baskets. After the dust, noise, and chaos of the road, the boat trip across the lake to Prek Toal was comparatively tranquil and took us to the floating village that was to be home for the next two weeks.

The floating village of Prek Toal is located on a river near the lake shore. Tonle Sap Lake and its surrounding floodplain experience a rise and fall in water level of up to 10 m (33 ft) in any one year, with the area of the lake changing from 3000 km^2 (1158 mi^2) in the dry season to 12,000 km^2 (4633 mi^2) in the wet season. While the wildlife and forest are naturally adapted to this dramatic seasonal flooding, so too are the resourceful Khmer people, having developed a community at Prek Toal that "floats" for the majority of the year. Everything except a secondary school, a new environmental center, and a temple (all built on concrete stilts) floats for most of the year, including houses, the police station and jail, petrol station, ice factory, dentist, restaurant/karaoke bar, homes, gardens, crocodile farms, and even livestock pens. Just like any other village it had a "high street." However, at Prek Toal the high street was a river and the transport of choice were boats of all shapes and sizes, some with engines and some without. The largest boats were the ferries transporting people and supplies between the capital and the principal provincial towns, while the smallest were flat-bottomed canoes that the children paddled to school. We discovered if you needed something, rather than going to the shop, the shop in the form of a boat came to you—you simply waved it over as it passed by. These "shops" were very distinctive as they resembled giant cigars and the onboard cooking fires left a trail of smoke in their wake. It was even possible to get some "fast food" from smaller boats that were paddled around the village by Vietnamese ladies (apparently you could tell they were not Khmer by the shape of their hat), which was very popular with our translator, who seemed to favor the half-formed ducklings in a hardboiled egg. Needless to say, neither of us had the "stomach" to try one of these delicacies, but we were quick to joke with our translator about avian flu being quite common in poultry and waterfowl in the region.

We stayed in the new permanent section of the environmental center, which was on concrete stilts. Being recently finished, it was a very smart-looking building, and with electricity generated by solar panels and running water filtered from the lake, it certainly stood out among the floating shacks that made up most of the village. However, like all new field centers it had some infrastructure issues to work through, and as some of the first people to stay there, we got to experience them. Apart from the electricity regularly cutting out at night, the far more inconvenient (and bigger risk to our health) was the water regularly smelling strongly of raw sewage. Clearly something was amiss with the filter system, and until this was resolved we collected water from the flooded forest each day for a rudimentary "bucket" shower in the evening. The center also had an excellent cook, who agreed to prepare us a meal each night. Following local advice we had arrived in the village with sufficient food for the duration of our stay, and so we duly handed over our supplies to her. Occasionally she supplemented our evening meals with a few of the local delicacies, but basically it was a somewhat repetitive diet of the rice, vegetables, and tinned fish that we had brought with us. We later discovered that there was a surprising variety of food available in the village (although the supply could be a little unreliable), including fruit, vegetables, fresh fish, and even pork. We became aware of the latter when every third day or so, our early wakeup call (at 5 a.m.) was the sound of a pig being slaughtered at a floating abattoir not far from our windows!

We knew that we had arrived at Prek Toal after the flood waters had reached their peak and the water level was now dropping. The watermarks left on the concrete stilts of the environmental center made perfect measuring posts, and each morning we noted how much the water level had dropped. This was important not just for us, since it affected the access we had to the flooded forest, but also for the villagers, because they moved their houses around according to the water level. As the water level receded, homes were towed by boats from the edge of the forest onto the main river channel so as not to become marooned in the mud. With the rapidly receding water this was a daily activity, and during our two-week stay we experienced a succession of neighbors, including one household that included a cage full of crocodiles. I guess that one advantage of this is that any neighborly disputes could be easily resolved by moving the house elsewhere.

While the forest is flooded, the only way to get around is by boat, so our days were spent in a small wooden boat locating and observing fishing eagles, accompanied by a boatman, a ranger, and a translator. The boat, like most in the area, was resourcefully powered by an old Toyota car engine mounted at the stern. This was not the only part of a car in the boat: the steering wheel (complete with switches for indicators, lights, and wipers!) provided the means of steering. Our ranger, Ly, was a former snake hunter, egg collector, and bird poacher whose knowledge of the flooded forest and wildlife proved invaluable. He was adept at spotting fishing eagles, knew the location of many of their nests, and always knew exactly where we were in the forest. Between his knowledge and our general observations, we managed to gather sufficient information to confirm the status of the fishing eagle in the protected area and document some aspects of its breeding biology and feeding habits. Fortunately the eagles seemed largely indifferent to five people in an "aquatic car," which allowed us some "up close and personal" behavioral observations. We observed several different styles of hunting techniques and learned that the "fishing eagle" might perhaps be better described as the "snake eagle," because all prey caught were water snakes. This was new information for us, but of course the locals were one step ahead, as usual; Ly informed us that one species of water snake was locally known as the "fish eagle water snake." Water snakes not only were eaten by the fishing eagles but also were harvested for local consumption (as we were to experience firsthand), as food for the farmed crocodiles, and for live export to other Asian countries.

In the flooded forest at that time of year there wasn't any dry land (no need to worry about stepping on a landmine!), so each day from 7 a.m. to 5 p.m., five of us were confined to a small boat while we studied the fishing eagles. All activities therefore had to be conducted on or over the side of the boat. This led to some rather comical and uncomfortable moments, usually at the expense of one individual. Being the only female team member, my friend Ruth was reluctant to relieve herself over the side of the boat, so by early afternoon each day, she was looking decidedly uncomfortable and did not seem to appreciate the humor of being repeatedly offered water. Surprisingly only one person fell overboard—our esteemed ranger, Ly (only his pride was damaged). More surprisingly, despite actually driving through the forest canopy in an area renowned for its venomous pit vipers and cobras, no snakes fell into the boat. If one had, then I suspect we all would have fallen overboard. We never managed to set fire to the (wooden) boat despite cooking breakfast and lunch on a gas fire, even though the cooker blew up once. The boat only broke down once, but some rope, wire, and a bit of paddling soon fixed that— Toyota reliability.

We did, of course, get the opportunity to see a lot of wildlife in addition to the eagles. The flooded forest supports a vast number of large waterbirds including storks, egrets, cormorants, and pelicans. We were privileged to witness a mixed flock following a shoal of fish through the forest canopy early one morning. The sizes of the shoal and flock were impossible to gauge, but for more than 10 minutes the water around us "boiled" as the fish passed by, followed closely by a whirling mass of birds. We even managed to see, perhaps a little too closely than is wise, a cobra.

Although poisonous snakes were high on our danger list, along with land mines, they didn't make the top position. That dubious honor was given to the Khmer Rouge, a genocidal regime responsible for the deaths of an estimated two million people during 1975–79, through execution, starvation, and forced labor. Although they were overthrown in 1979, small pockets of guerrillas were still thought to exist in remote areas of western Cambodia, as demonstrated by the kidnapping and murder of British, Australian, and French tourists in the mid-1990s. Ruth had spent a good deal of our trip reading up on the activities of the Khmer Rouge, and we'd made a sobering visit to the "Killing Fields" just outside Phnom Penh, where thousands of Cambodians were executed (with pickaxes, to save on bullets) and buried in mass graves. During a lunchtime break in the boat one day, Ruth asked Visal, our Cambodian colleague, about what had happened to the Khmer Rouge guerrillas after the collapse of the regime and how they were received by local villagers, many of whom had been personally subjected to the regime's extreme brutality. Visal's reply was unnerving, to say the least. He said that the region we were working in had been the heartland of the Khmer Rouge, and that many of the guerrillas had returned to their villages to live "normal" lives after the conflict. He told us that the locals felt no animosity toward the guerrillas because they believed they had been "brainwashed" into working for the Khmer Rouge. Ruth then asked Visal whether there were any former members of the Khmer Rouge in the village. He told us that there were and that we were closer than we thought to several of them. This proved to be a rather sobering thought and signaled a prompt end to our discussion on the Khmer Rouge.

The more we watched the grey-headed fishing eagles, the more we began to realize that water snakes could be a fundamental part of their diet. As we knew next to nothing about water snakes, however, we resolved to find out as much as possible in our last few days. We recorded the different species of snakes caught in fishermen's nets along the main river channels, we had numerous discussions with people who harvested or studied water snakes in the area, we acquired a few live specimens of the different species, and we even ended up eating a few of them. In the local villages, water snakes are a regular source of protein, along with fish, and we returned back to the environmental station one evening to find a simmering pot full of water snakes on the open fire on the deck. We were presented with several species cooked in a variety of ways, much to the amusement of our local ranger team. To be honest neither of us could tell one species from another by taste, but fried snake was definitely better than stewed snake, largely because it was cooked with excessive amounts of ginger and therefore tasted less of mud and lake water.

Our time spent in the flooded forest allowed us an insight not only into Khmer culture but also, more importantly, into the lives of these fishing eagles. Large Chinese hydropower dams are currently under construction in the upstream reaches of the Mekong River, with potentially disastrous effects on the people and wildlife of the Tonle Sap Lake. The fishing eagles are now being used as an environmental indicator of ecosystem health, so by watching the eagles, we can watch (and monitor) the changes that occur to this unique floodwater environment.

15
Wahlberg's Eagle

COMMON NAME: Wahlberg's eagle

SCIENTIFIC NAME: *Hieraaetus (Aquila) wahlbergi*

OTHER NAMES: None

IUCN CONSERVATION STATUS: *Least Concern (population stable)*

DESCRIPTION: A generally small eagle with relatively long, narrow wings and a long squared tail. Has a small head and face and well-feathered legs. Light brown morph appears most commonly, but coloration may be dark brown or very light, almost white. Preadults are difficult to distinguish from adults.

SIZE: 53–61 cm (21–24 in); Wingspan: 130–146 cm (51–57 in); Weight: 0.85–1.5 kg (1–3 lb)

THREATS: Threats appear minimal, but this species is impacted by hunting and poisoning.

DISTRIBUTION: Occupies most of sub-Saharan Africa. Breeds in southern and central Africa, migrates north, crossing the equator, and winters north of the equator but south of the Sahara desert.

MOVEMENTS: Most are migratory, although some populations may be non-migratory. Adults arrive in southern Africa in August or September and depart again in March or April. Timing of migration appears to coincide with weather, such that the birds experience the rainy season during breeding and nonbreeding seasons.

HABITAT: Woodland savanna. It avoids deep forest with closed canopy and open arid or mountainous areas and prefers a mosaic of open grassland and woodland.

DIET: Wahlberg's eagle has a highly varied diet, taking mostly reptiles but also mammals and birds with regularity. Is known to take the young of many species, including hyrax, francolin, and herons.

NOTES: In 1994, researchers in Namibia attached a satellite transmitter to a Wahlberg's eagle for the first time and tracked its movements from February to November. During this time it migrated north to western Chad and flew at least 8816 km (5478 mi). It was rediscovered back in Namibia incubating close to where it was originally captured.

Author's Biography

ROBERT E. SIMMONS on
the banks of the Orange
River, South Africa.
Photo by Hannah
Thomas

Rob Simmons grew up in southeastern England, which was then the most raptor-depauperate piece of real estate in the world; a combination of DDT and gamekeepers had managed to exterminate all the buzzards, all the sparrowhawks, and most of the kestrels. It was actually 20 years before the first sparrowhawk reappeared, but by that time Rob had given up to try his luck in Canada, where he simultaneously met his wife, Phoebe, and studied for his MSc degree, on harriers. Seeking greater adventures and lured by a possible study of pesticide uptake in raptors in Zimbabwe, he winged his way to southern Africa and has been there for more than 25 years. It was a case of raptor rags to riches, since southern Africa offers no less than 80 species of raptors and vultures, despite the attempts of chemical manufacturers and some landowners to reduce that number to levels found in southern England. In Namibia, Rob was the state ornithologist for 14 years, working on cranes, penguins, parrots, and endemics and grappling with biodiversity issues within Namibia's progressive Biodiversity Program. Most of his interest lies with harriers and especially their mating systems and rarity. Following his doctoral work on African marsh harriers, he wrote all his thoughts into one book and sold it to Oxford University Press; amazingly other people bought it and now he is seen as the world authority on harriers. The eagle part of the story started as an afterthought, when he found that eagles were easier to find, were easier to watch, nested in accessible places, and people had heard of them. He studied Wahlberg's eagles in the lowveld of South Africa for four years and survived the experience, living with Phoebe and his 6-week-old daughter in a ramshackle railway station with cobras in the roof and scorpions in the bedroom. Rob now lives in a safer house in Cape Town, where he body surfs with two daughters and the same (lovely) wife, alongside whales and great white sharks, while watching Verreaux's eagles and peregrines sail overhead.

WAHLBERG'S EAGLE, SOUTH AFRICA

Robert E. Simmons

It was at an international meeting of ecologists in Princeton, New Jersey, United States, where I first met the imposing figure of Doug Mock. Doug is a disconcerting character with his broad American accent, his esteemed reputation as the doyen of sibling aggression studies, and his habit of looking at you with first one eye then the other. Doug's squint makes it impossible to know whether or not he's concentrating on you, but one thing he said in jest irritated me and stuck in my memory long after our meeting. He said that most people who study raptors do so just because they are stunning, spectacular birds and not because they can tell us anything interesting that other commoner species cannot. He laughingly labeled raptor biologists as "raptor bozos." This one remark galvanized me to prove him wrong—to make sure that even though I loved the thrill of chasing and studying such spectacular birds, the raptor studies I did in Africa had a worthwhile scientific goal.

I met with Doug because I was passionately interested in solving the mystery of why some large eagles allow the killing of their second chick in the nest. This behavior is called "siblicide," and describes the killing of a sibling shortly after the second egg hatches. The senior chick mercilessly attacks its newly hatched kin until it is either dead or so intimidated that it no longer calls for food and starves to death. This behavior has been described as "biological waste" by some. This I knew (in my arrogance) to be wrong, and Doug's mocking pushed me to study a species that bred in large numbers so that I could undertake some simple field experiments to help solve the mystery of siblicide.

Wahlberg's eagle is probably Africa's most common eagle—it is relatively small, migratory, occurs at high densities, and breeds in some of South Africa's major reserves. There was only one problem for a study of siblicide in this species—it lays but a single egg!

So it was in 1988 that I first set foot in the hot and somewhat bizarre environment of the Sabi Sands Game Reserve in northeastern South Africa. This reserve abuts the more famous Kruger National Park and has the full complement of predators and big game for which Africa is famous. Arriving there, green behind the ears, with a wife and month-old baby meant learning quickly. Getting stuck far from our converted railway station home and avoiding venomous snakes and large predators were the least of my worries. The landowners were by and large much more unpredictable. The reserve is famed for its amalgamation of the wealthiest businessmen and women in South Africa. It provides an escape from their high-pressure lives, and, of course, it makes money by providing high-paying tourists with access to the big five (lion, leopard, elephant, rhinoceros, and buffalo). Paying US$1000 per night was not unusual then, and fees are much higher today. Most landowners were indifferent to me studying a bird most of them hadn't heard of—as long as I didn't upset the guests, stuck to the rules, and reported my findings at the end of my research.

Studying Wahlberg's eagles in this environment rich in wildlife was exhilarating and tense at the same time. I was wary of breaking the rules and of taking my wife and baby into the bush, but I was just as wary of breaking down in the borrowed Land Rover far from home and having to walk out. The one evening that I did run out of fuel, 3 km (1.9 mi) from home, proved more adrenaline-pumping than precarious. My nerves tingled like never before as my eyes nervously scanned the ground for telltale tracks and I searched ahead and all around for a swishing tail or a movement in the grass. I used my nose for the first time in my life, sensing the pungent smell of buffalo or lion, and my heart rate never fell below about 150. I have run harder, more strenuous jogs, but I have never before or since used more nervous energy in such a short run.

Eagle watching starts early in southern Africa, well before the sun rises, to beat the heat. My approach was to find as many eagle nests as possible, and to monitor their progress either by climbing to the nest and measuring the egg or chick, or by using a long extendable mirror to check the contents of the nest 5 to 15 m (16 to 49 ft) above the ground.

There still remained the problem of studying siblicide in a species that lays only a single egg. To resolve the issue I conducted an experiment. I found nests that had similar-sized young, and I brought the young into a makeshift laboratory in one of the railway station's several rooms. There their interactions with other young eagles could be studied firsthand. Those eaglets may well have been the first Wahlberg's eagles observed exhibiting sibling aggression. Young birds that could barely hold up their heads fought with their nest mates until my assistant, Colleen Begg, parted them to avoid any sustained injury. Some older nestlings even clambered out of their makeshift nests to have a go at the neighboring chick. Even this simple experiment showed us something new—that Wahlberg's eagles do exhibit sibling aggression and join the list of many other large eagles that show this strange behavior.

My hunch for why sibling aggression occurs at all is that parents set up a kind of contest in which the winner takes all. In this case the winner is the chick that survives—usually the senior chick. By doing so the parents can be assured that they have the highest-quality offspring into which they pour all resources and raise it to be a robust and well-fed eaglet—improving its chances of surviving the rigors of adult eagle life. Simultaneously they can ensure that if the first egg does not hatch, then a second egg can act as insurance against complete failure.

The question then becomes, Why doesn't Wahlberg's eagle lay a second egg?—which is actually just another way of asking, Why do the other eagles lay that second egg? I set about answering this question in two ways. First I asked, Is there a cost to a bird laying two eggs rather than one? I studied this question by comparing the size of the eggs of all eagles that lay only one egg, with the size of the eggs of eagles with the same body size that always lay two eggs. Birds of similar body size are expected to lay similar-sized eggs so any difference in egg size is likely to be due to other factors. I found that the first egg of the two-egg eagles was smaller than it should be. So what? Well size is important—and in eggs it is very important. A small Wahlberg's eagle egg has a very high chance (more than 50%) of failing to hatch. So one viable strategy would be to lay the largest single large egg that it can, rather than compromise the hatchability of that egg by laying a second one.

Second, I asked if the parents could rear a second chick if it did hatch. To do this I added a second nestling of roughly the same size to an active nest with a single chick. By doing so about 4 to 6 weeks after hatching, I was able to avoid any form of sibling aggression and siblicide, which, in this species, disappears at around this age. If pairs couldn't rear the second chick, then I could conclude that another reason why these eagles normally laid a single egg was because they could only rear one chick. This hunch was indeed correct: of the eight pairs that I gave a second nestling to, none could rear both chicks. In all cases the second starved to death (this occurred because the parents did not increase the amount of food provided). This outcome is different from eagles that lay two eggs. In these species, experiments have shown that they can sometimes rear an additional chick if the sibling aggression stage is avoided. I concluded that eagles lay the number of eggs they can normally rear. The species that always exhibit some siblicide in the nest, however, do not rear both chicks because they have set up a contest to eliminate one chick to produce the strongest, highest-quality nestling they can. For some eagle species (typically Northern Hemisphere ones) in which clutch size is more than two eggs, siblicide may be dependent on resources such as food, and several chicks can be reared in good years.

After four years' work, I was in for one more surprise from these eagles. I had spent some time marking the eagle pairs with small plastic wing tags to uniquely identify individuals. Catching the birds was relatively simple but time-consuming. A small cage containing an active mouse and covered in nylon nooses was dropped under the nose of a hunting bird. Hungry eagles usually came down immediately to these traps (called a *bal-chatri*, or "BC"), flapping around on top in a futile attempt to capture their prey inside and, in the process, entangling their legs and feet in the nooses. With this system I caught and tagged 45 adult eagles. Watching eagles hunt is a rare occurrence, so seeing a bird come down to a trap was always incredibly exciting and gave me great insight into the supreme abilities of these amazing predators. On one occasion I spotted, through the large game fence that surrounds the Sabi Sands Game Reserve, a perched eagle. I quickly readied the trap, dropped it over the side of the Land Rover on the track, and backed off. I was in luck—the bird soon bobbed its head, shifted position, and with a couple of flaps took off on the long low glide that was characteristic of a hunting eagle. It was at this point that I realized with horror that he was heading directly for the top of the taught, barbed-wire fence that borders the reserve. I could barely watch as the bird closed in on my trap—and the fence—anticipating the bloody and tangled end that I had so stupidly masterminded. I hadn't reckoned on the astounding aerial agility of the Wahlberg's eagle as he deftly shot through the gap between the top strands of the fence and straight onto my trap. Once my adrenaline levels had returned to normal and I processed and tagged my prize bird, I inspected the fence strands it had casually sailed through—there was a space no more than about 13 to 15 cm (5 to 6 in) wide. My appreciation for the aerial agility of these unpretentious brown eagles had just gone up a quantum leap.

All this excitement had an end and a purpose, and that was to see if the tagged birds returned to their territories after migration. To my surprise and relief, they did—on average 80% to 85% of the adults returned to their territories each September. Sometimes they re-paired with their mates even if they didn't breed that year. As a bonus they even revealed where they went when they left South Africa's Lowveld. A tagged bird was picked up—dead—over 4000 km (2485 mi) away, near Khartoum, in Sudan, and the ring returned to me by a South African businessman who was shown the ring by the kids who had found it.

The most interesting finding, however, was hidden in the data on the tagged birds that I had tried to get to rear the second chick. Looking for other answers to why these birds would lay just a single egg, I returned to the question: Are there any hidden costs to this lifestyle that might explain why these birds lay just one egg? It seemed there was. Of the eight pairs that I had given the twin eaglets to rear, only one attempted to breed the next year. In other words they took a year off, despite returning to the same territory. In contrast, most of the other pairs that had reared a single nestling the previous year bred the following year. This suggests that there may be a substantial cost to rearing young, and if a bird was to continuously attempt to rear more than a single egg, it would, over the course of its life, consequently leave fewer offspring. What the immediate costs were is unknown.

In addition to publishing my results, I went to bed happy that year, content in the knowledge that despite the small samples and despite working with a species that only raptor bozos would ever work with, I had learned something new about the life of an African eagle that could be useful to other ecologists working on similar topics.

16
Solitary Eagle

COMMON NAME: Solitary eagle

SCIENTIFIC NAME: *Harpyhaliaetus solitarius*

OTHER NAMES: Black solitary eagle

IUCN CONSERVATION STATUS: *Near Threatened (population trend unknown)*

DESCRIPTION: A large, dark gray hawk-like eagle with relatively long and broad wings. Tail is black with a white band across the middle. Legs are long and bare. Juveniles are dark brown above, with pale heads, and below are buffy with dark brown streaks, making them easy to distinguish from adults.

SIZE: Length: 65–75 cm (25.5–29.5 in); Wingspan: 157–180 cm (62–71 in); Weight: ~3 kg (~6.5 lb)

THREATS: Unknown, likely habitat loss and disturbance or hunting

DISTRIBUTION: Occurs locally from northern Mexico across Central America through South America east of the Andes to northern Argentina.

MOVEMENTS: Nonmigratory, but movements generally unknown.

HABITAT: Hilly and mountainous forested areas. Only crosses lowlands and open areas.

DIET: Poorly known but limited observations suggest that snakes are an important part of the diet.

NOTES: This is one of the least studied eagle species in the world.

Author's Biography

BILL CLARK lives in the Rio
Grande Valley of Texas,
United States, and is often
out watching raptors.
Photo courtesy of the author

Bill Clark coordinated the Cape May Raptor Banding Project (focusing on raptor migration) in New Jersey for over 30 years, and worked for 5 years as Director of the National Wildlife Federation's Raptor Information Center, where he developed courses in raptor field and in-hand identification. After leaving the National Wildlife Federation, he wrote his first raptor field guide, published in the Peterson field guide series, called A Field Guide to *Hawks: North America*. Later he coauthored *A Photographic Guide to North American Raptors*, the *In-hand Identification Guide to Palearctic Raptors*, and *A Field Guide to the Raptors of Europe, the Middle East, and North Africa*. He is currently writing two more raptor field guides, one for Africa and the other for Mexico and Central America. Bill has traveled worldwide studying, observing, and photographing raptors, and he regularly leads raptor and birding tours and workshops, both at home and abroad, with his company, Raptours. He has undertaken raptor fieldwork in many countries, including Europe, Israel, India, South America, Africa, and Central America. Most of this was oriented to learning more about raptor field identification, but much was for banding or ringing raptors, some 84 species to date. Bill has published numerous articles, both popular and scientific, on many raptor subjects, including ageing and sexing, color morphs, taxonomy, field identification, and migration. He regularly teaches evening and weekend courses on raptor field identification and biology, and frequently presents illustrated lectures on raptor subjects. Bill has been living in the Rio Grande Valley of south Texas since 2002 and has a personal goal to see and take photographs of all of the world's diurnal raptors.

SOLITARY EAGLE, MEXICO

Bill Clark

The first steps on the road to becoming a successful eagle watcher are to learn where to find your eagle and then to learn how to identify it once you have located it. This may sound obvious, and for many well-known eagle species it is indeed a relatively simple task. However, even today, at the beginning of the twenty-first century, there are still several eagle species of which we know very little, even the details of their appearance. One such eagle, the rare solitary eagle, has been my nemesis for many years.

Advancing the art of raptor field identification has occupied much of the last 35 years of my life. Wherever I travel in the world, I assess which species cause the most identification problems in that country or region and try to come up with field marks that will distinguish one similar raptor from another. I do this by studying the written descriptions, illustrations, and photographs of the species involved, as well as by visiting museum collections to examine historical specimens. I realized early on that the solitary eagle would be one of those "difficult" raptors to identify in the field, and was curious as to whether I could determine any characteristic field marks. As it turned out, field marks were the least of my worries; the first problem was to actually find a solitary eagle.

The solitary eagle lives in Central and South America, with a range extending from northern Mexico to northern Argentina, but it is extremely rare and patchily distributed. According to the available information, the adult solitary eagle appears almost identical to the adult common black hawk and the adult great black hawk. All three species have an overall dark blackish-gray plumage with a wide, white band across the middle of the tail. Likewise, the immature plumages of all three species are similar. Until recently, there was only one published photograph of a solitary eagle, that of a perched adult. The illustrated drawings of this species in regional bird field guides differ greatly between books and show a bewildering range of color variation and shape, making identification difficult for even the most experienced observer.

Eagle watchers who believe they have seen solitary eagles often have had difficulty in convincing others of their sightings, as there were no published definitive field marks to separate the eagle from the black hawks. Most supposed identifications of solitary eagles had relied on the field marks of large size and grayish coloration. Solitary eagles in the Andes of South America are a paler gray than are solitary eagles elsewhere and can be distinguished from the black hawks based on color. However, most solitary eagle sightings have come from other areas, where the birds are darker and not much different in color from the black hawks, which occur commonly in those areas. Additionally, we humans are not very proficient at judging the size of raptors when they are flying alone. Both of these factors conspire against wanna-be solitary eagle watchers.

My quest to find and observe the solitary eagle in the wild has been a long and frustrating one. I began by studying the few solitary eagle specimens that are held in museum collections, to familiarize myself with the bird's shape, size, and plumage characteristics, hoping that this would give me a head start in the field. I then traveled to two locations in Mexico and one in Belize where solitary eagle sightings had been reported. Even though I spent many days searching, I left without seeing the bird. My crusade then took me to Venezuela and Costa Rica, where experienced professional bird tour leaders had told me that they regularly saw solitary eagles in flight. Again, many days in the field ended in disappointment. I did see great black hawks at both locations, and wondered whether the tour guides were confusing these hawks with the solitary eagle. I had a recording of the solitary eagle's call and I played it to a colleague from Venezuela, to see whether he recognized it. He told me that his recording of the solitary eagle was different from mine. He pulled out his CD of Venezuelan bird songs and clicked on the track that was listed as the solitary eagle. Lo and behold, it was actually the call of the great black hawk. We then looked at the bird field guide books for that area, and the artist's impressions showed the shape of the eagle as being almost identical to the shape of the great black hawk. I concluded, downheartedly, that the bird tour leaders had not been seeing solitary eagles. My searches continued.

When I learned of a solitary eagle sighting from Mountain Pine Ridge in Belize, I contacted the bird tour leader who had reported it and he sent me a detailed description of what he and his group had seen. After reading this, I replied to him that I thought it was possible that he had seen a solitary eagle, but that it wasn't definitive. Then he remembered that one of the tour participants had taken some distant in-flight photographs of the raptor in question. After looking at these photographs, I realized that the eagle had uniquely shaped wings and tail that differed noticeably from those of the black hawks.

I also learned of a Web site where video of a flying solitary eagle from Peru was posted. This was definitely a solitary eagle, as it was overall pale gray, and neither of the black hawks occurs in that area. After studying the video of the flying eagle, I noticed field marks, including wing shape and leg length, which would serve to separate flying solitary eagles from the two black hawks. It was also apparent that the solitary eagle differed from the black hawks by having wingtips that extended past the tail when the bird was perched, a feature not shown on either black hawk.

Although I was now closer to knowing how to identify a solitary eagle, I still hadn't had any sightings of this elusive raptor, despite spending years in hot pursuit. When my first sighting finally happened, it was more by luck than design. In October 2006 I was leading a raptor tour after a conference in Veracruz, Mexico. On the next-to-last day of the tour, we were on a mountain ridge in northern Oaxaca. It was an overcast day with occasional breaks in the clouds, where the sun showed through. We were watching a pair of white hawks soaring down in the valley below us when one of the tour participants shouted, "What is that large raptor?" A third raptor was soaring with the white hawks. I quickly found it in my spotting scope and zoomed up to the maximum 60 power magnification. Was I finally seeing the eagle? Time passed slowly as I verified all of the field marks we had advocated in the recent identification article that I coauthored, from wing shape to wing pattern. The raptor cooperated. I had time to watch this magnificent bird; it perched three times, and each time I verified that its wingtips extended beyond its tail tip—that telltale distinguishing feature. The endorphins flowed—at last my first solitary eagle!

I also noted a new adult field mark: the upper sides, when viewed in sunlight, were quite pale gray with noticeable black wingtips. This is the sort of detail that is impossible to attain from studying museum specimens alone.

Ironically, after spending many years looking for this eagle, I saw more within six months after the initial sighting. On a birding trip to Manu, Peru, in February 2007, I encountered an adult pair of solitary eagles soaring. I saw them in flight on two days for minutes at a time in this mountainous area. As my group was leaving on the morning of the fourth day, we found one of the adults perched right beside the road, giving alarm calls. It allowed me to take many digital photos of it through my telescope, while a colleague recorded its vocalizations.

Slowly but surely the solitary eagle is revealing its secrets to the world. A recent scientific paper reported that, based on DNA sequences, the solitary eagle is more closely related to the great black hawk than is the common black hawk. The solitary eagle then is just an overgrown black hawk and should be reclassified in a more appropriate genus. If that's the case, what do we call it now? No doubt there will be a long and protracted debate within scientific and birding circles, but personally, it will always be the solitary eagle to me.

17

Javan Hawk-Eagle

COMMON NAME: Javan hawk-eagle

SCIENTIFIC NAME: *Spizaetus bartelsi*

OTHER NAMES: Java hawk-eagle, Elang jawa (Bahasa Indonesia)

IUCN CONSERVATION STATUS: *Endangered (population declining)*

DESCRIPTION: A small to medium-sized eagle with a long, noticeable crest. Like many large tropical forest raptors, the wings are relatively short and rounded and the tail is long and banded. Adult is dark brown above, and light with brown-streaked breast and barred belly and legs. Legs are well feathered. Pre-adults are dark above but often rufous below and without adult dark streaking and barring.

SIZE: Length: 56–60 cm (22–24 in); Wingspan: 110–130 cm (43–51 in); Weight: unknown

THREATS: Habitat loss is the greatest threat to this and many other Indonesian species. Javan hawk-eagles also are trapped and sold in markets each year. An estimated 600 to 900 individuals remain in the wild.

DISTRIBUTION: Indonesia. Endemic to Java.

MOVEMENTS: Nonmigratory; juveniles appear to disperse long distances.

HABITAT: Primary tropical rainforest. Birds have been recorded in second-growth stands and in plantations, but only rarely.

DIET: Primarily small to medium-sized mammals, but birds and reptiles are also taken.

NOTES: It is thought that this species became Indonesia's national bird because of its resemblance to the legendary birdlike creature the Garuda, which appears in Hindu and Buddhist mythology and features on Indonesia's coat of arms.

Author's Biography

VINCENT NIJMAN has to protect his identity for his undercover investigative work in Asia. This is a picture of a Javan hawk-eagle, Vincent's study species. Photo by Bas van Balen/BirdLife

Born in the reclaimed lands, or "polders," of the Netherlands, Vincent became interested in wildlife from an early age. He first started to observe eagles while undertaking his BSc in biology at the University of Amsterdam, and then later in Scotland while undertaking fieldwork for his MSc in behavioral ecology at Manchester University. Vincent began his studies on the Javan hawk-eagle in 1993. With Bas van Balen, Resit Sözer, and numerous Indonesian students, he tried to assess the status of the eagle and, with mixed success, tried to implement a management strategy to safeguard the species from the threat of extinction. During those first years in Indonesia, he typically spent half of his time in the field. As forest-dwelling eagles appeared to be late risers, he studied forest primates during the early parts of the day and subsequently earned his PhD in primate conservation and ecology in 2001. In 1998 while studying the resident eagles of the Dieng Mountains in central Java, Vincent noted the arrival of dozens (and later hundreds) of migrant sparrowhawks and honey buzzards, and this sparked a series of studies on the magnitude and timing of raptor migration in Indonesia. Vincent is currently employed as head of the Vertebrate Section of the Zoological Museum of the University of Amsterdam and continues his interest in birds of prey.

JAVAN HAWK-EAGLE, INDONESIA

Vincent Nijman

I write this from behind my desk at the zoological museum in Amsterdam, surrounded by old jars with pickled bats and primates and parts of a whale's backbone. In a similar environment, almost 15 years ago, I rested my eyes for the first time on a Javan hawk-eagle.

In the early 1990s, the Javan hawk-eagle was considered one of the least known and most rare eagles in the world. Fifty to 80 pairs were thought to remain. Endemic to the island of Java, Indonesia's political, industrial, and economical center, few ornithologists had observed the eagle firsthand. Photographs of the Javan hawk-eagle were nonexistent, and illustrations in field guides and books varied so much that it was difficult to picture what the bird would look like in the wild. Despite the fact that so little was known about the species, in 1993, President Suharto declared the Javan hawk-eagle "Indonesia's National Rare Animal." With that designation, increasingly strange-looking eagle-like birds were depicted on stamps, telephone directories, and in children's magazines. With its fame came special protection. Keeping a Javan hawk-eagle as a pet required special permission from the president, permission that was never granted to anyone. Furthermore, trading in Javan hawk-eagles was declared illegal, resulting in fines of US$10,000 and imprisonment for up to five years. With the eagle now a star among Indonesian birds, it was recognized that there was an urgent need to collect the most basic data on its identity and whereabouts.

Having finished my master's degree in biology with a year and a half of government funding remaining, I decided to conduct extra studies in tropical ecology. With fellow student Resit Sözer and under the guidance of the BirdLife Indonesia office, I embarked on a nine-month field study of the Javan hawk-eagle in central Java, an area where the species had not yet been recorded. Back home in the Netherlands, we felt that the best way to prepare ourselves for our trip was to get familiar with the specimens and data collected at the beginning of the twentieth century, a time at which Java and the rest of Indonesia was a Dutch colony. One important source for those specimens was the National Natural History Museum in Leiden.

There were 18 Javan hawk-eagle skins in the museum that had been collected over a 150-year period. The differences between the 18 specimens made clear that the Javan hawk-eagle showed quite a bit of external variation. One visit to the museum taught us more about how these birds look than all the field guides and books, and thus we felt confident that we could identify a Javan hawk-eagle if we saw one.

Having prepared ourselves as thoroughly as possible, we left for Java in early 1994. Only a few short weeks later, Resit and I saw our first pair of Javan hawk-eagles and their nest, in a remote valley of Mount Pangrango in west Java. For the next three months we spent our time surveying forested areas in central Java and studying the nest we had first found in west Java. We quickly learned that the Javan hawk-eagle was indeed a very rare bird, difficult to observe in its rainforest environment and with a low reproductive output of approximately one fledgling every other year. If the estimate of 80 pairs remaining was indeed correct, this meant that only some 40 young were produced every year. The world could not afford to lose even a single chick.

We were therefore genuinely shocked when we heard that the director of BirdLife Indonesia had seen not one, but two, young Javan hawk-eagles for sale in a small village in the southern part of west Java. He informed us about his findings but immediately warned us not to do anything stupid. This was the time when Indonesia was still firmly ruled by the autocrat Suharto, and when it came to politically sensitive issues, international nongovernmental organizations had to be very careful.

We decided to follow our hearts and distracted the BirdLife office by announcing we would take a day off. Having worked hard for the last couple of months, we thought a visit to the southern beaches was timely. The next day we headed southward with our swimming gear, our permits, and copies of the president's declaration that the Javan hawk-eagle was the National Rare Animal. A few hours later, in the small village of Boyong Galeng, we stepped out of the bus for some refreshments, and lo and behold, we saw the two Javan hawk-eagles. Hatchlings still, they were being offered for sale on the side of the road, together with two adult crested serpent eagles. We quickly enquired where the birds came from, at what price they could be purchased, and whether or not the vendor had sold these kinds of birds before. From this it became clear that in his mind, these birds were nothing more than just the young of a large eagle and nothing to get excited about really. He informed us that he sold eagles on a regular basis and that he was fully aware that all eagles were protected by Indonesian law.

We felt that we needed to report this to the nearest branch of the Ministry of Forestry, and this happened to be in Palabuan Ratu, a town 30 minutes or so to the south. We finished our coffee, jumped on the next bus, and before midday, found ourselves reporting the illegal sale of Indonesia's National Rare Animal to the forestry department. All things take time, and yes, surely, the officer would visit the village the next day and take subsequent action; "Leave it all to us, trust us, don't worry." We did worry, we did not trust them, and we wanted action to be taken now. After all, we were studying this species and had firsthand experience how rare the eagle was. We worked closely with the bosses at the head office in Jakarta ("How do you feel about this lack of initiative?" and "Since there are two eaglets, wouldn't it be a great idea to present one as a gift to the president? A rare chance for him to see the National Rare Animal up close."). This surely would make the headlines, with all the credits going to the Palabuan Ratu forestry department. By this time the police had arrived, and after having assured themselves that we were indeed who we said we were, the idea of confiscating the two eaglets started to grow on them. A bit of positive publicity could only bring good things.

After lunch we got in the car with two forestry officers and two policemen, and we set off to confiscate the two eaglets. Within minutes upon arrival back in Boyong Galeng, all the villagers had gathered around us and the two eaglets. It was at this point that negotiations began. Not wishing to interfere in this delicate process, we three foreigners stepped aside. After half an hour, one of the police officers came to us with the first offer. The two birds were to be confiscated, all we had to do was to reimburse the bird seller—after all he had made efforts to obtain these birds and he had fed them good meat for the last week. Clearly someone had to pay for that. We discussed this option with the police and the forestry officers, but we noted that we could not pay for the birds, as then we would be in breach of the law. The birds had to be confiscated without an exchange of money, and we asked, "Shouldn't the vendor be taken to the police station for questioning?" While we were discussing this, the bird seller decided that a timely visit to the mosque was in order. This left us with nothing to do other than wait, and wait, and wait. Surely, we could not take the birds without the vendor being present. In the meantime, the crowd of villagers around us was getting noticeably annoyed with the three foreigners wanting to do this injustice to one of their community members. Finally, after another negotiation session, just before darkness fell, the vendor came out of the mosque. He and the eaglets were taken in the car, and we all left to return to the forestry office in Palabuan Ratu.

After a communal dinner with all the enforcement officers involved in the confiscation, the tables turned. The police became suspicious about our motives, and instead of watching the vendor face the heat, we found ourselves being taken into the police office for interrogation. Since we were law-abiding citizens, little came from this questioning, and finally, nearly at midnight, we left Palabuan Ratu, leaving the eaglets at the mercy of the police officers.

The next day we informed the BirdLife Indonesia office about our unexpected adventure, and after some quibbling among the staff there, it was decided that action needed to be taken. The eaglets had to leave the police office as soon as possible, in large part because we were worried that the birds would be brought back to the vendor. Action was indeed taken, and in the end the birds were taken to Taman Safari zoo. No charges were filed against the vendor. Furthermore, by the end of the next month, the then 6-week-old eaglet we had studied in the rainforest of Mount Pangrango had disappeared, quite possibly taken by poachers.

In the years that followed, we continued our studies on the Javan hawk-eagle and broadened our work to include other forest eagles. We found the hawk-eagle to be more common than initially thought, and working with the Ministry of Forestry and other government agencies, we prepared a recovery plan. Our experience in Boyong Galeng was a harbinger of our future work, and our recovery plan identified addressing the wildlife trade as the top-priority action. Ironically, the declaration of the Javan hawk-eagle as the National Rare Animal not only made clear that this was indeed a rare bird worthy of protection, but also introduced the eagle into the world of bird keepers. It was only after the mid-1990s, when the species became politically important, that zoos and private collectors felt a need to display them. Since the confiscation of the two eaglets in Boyong Galeng, at least a dozen Javan hawk-eagles have been confiscated, yet none of the owners or traders has been prosecuted. Thanks to a large amount of research (it appears that this is the most popular bird to study for Javan biology students, and also several international teams have worked on aspects of the eagle's biology), we now know more about the Javan hawk-eagle than ever before, yet due to a lack of serious protection and institutional deficiencies, we still run a serious risk of losing this ambassador for the Javan rainforest and all its rare animals.

What lessons can be learned from the above experiences? First and foremost is the sobering lesson that making a threatened species a focal point for conservation may also draw the attention of others with less noble intentions. Merely putting a species on a protected-species list, without a proper strategy as to how to implement this protection, may directly contribute to the extinction of a species. Demand increases, prices go up, supply decreases, prices go up even more, and the inevitable vortex toward extinction sets in. Although this might suggest that oblivion and obscurity provide effective protection, there is also a real possibility that little-known species might go extinct for reasons that could have been solved easily, had we only known. I do not know what to prefer—a species heading toward extinction simply because we do not know, or a species heading to extinction with all of us watching.

18
African Fish Eagle

COMMON NAME: African fish eagle

SCIENTIFIC NAME: *Haliaeetus vocifer*

OTHER NAMES: River eagle, West African river eagle, fish eagle

IUCN CONSERVATION STATUS: *Least Concern (population stable)*

DESCRIPTION: A striking medium-sized eagle with long rounded wings and a short tail. Has a brown and rusty body, with a white tail and head and breast and long legs. Slightly larger and relatively longer winged and shorter legged and tailed than the closely related Madagascar fish eagle.

SIZE: Length: 63–75 cm (25–30 in); Wingspan: 175–210 cm (69–83 in); Weight: 2.0–3.6 kg (4.5–8.0 lb)

THREATS: This species was significantly impacted by DDT-induced eggshell thinning. However, it rarely suffers from direct persecution by humans.

DISTRIBUTION: Throughout sub-Saharan Africa where water is found

MOVEMENTS: Nonmigratory, although juveniles may disperse long distances, and adults and juveniles may become nomadic in response to changing water conditions.

HABITAT: Breeds near water—lakes, rivers, floodplains, and human-built impoundments. Also observed in coastal environments. Juveniles may be observed long distances from water, particularly when dispersing.

DIET: Primarily fish. Also known to take birds, mammals, reptiles, and even insects. Juveniles especially sometimes observed to take carrion.

NOTES: This species' distinctive and far-reaching call, *Koy-koy-koy-koy-koy*, is so well known it is considered to be "The Voice of Africa."

Author's Biography

MUNIR Z. VIRANI with an
African fish eagle trapped
at Lake Naivasha, Kenya.
Photo by Paolo Torchio

Munir Virani was born and raised in Nairobi, Kenya. As a teenager, he played cricket most of the time, and was fortunate to play for one of the top cricketing clubs in Kenya, for which the reward for winning a tournament was usually a couple of nights in Kenya's elite game reserves and national parks, which he utilized to nurture and cultivate his interest in wildlife. In 1990, Munir was selected for the Kenya Cricket Team to represent Kenya in the ICC World Cup in Holland, but he knew he had to make a decision between his passion for cricket and wildlife, and he ultimately chose studies over cricket. He graduated from Nairobi University with first-class honors in zoology and was selected by The Peregrine Fund to train as a raptor biologist under the legendary Simon Thomsett. Munir registered at the University of Leicester (United Kingdom) and did his master's thesis on the endangered Sokoke scops owl. He successfully conducted his PhD research on augur buzzards at Lake Naivasha, where he also studied African fish eagles. In 2000, Munir was sent to South Asia by The Peregrine Fund to evaluate the magnitude of declines of populations of critically endangered *Gyps* vultures in the region. He set up a team of biologists and technical staff in India, Nepal, and Pakistan and established a successful field and diagnostic research project that helped to identify the pharmaceutical drug Diclofenac as the cause of the catastrophic crash of vulture populations there. Munir also runs raptor research projects in East Africa. He currently lives with his wife and sons in Nairobi, where his interests are cricket, squash, singing, raptor watching, and photography.

AFRICAN FISH EAGLE, KENYA

Munir Z. Virani

Gandhi said, "It takes only one moment to change your life." My moment came when I was 13 years old. Diana and Mirko, friends of my parents, took me and my brothers on a fishing trip at Lake Naivasha in Kenya's Great Rift Valley. At the risk of sounding old, the lake in those days was a portrait of wild Africa—crystal clear waters dotted with tens of thousands of water-fowl floating among a mosaic of water lilies. Pods of grunting hippos emerged from huge papyrus-fringed swamps while buffaloes and giraffes watched from a distance, wary of stalking predators among the thick *Acacia* woodlands. Confined in the boat, we kids screamed and yelled with excitement while the adults did their best to shut us up so they could fish. We caught bass and stuffed ourselves with sausages as the adults drank beer. Late in the day, finally exhausted we drowsed in the boat. Then, Mirko hurled a fish into the water. *Splash!* Seconds later, with a nearing whooshing sound, Africa's most majestic eagle shattered the stillness of the lake as it folded in its wings and cut through the air. With the powerful grace of a ballet dancer, it threw its wings wide, flung its feet forward, and snatched the floating fish from the water before flying to a snag to devour its catch. I was stunned. I had never seen anything so menacing yet graceful. The eagle then flew to a tall *Acacia* tree and preened itself with avian arrogance. If looks could kill, then this eagle had the power to do so. Throwing its head back, it let out one of the most powerful, piercing sounds I have ever heard—the call of the African fish eagle—the call that symbolizes Africa. Sitting in the boat, mouth agape, I felt a chill so strong, I shuddered. I felt as if the spirit of the eagle had entered my body. Little did I know that I would return sometime in the future to repay a debt owed, perhaps during my previous life? Now many years later, these poignant cries have become part of my daily existence. For me, it is not a cry as much as it is a prayer, or rather, a plea for help.

I had always been married to cricket (for American readers, this is a very civilized version of baseball that includes a tea break with cucumber sand-wiches) but began a wild and cherished love affair with raptors, particularly with fish eagles since the day I was introduced to one Simon Thomsett, raptor-guru extraordinaire. Mentor, friend, and confidant, Simon injected me with a lethal addictive dose of his passion for raptors. Now I am a pa-thetic addict. One glorious morning, I heard a BBC news story on the radio that Kenya had caused an upset in the 1996 Cricket World Cup by beating the mighty West Indies in India. I smiled wryly and felt a sense of national pride, for this was indeed a great achievement. From the verandah of my cottage at Lake Naivasha, I saw an eagle returning with nesting material to line its nest. Instinctively, I rushed out with my binoculars. Watching the pair engaged in copulation and soaking up the sounds of their calls, I reassured myself that I did the right thing by giving up professional cricket to take up a career in raptor biology.

In 1994, following a year-long nocturnal foray in Arabuko-Sokoke Forest chasing Sokoke scops owls in the dark, I was asked to assist a graduate student, Maureen Harper, to census fish eagles. Browsing through her literature collection, I read with fascination all the outstanding work done on fish eagles by the late Dr. Leslie Brown. Little was I to know that my time in the Lake Naivasha area was going to be a critical phase in my life, for this is where I conducted my PhD field research on augur buzzards. Without a doubt, the fish eagles were going to be the stars of the show. Despite being busy with buzzard fieldwork, I managed to find time to survey the lake on a monthly basis and map out fish eagle territories. My ever reliable boatman, Chege, and I would depart the Elsamere jetty at 6:00 a.m. and head out toward the mouth of the Karati River on the eastern side of the lake. Despite being in the floor of the Rift Valley, Naivasha lies at 1.8 km (6000 ft) and it was usually pretty cold at dawn. I always got a kick from preparing a fresh cup of Kenyan coffee on the boat using my newly acquired gadget—a French press. This was a priority. The counts began at about 7:00 a.m. and Chege very expertly maneuvered the boat in the shallows close to the shore without running over any hippos. With their chestnut bellies and brilliant white head and chests set against a milieu of *Acacia* trees, African fish eagles are one of the easiest birds to census. They are virtually "nailed to the perch." Without trying to exaggerate, I honestly cannot think of anything more relaxing than watching fish eagles on Lake Naivasha.

Lake Naivasha conjures images of history, romance, decadence, and wilderness. It is where I wanted to exchange my wedding vows, though my wife had different ideas. I have colorful memories of waking up at dawn one day and sauntering toward the lake shore, cup of coffee in hand and binoculars strapped around my neck. Sunrises were always spectacular—fire-lit, shimmering skies anointed with flocks of birds, mainly herons, cranes, cormorants, and flamingoes going about their morning rituals. The tranquility of the lake was captivating. Like a giant painting against a colossal backdrop of the Rift Valley escarpment, the lake stood motionless and resplendent.

Time had stopped. Not on this day, however, as within the acacias above me, a pair of fish eagles emitted their haunting thunderous call, in unison and then in turns. One of the eagles, a male, suddenly flew toward the lake in a focused quest. He had seen a subadult fish eagle soaring over a flock of coots. The pursuit was choreographed to perfection as the male met head-on with the intruder, the two birds locking talons in a deadly grip. Fish eagles began calling from every direction as these two cart-wheeled nose down in what could only result in death. Barely centimeters (inches) from the lake's surface, they suddenly let go, both unscathed, flapping strenuously, with the male escorting the intruder away from his territory. Fish eagles are highly territorial, and it is perhaps because of this constant aggressive interaction with their neighbors that fewer chicks are produced per year at Lake Naivasha than elsewhere in the fish eagle's range. Such treats were rare and only reinforced my enthusiasm to understand more about the eagles.

So apart from the relaxation aspect of watching these birds, our counts yielded some startling yet concerning results. I began to note that the fish eagle population was declining alarmingly. From Leslie Brown's counts in the early 1970s of over 200 birds, I counted a meager 67 individuals in 1997. What's more, during this time, only one pair of fish eagles had produced young. Something was clearly affecting the behavior and ecology of these majestic eagles. Around this time, flower-farming on the lake shores had increased exponentially, and water was being uncontrollably extracted to quench the thirst of these hungry farms. Furthermore, the human population around the lake skyrocketed to meet the demands of a labor-intensive industry. Lake levels dropped drastically and illegal fishing was on the rise until fish stocks were exhausted. We began trapping and ringing the eagles to determine what was wrong with them. At least 75% of the birds we trapped were underweight, suggesting that they were suffering from lack of food. Early Naivasha settlers used to call the fish eagle the "coot eagle" because that is what the birds mainly ate (all the fish species in the lake are alien introductions, and we have President Roosevelt to thank for introducing the American large-mouth bass in the 1920s). However, coots also completely disappeared as a result of their food source—submerged plants—being depleted by the Louisiana crayfish, another alien introduction in the mid-1970s to enhance the fishery. To cut a long story short, the fish eagles were starving to death and as a result either disappeared or were unable to produce young.

My suspicions were confirmed when in 1998 heavy El Niño rains raised the lake's water levels by 3 m (9.9 ft). The consequence was crystal clear lagoons and thousands of fish with very large gonads just waiting to explode. The fish boom resulted in the fish eagle population increasing to 100 individuals. With now nearly everything exotic on Lake Naivasha, a further accidental introduction of the common carp raised the fish eagle population to 150 eagles by January 2009. Never before have I seen every pair of eagles with chicks. But this boom may be short-lived. While fish eagles are remarkable barometers of the health of aquatic systems, they are succumbing to the pressures of human-altered habitats. By mid-2009, Kenya is facing its worst drought and lake levels are fast receding—the lowest I have ever seen. Illegal fishing by poachers is at an all-time high, nesting habitats have been destroyed, and dispersal areas have undergone major land transformations—all to the detriment of fish eagles.

With a myriad of problems, Lake Naivasha, once the jewel of the Great Rift Valley, is fast sinking into oblivion. Recently, I attended a memorial service—a celebration of the life of Joan Root, wildlife filmmaker, conservationist, and friend. She was brutally murdered at her residence on the shores of Lake Naivasha. As I listened to the service, I couldn't help but look upward where Joan's fish eagles circled, perhaps their way of showing respect. Then as soon as the service ended, the earsplitting calls of the fish eagles began . . . first in unison and then in turns. Their prayers remain unanswered.

19
Bateleur

COMMON NAME: Bateleur

SCIENTIFIC NAME: *Terathopius ecaudatus*

OTHER NAMES: Bateleur eagle, bataleur

IUCN CONSERVATION STATUS: *Near Threatened (population declining)*

DESCRIPTION: A medium-sized but uniquely formed eagle. The bateleur is behaviorally related to vultures and has a black body with gray on the outer (upper) wings and white below the wings with a black trailing edge. Back is either rufous brown or cream white; face is featherless and a variable red to orange color. Wings are long and pointed; tail is the same color as the back and exceptionally short, appears almost tailless. Juveniles are uniformly dark, without the light-dark contrasts.

SIZE: Length: 55–70 cm (21.5–27.5 in); Wingspan: 168–190 cm (66–75 in); Weight: 1.8–3.0 kg (4.0–6.5 lb)

THREATS: Habitat loss and poisoning are the greatest threats.

DISTRIBUTION: The species has a widespread distribution throughout much of sub-Saharan Africa in open woodland and savanna.

MOVEMENTS: Nonmigratory. Some adults and immatures have large home ranges and may be nomadic in response to climatic variation. Vagrants can travel as far as Iraq.

HABITAT: Open country, ranging from savanna grasslands to open woodlands, and only in deserts with trees along watercourses; not thick forests.

DIET: Bateleurs feed on small vertebrates of many types—mammals, birds, reptiles, fish—as well as invertebrates (crabs, insects). Carrion is important to the species, representing as much as two-thirds of their diet.

NOTES: The bateleur is an interesting species because it behaves much like a vulture, in food-searching and -foraging behavior. Likewise, its body form shows several adaptations—especially in wing shape and flight behavior—for this lifestyle.

Author's Biography

RICHARD T. WATSON on the
shores of Lake Llanquihue,
Chile. Photo courtesy of
the author

   Richard Watson was determined to pursue a life of undersea study and
adventure after being inspired by Jacques Cousteau's TV documentaries
in the 1960s and 1970s. Richard completed an undergraduate degree in
marine zoology, only to be told, and to learn through bitter experience,
that jobs for marine biologists in the 1980s were hard to come by. However, by this time, his interests had broadened to include the dire need
worldwide to conserve endangered species, and he realized that a postgraduate degree would be helpful in such a career, so he embarked upon a
PhD in animal ecology, with the main criterion being that the research
topic had to contribute meaningfully to conservation of an endangered
species. That's how Richard came to study bateleurs in South Africa, where
the species had undergone an 80% population decline in the previous few
decades. After doing postdoctoral work studying insects in Namibia,
Richard steadily followed a career dedicated to wildlife conservation, from
banding roseate terns on an island in Long Island Sound, and hooting
surveys for Mexican spotted owls, to working for The Peregrine Fund, a
United States–based raptor conservation organization. He has worked for
The Peregrine Fund since 1990, initially as Africa Project Director, then
International Program Director, then Vice President. Richard currently
supervises 15 projects on three continents, which vary from captive
breeding and release of harpy eagles in Central America, to researching
the catastrophic decline of *Gyps* vultures in South Asia. He has also
supervised national and international graduate students at master's and
doctoral levels and was appointed adjunct faculty at Boise State and Idaho
State universities.

BATELEUR, SOUTH AFRICA

Richard T. Watson

"All you really need is a decent pair of binoculars, good boots, and determination," said Warwick Tarboton, my PhD supervisor. He was right, of course, but I was determined to use the latest technology in my research by employing VHF radios to locate and track my study subjects, bateleurs, as they traversed their home range in search of food and defense of mate and territory. It took me about six months of frustrating effort to understand that scavenging raptors, such as bateleurs, are really hard to catch. And, unfortunately, you have to catch them to attach a transmitter! After I tried that route and failed, it took me only about a week to figure out that all I really needed was a good pair of binoculars, a spotting scope, a high observation point, and lots of stamina to watch them as they soared across their home range in pursuit of love, life, and happiness. And by doing so, I learned far more about their behavior, foraging, and ecology than I would have done with all the technology in the world.

The best lessons in life are the hardest to learn, they say, but I wish I had listened to Warwick in the first place. I have repeated his advice, and my lesson, to every student I have supervised since then. Do they listen? You can guess. In all fairness, though, technology has advanced tremendously since then. The latest satellite-tracked GPS transmitters have the capacity to provide inordinate amounts of precise, quantitative data, including flight speed, direction, altitude, ambient temperature, physiological data, and much more. But the truth of my lesson still remains intact; unless you can see them, you don't really know what they are doing, and that's often more important to know than simply where they are.

Much information has been collected on the breeding behavior of many species of birds, but most of these studies have concentrated on courtship and nest-related activities. This was particularly true of the bateleur, where nest observations had been made, yet little information on behavior away from the nest existed. What did exist was anecdotal, tending to emphasize the unusual and spectacular, and the function ascribed to the behavior was largely based on the observer's subjective opinion, often heavily influenced by anthropomorphism.

The reason for this gap in our knowledge is related to the relative difficulty of observing eagles away from the nest. The bateleur, in particular, is known for its habit of flying fast in one direction and disappearing rapidly from view. Add to this habit the difficulties of terrain and weather (heat haze, rain, mist, cloud, wind), and you can begin to understand why ornithologists hadn't tried to watch them other than at their predictable nest sites. However, when faced with my lack of success at trapping bateleurs and with no way to utilize VHF radio technology, I began to explore, with some desperation, the idea that I might be able to watch bateleurs from a high vantage point using a reasonably powerful telescope.

My first choice of observation site was Matikiti (*Ma-tik-eet*), an isolated granite kopje (hill) situated in the middle of my study area in the heart of Kruger National Park, South Africa. From here I discovered that the bateleur's habit of flying at relatively low altitudes (roughly two or three times treetop height) for hours on end actually allows for observation from a high vantage point with a telescope. Its characteristically unstable, rocking flight pattern, and its silhouette and sexually dimorphic plumage help make it easily identifiable to species and gender from a distance of several kilometers. A rare cream-back plumage polymorphism in less than 5% of the Kruger Park's bateleur population even helped identification of individuals at a distance, as did other individually unique characteristics, such as the permanently missing outer feather in the right wing of one of my study eagles.

From its 40 m (130 ft) elevation, Matikiti provided an unobstructed view for at least 10 km (6 mi) to the horizon in all directions. My second study site, Sweni, was a smaller rock outcrop on which I built a temporary scaffold and platform to elevate me and my telescope to about 20 m (65 ft) above surrounding ground level. From both sites I could see the nest-trees of at least two adjacent breeding pairs of bateleurs and, it turned out, the entire home ranges of each pair.

At first I was nervous about standing alone on the top of a rocky outcrop for days on end; leopards were known to inhabit the area, black mambas were not uncommon, and herds of elephant and buffalo were frequently seen in the area. But as the days went by, I became more at ease, feeling only the occasional adrenaline rush as a predator walked between me and my safe haven, my vehicle parked 274 m (300 yd) away. About six months into the observations, an entry in my notebook reveals my increasingly laissez-faire attitude:

> *I saw several hyenas and jackals in the area, which made me wonder if there'd been a lion kill, but I didn't see any signs of one. Halfway through the morning, the hyenas came running out from under a bush where they had been sleeping and straight towards me—they were obviously more scared about something else in the*

bush than they were worried about me! Then an elephant wandered out of the
bushes nearby, so I guessed that was what had startled the hyenas. When I left at
the end of the day, I checked out the bushes and discovered a lioness laying there—
she'd probably been eyeing me up for dinner all day!

Most of my wildlife encounters, however, were more of the nuisance kind, like the bees from a nearby hive that insisted on buzzing circles around me as I tracked a bateleur through my telescope. On several occasions this problem was solved with the help of a wintering European bee-eater, which would spend a happy day swooping by me snapping bees with its bill. So still was I, as I concentrated on my task, the bee-eater seemed not to notice that I was alive, even sometimes touching me with its wings as it swooped for its prey.

Maintaining sight of the focal bateleur as it flew over its home range required that it be kept in constant view through the telescope mounted securely on a tripod. Even the briefest loss of visual contact could result in losing sight of the bird for hours until it returned to its nest. To help maintain constant visual contact while collecting data, I mounted a compass above the telescope's eyepiece so that the bird's direction could be measured with minimal break in visual contact. A screen was mounted around the eyepiece to obscure vision through the eye not in use, which allowed me to keep both eyes open to reduce muscle fatigue. My observations were recorded on a tape-recorder and later transcribed to paper data-sheets and eventually to a computer database. The bird's compass bearing, estimated distance, and activity were recorded at one-minute intervals, and behavioral events and interactions were timed to the second using an audible time signal broadcast on short-wave radio. Distance was based on estimates of the bird's position relative to landscape features at known, measured distances from the observation point. Focal birds were observed for as long as they remained in sight or until fatigue overcame me and I simply had to stop. Most observation bouts lasted at least 30 minutes; the longest I managed was 3½ hours, by which time I was exhausted.

By naked eye, I could usually see a bateleur up to 1 km (0.5 mi) away, and with binoculars I could identify its age and gender. Most observation bouts started by spotting the bird by eye, then following it with the telescope. Apart from two individuals that I could recognize from unique plumage characteristics, the identity of the bateleur could only be deduced when it visited or flew over its nest. If it did neither during an observation bout, then its identity remained unknown and that observation bout had to be discarded.

Observations were made over six consecutive days each month for a year and resulted in 223 observation bouts totaling 172 hours of recorded bateleur behavior, each bout averaging 46 minutes. On each day I accumulated several usable observation bouts, averaging 4 hours and 47 minutes. Those were hard-earned data, requiring 12 hours per day of sitting under the grueling sun either making observations or waiting for a bateleur to come within sight.

Heat and heat haze were the most frustrating things to deal with. Standing in the midday African sun, one had to cover up or burn and risk skin cancer. After the first few days of bearing the summer heat, I built a canopy to shade myself, which helped, but sometimes the air temperature felt like a blast furnace, even under the shade. Such days were the worst, with nothing to do but bear it.

Apart from the physical discomfort, the most difficult thing to deal with was the tedium of watching birds fly for hours on end, apparently doing nothing much in particular. However, the occasional startling event would occur at least once in a day's observation and was always worth waiting for. Such events included dramatic displays and interactions with other bateleurs, often of the same gender or a juvenile that was clearly trespassing on the owner's territory. Spectacular displays and important new insights into behavior and ecology were the reward for the effort and the reason why I tolerated the discomfort and hazards of working in the African bush. Through careful observation, I learned that bateleurs spend the vast majority of their day in flight, traversing a fairly limited home range of about 25 km^2 (10 mi^2) in search of food and occasionally defending their territory from an intruding bateleur. This territorial defense was among the most spectacular of behaviors to watch and complex to analyze. However, because it almost always involved a bateleur of the same gender or a juvenile, and always resulted in the intruder departing rapidly from the resident's nest area, interpretation of territorial aggression was justified. One such display began in gliding flight with wings held out, rigid and not flapping, while the legs were extended down below the body, talons spread, and the head thrown backward to call the characteristically raucous *kaaw* of the bateleur. Another that I named the "flip-flip flight" was the most spectacular and rarely seen. It began with the eagle taking a shallow but high-speed dive from about treetop height to only 1 to 2 m (1 to 2 yd) above the ground while executing a series of about 10 half rolls with first one wing and then the other pointed rigidly skyward. The visual result was stunning, with the bateleur's brilliant white feathers under the wing flashing alternately with its black and dark gray upper wing all at high speed and with an anthropomorphically death-defying recovery just when collision with the ground seemed certain.

I also learned that bateleurs are not dashing hunters that stoop to kill their prey with spectacular aerial dexterity like falcons and some other eagles. Rather, with their short tail and long thin wings designed for efficient gliding flight, more like an albatross of the land, bateleurs lack the flight control needed to stoop and stop. (With a short tail they cannot stop quickly; but, in flight, they are very aerobatic—almost unstable like some fighter jets—but require space to maneuver.) Instead, a typical bateleur stoop consists of circling while descending with wings held aloft, rather like a parachute. Most prospective prey must easily see the descent, as I only rarely observed such maneuvers result in the capture of live animals. The bateleur's diet consists of a broad range of mammals, birds, and reptiles, most likely as carrion. In fact, bateleurs are well adapted to finding and quickly consuming small dead animals. They found 67% of small baits (about 500 g, or 1 lb, of meat with feathers scattered around to make it more visible) that I had set out in feeding trials for diurnal scavengers, and of the baits found, they were the first animal to arrive 92% of the time. This amazing ability renders them extremely vulnerable to poisoning by farmers who attempt to kill feral dogs and other predators that attack livestock. Yet, there was a curiously consistent array of animals in the diet (determined from over 4000 prey remains collected at the nest, another eagle watcher's strategy for understanding their subject), which suggested that bateleurs might be able to capture their own prey. The animals that consistently cropped up among prey remains could be broadly described as nocturnal mammals, insectivorous birds, and lizards. Each prey type, in its own way, may become vulnerable to the bateleur when, respectively, it is disturbed from a daytime lair, focused on capturing its own prey, or basking in the sun. Such kills were so rarely seen, however, that I can only speculate.

Despite its penchant for carrion, which, incidentally, is shared by many eagles, including such noble characters as the American bald eagle and golden eagle, the bateleur commands the respect of eagle watchers around the world for its bright coloration and spectacular aerial displays. I feel very fortunate to have been inducted into a career of raptor research and conservation with this species as my tutor. Now employed in a "real" job, I have continued to watch many eagle species since then, typically as a part of projects aimed to conserve endangered species or find out at least the basic biology of species that are little known. There is still plenty of original research and new insight to be gained about eagles and many other birds of prey for people willing to take the time, make the effort, and tolerate the discomforts. All you really need to get started are a decent pair of binoculars, good boots, and determination.

20

Harpy Eagle

COMMON NAME: Harpy eagle

SCIENTIFIC NAME: *Harpia harpyja*

OTHER NAMES: American harpy eagle

IUCN CONSERVATION STATUS: *Near Threatened (population declining)*

DESCRIPTION: A massive eagle, one of the world's largest. Adults primarily have a gray head, gray-black back, black upper breast band and white lower breast. As is the case for so many other tropical forest raptors, it has relatively short, broad, and rounded wings and a large visible crest. Legs are bare, yellow, and enormous. Juveniles are largely pale, even almost white.

SIZE: Length: 89–102 cm (35–40 in); Wingspan: 176–201 cm (69–79 in); Weight: 4.0–9.0 kg (8.8–20 lb)

THREATS: Persecution by humans occurs regularly, especially by shooting. Harpy eagle population density tends to be inversely related to human population density.

DISTRIBUTION: Formerly from southern Mexico throughout tropical forests in the Amazon. Has been extirpated from much of its Central American range as well as from western Colombia although recently re-established in parts of Ecuador.

MOVEMENTS: Largely nonmigratory. Some short-distance group movements have been observed, but these are not understood.

HABITAT: Lowland tropical rainforest. Most frequently occurs in primary forest but can persist in small fragments or second-growth forest, if there is suitable prey and individuals are not persecuted.

DIET: Large to medium-sized mammals, birds, and reptiles, especially arboreal species. Prey includes sloths, deer, monkeys, curassows, and large lizards.

NOTES: Harpy eagles are famed for picking large prey from trees and are even reputed to have, in a defensive action, knocked the occasional human from a tree near an eagle nest.

Author's Biography

JANEENE TOUCHTON radio-
tracking harpy eagles on
Barro Colorado Island,
Panama. Photo by Christian
Ziegler/STRI

Janeene Touchton grew up with a love for wildlife and appreciation for nature, spending countless afternoons as a child in her backyard poking at flowers to see if she could find a beetle inside, chasing dragonflies, catching unsuspecting tadpoles, and keeping an ever-watchful eye for that red-tailed hawk that sometimes foraged nearby her Boulder, Colorado, home. At the age of six, she declared that she would become a biologist and would work with the emperor and king penguins of Antarctica. Janeene began her academic pursuits by obtaining a BSc at the University of Oregon, where she spent a memorable period of time at the Oregon Institute for Marine Biology developing a passion for field research and discovering the exciting world of microscopic organisms. Although she was enamored with her work on phytoplankton and cyanobacteria, Janeene realized that she would rather look through binoculars than a microscope, so after graduating, she took a job with The Peregrine Fund in the lowland rainforest of Central America instead of in the Dry Valleys of Antarctica. Despite the penguins that Antarctica had to offer, running around through a warm, moist, lush tropical landscape chasing harpy eagles seemed more appealing than fighting the freezing cold in quest of rare cyanobacteria. This decision forever changed Janeene's way of thinking about ecology and biodiversity, as she quickly appreciated the role that one species like a harpy eagle could have on an entire community, and began to appreciate the many complex interdependences fundamental to tropical forest ecosystems. Following her work with harpy eagles, Janeene decided to dedicate her research efforts to better understand the various mechanisms underlying the structure of tropical communities, and undertook her MSc studies on ant-following birds at the University of British Columbia. Currently, Janeene is continuing research with ant-following birds for her PhD dissertation at Princeton University. Although she is no longer working directly with eagles, she is still awed by the role that these magnificent birds play in their respective communities, and hopes to maintain an active role in the understanding and conservation of eagles.

HARPY EAGLE, PANAMA

Janeene Touchton

As I stepped off the boat, *The Jacana*, onto Barro Colorado Island (BCI), the deafening roar of the howler monkeys nearly knocked me over backward. I quickly looked around; the forest was still dripping from the torrent of Neotropical rain that fell the night before and the sun was just beginning to burn away the mist that had hung low all morning. Although I wanted to take in all my surroundings—the lush greenery, the unfamiliar sounds and smells, strange colorful insects, the Amazon parrots flying overhead, all the crazy scientists running about—I could not be distracted. Today I was going to see my first wild harpy eagle.

BCI, an artificial island, was formed with the damming of the Chagres River and subsequent formation of Gatun Lake during construction of the Panama Canal, between 1907 and 1913. Arguably the world's most intensively studied piece of tropical forest, scientists have been working on the island since the 1920s. When captive-bred harpy eagles were released in Panama, the great benefits of reintroducing a pair of these elusive birds onto BCI were quickly realized. The last sighting of a harpy eagle on the island had been in the mid-1950s. BCI was a good place for harpy eagles because, on the one front, tireless game wardens were there to keep poachers at bay, and on the other, decades of mammal census data provided the rare opportunity to actually quantify the impact of free-ranging harpy eagles on prey populations. Historically, the amount of prey a harpy eagle consumed had only been inferred from prey brought back to nests.

With this in mind, a subadult eagle named James was released on Barro Colorado in 1999. James was outfitted with a radio transmitter and followed for four months by the use of radio-telemetry. By the time I arrived, another captive-bred harpy eagle, a subadult female named MV (after the letters engraved on her large metal leg band), had just been released. My job was to take over tracking, to learn all I could about these fantastic eagles, with a focus on the female, MV.

As I followed my predecessor into the forest on his last day in Panama, I felt the early-morning bits of civilization slip away—the old army base where I had slept the night before, the massive ships awkwardly gliding through the Panama Canal, the insane drivers of Central America. It felt so wonderful to be surrounded by the giant trees characteristic of Neotropical rainforest and to feel the soft weathered soil underfoot. After walking along one of the island's many well-marked trails for several hundred meters, we scanned first for James's radio frequency, then for MV's. Static. We walked farther. Again, static. Farther yet. And then, a beep started to sound from our small handheld receiver. We headed off the trail in the direction of the strongest beep. "She is close." I think my heart skipped a beat. I scanned the trees in front of me down the slope. I keyed onto her because of her "head-bobbing" movement, a technique that raptors use to gauge distance. MV's stare pierced through the leaves in the mid-canopy, and locked with mine somewhere in the space between us. Obviously, she had been aware of our presence long before we could see her. She was beautiful. At that moment, I had no concept of the time I would soon share with MV—observing her hunt, bathe, and pass the hours in the sun-drenched forest-canopy watching butterflies fly about.

We first had to get to know each other. How do you introduce yourself to a harpy eagle? I quickly realized that there was no possibility of making my presence unknown to MV. I therefore had to get her accustomed to me, all within a respectable distance, of course. My biggest concern was interfering with MV's ability to capture food. After just a few weeks, however, MV stopped paying much attention to me and quieted my concerns.

One day I had tracked MV into a quiet valley on the island. She perched atop a branch typical for her—thick and horizontal, situated in mid to low canopy. Harpy eagles do not soar to search for prey like some other eagles. Rather, being forest-interior hunters, they sport short broad wings and a long tail, making them apt at maneuvering through the trees, where they catch their prey.

I scanned the area to determine if I could spot any prey that MV could have been hunting. Admittedly, in the case of a sloth (one of the harpy's preferred prey), my eyes were useless, and I had to rely on MV to point it out for me. But, she didn't appear to be looking in any one direction, and I couldn't see any likely candidates. So, I gave MV some distance, plopped down my small camping stool, and prepared myself for many hours of sitting in this peaceful valley in the company of a glorious eagle. Then, MV flew closer to me and landed on a low branch. As she appeared quite uninterested in anything, I decided to stay put. A moment later, and two quick movements of her head, she plunged to the ground just 5 m (16 ft) from me. I heard the cry of a white-tailed deer fawn, which had earlier escaped my notice. The fawn's mother ran toward her young but hesitated as soon as she saw the large eagle. The mother took a step forward, and then back—looking at her fawn, to

MV, to me, and back to her fawn again. MV stolidly held the fawn in her talons, unwilling to let go despite the mother's silent pleas. MV looked from the mother, to me, and back to the mother, never once looking at the fawn or loosening her grip.

After what seemed an eternity but in reality was less than a minute, the fawn ceased to struggle and the fawn's mother slowly turned around. Her head hung low, she began to walk away, turned around again and stared at MV, and took another step toward her fawn as if to make certain there was nothing she could do to reverse what had just happened. No. She started walking away again, head hung even lower, turned back one more time, and then was gone. After she left I realized tears had been streaming down my cheeks and I secretly wished that MV hadn't included me in this intimate event. Before, I had just been an observer at a distance. Today my ability to maintain a detached point of view had been challenged.

I quickly learned that MV preferred to hunt for prey in the trees rather than on the ground and that the fawn was an exception. I discovered that over 53% of the prey items MV captured were sloths. At first I thought perhaps sloths were simply easier to catch, but after watching MV capture and kill a couple of them, I soon thought otherwise. One day MV was intently watching a two-toed sloth hanging upside down from a low horizontal branch. She looked straight at the sloth. Then, she tilted her head to the right, to the left, and nearly all the way around. Hopping back and forth on her perch she looked at the sloth from what seemed every angle possible. She repeated this exercise so many times that I soon began to think she was trying to make up her mind about whether she was actually hungry after all. I recalled the close call that she had experienced recently when trying to catch a three-toed sloth, however, and understood her calculated precautions. She had come a little too close and the three-toed sloth swiped at her with his long claws, catching some of her chest feathers. Now I could see that she had learned from that experience and I stopped questioning her approach. What she did next, however, was a total surprise. MV sprang off her perch, flew toward the sloth, and flipped upside down in the air, reached up, and grabbed the sloth. But the sloth hung onto the branch. MV also hung on—to the sloth—her giant wings draped below her. Eventually she tired, let go, and flew back to her perch. Not for long though. She flew in again with the same aerial roll and grabbed the sloth for a second time. The sloth still resisted and didn't let go. MV started pumping her wings, using all her force to pull the sloth off its branch. A risky venture I thought. If the sloth suddenly let go, I wasn't certain MV could right herself and the sloth before hitting the ground. The sloth hung on. Twice MV flew back to the sloth with no success. Back on her perch MV looked at the sloth, let out a faint song that sounded half-pleading, half-disappointed. Then, she flew away. What happened to the sloth, I do not know. My task was to follow MV. When I later returned to check on the sloth, it was gone.

Soon thereafter, the first rains of a new wet season began. The forest seemed to change overnight. The moistened leaf litter nearly vanished before my eyes. Rather than crunching through what seemed almost 30 cm (1 ft) of very large leaves, I now had to traverse on a veritable "slip and slide." It was certainly easier to walk quietly—when I wasn't falling, of course. Much of the light that used to hit the forest floor had been gobbled up by new greenery. Howler monkeys roared more frequently, publicly sharing their disgruntlement about getting wet every time it began to rain. Songbirds flew around in a frenzy of activity, often trying to feed potential mates showy items like large katydids and wolf spiders. Around this time MV decided to focus her hunting pursuits on howler monkeys and to give the sloths a break.

For me, this meant covering a much larger part of the island as MV began flying more. It also meant spending endless hours tucked under my poncho when the rains were too heavy for her to hunt. If we were on the move, I could never be quite certain that when the howler monkeys roared, it was simply because they saw MV or because she had attempted to catch one. Keeping up with MV when she was in "monkey mode" was quite a challenge. Too often I arrived late, only finding MV with a recently killed monkey, not in time to actually witness the kill.

One morning, MV sat in the top of a dead tree with her feathers spread, soaking up sun and drying off. It appeared it was going to be one of those days when not a lot would happen. If I was lucky, some interesting animals might traverse by, like the *Tamandua* anteater that almost ran into me the day before. Minutes, then hours passed. The buzzing of cicadas started to come and go in intensity. MV hadn't moved. I felt my eyes begin to droop. My head fell out of my hand, which had been propping it up. Had I fallen asleep? I quickly looked up to the perch where MV had sat all morning—she was gone. It appeared she knew exactly when to escape my presence. Feeling slightly shafted, I sprang to action.

Luckily, she hadn't gone far. I quickly caught up, and was greeted by a nonchalant glance. "Sorry," I said. "It appears as though you may decide to go hunting today after all, and I don't want to miss it this time." Sure enough, she headed directly toward the area where I had heard howlers calling earlier that morning. Seconds later, I was hit by the howlers' deafening roar. Running, I saw MV fly over a valley past a very upset bunch of howlers, which were also watching her. She flew on. I followed. Landing quietly, she clearly was watching something. Howlers again. Busy foraging in a fruiting tree, they still seemed unaware of the eagle just 10 m (33 ft) away intently watching their every move. Head-bobbing more rapidly than I was accustomed to, she was fixated on a female howler somewhat isolated from the rest of the group, foraging out on the end of a branch. As if in slow motion, MV sprang off her branch, one strong flap of her wings downward, then two. Her talons reached out for the howler. In just that moment, another howler called out in alarm, sending the female howler scrambling out of reach. In an instant, MV went from graceful predator to whiney teenager, giving out a series of frustrated calls. Although I felt for her, and the howlers, I couldn't help but laugh.

After exhausting her options with that group of howlers, MV finally decided it was time to move on. Clearly, she meant business. Several long flights later, I began to worry I wouldn't be able to stay with her. Approaching another large valley on the island, I relocated her with my radio receiver. Just as I looked up, I saw the silhouette of a harpy eagle flying toward the outline of a sleeping monkey. With great speed MV stretched out her talons, grabbed the howler, and dropped it to the ground. I could not discern whether the howler was stunned or dead. When I had found MV with howler prey in the past, she was always on the ground. I thought she must have flown to the ground with the howlers, much like she did with sloths. But to do so would be risky because after MV dropped the monkey, several adult male howlers ran to mob her. She was out of reach, however, already astutely perched in another tree with her gaze on the monkey she had just knocked to the ground. The troop eventually left, and MV flew to the ground to claim her prize. The day was nearly over; I left her in peace.

My experiences with MV gave me cause to reflect on the relationship between harpy eagles and the large tracts of old forest they rely on for nesting and foraging. Neotropical forests are becoming more and more fragmented, and to add to their problems, harpy eagles are under constant threat from poachers. Hopefully, MV and her kin will not become ghosts of our past, ancient symbols of what our forests used to be. I, for one, will keep watching and waiting for those rare and special moments when a harpy eagle just might fly by.

21

White-bellied Sea Eagle

COMMON NAME: White-bellied sea eagle

SCIENTIFIC NAME: *Haliaeetus leucogaster*

OTHER NAMES: White-bellied fish eagle, gray-backed sea eagle, white-breasted fish eagle, white-breasted fish hawk, white-breasted sea eagle

IUCN CONSERVATION STATUS: *Least Concern (population stable)*

DESCRIPTION: A large but thin-looking sea eagle with long broad wings and a diamond-shaped tail. Adults are striking with a white head, breast, and underwing feathers; body slate gray. Preadults are brown.

SIZE: Length: 70–85 cm (27.5–33.5 in); Wingspan: 178–218 cm (70–86 in); Weight: 1.8–3.9 kg (4.0–8.6 lb)

THREATS: Human disturbance, shooting, poisoning, and habitat loss have caused declines of this species in parts of its range.

DISTRIBUTION: Coastal areas and inland lakes throughout southeast Asia, Australia, and islands of this region

MOVEMENTS: Generally nonmigratory, although adults and juveniles may travel long distances in response to environmental conditions, especially food shortages. Juvenile dispersal may be extremely long distance—up to 3000 km (1864 mi).

HABITAT: Coastal areas and large inland lakes and rivers. Ranges over woodlands and open country near to nesting areas.

DIET: Forages on a wide range of aquatic and terrestrial vertebrates, including fish, sea snakes, birds, mammals, and turtles. Also scavenges floating carrion or other aquatic animals and takes a wide variety of young birds from colonies. Known to pirate food from other birds of prey and seabirds.

NOTES: White-bellied sea eagles have been observed dropping large crabs and turtles from 40 m (131 ft) high onto rocks below, to smash open the carapace for access to the flesh.

Author's Biography

JASON WIERSMA in the field
in Tasmania, Australia. Photo
by Debbie Thoy/Wizard
Corporation Productions

Jason Wiersma lives in Tasmania, Australia, and developed an interest in predatory birds at the age of 15. His first paid job studying raptors began when he entered the Australian National University and studied peregrine falcons under the guidance of Dr. Penny Olsen and Nick Mooney. Jason also developed a keen understanding for raptor rehabilitation, spending several years as a raptor rehabilitator. At the beginning of his university study, Jason, in consultation with Wen and Julie Nermut, developed a study on the white-bellied sea eagle that considered mortality factors of sea eagles over a 12-year period. Through his private study and raptor rehabilitation efforts, Jason was nominated and granted the Young Australian of the Year Environment Award, and used the $2000 grant award to continue his study on the white-bellied sea eagle. He also worked on the Regional Forest Agreement Study, which looked at assessing the status of the masked owl in Tasmania, and spent three years as a private consultant to Forestry Tasmania and the Forest Practices Board, conducting pre-logging nest site surveys. Jason completed his BSc (Honours) degree and was granted a $7000 scholarship to study sea eagles during his honours year through private funding, the university's first privately funded grant. Jason's enthusiasm for eagles extends to the United States, where he has been involved in monitoring migrating bald and golden eagles in Montana with Al Harmata (US Fish and Wildlife Service) and Marco Restani (St. Cloud State University). Jason currently works as a field scientist on the Tasmanian Devil Facial Tumor Disease Project, where he has developed a special remote camera system to monitor the spread of the disease across the state. While he currently works on carnivores, Jason continues to study white-bellied sea eagles when time permits.

WHITE-BELLIED SEA EAGLE, TASMANIA

Jason Wiersma

At the age of 15 I was a keen raptor enthusiast. I wasn't much keen on loitering at the local mall and just hanging out. Instead, I spent most of my spare time wading through glossy raptor books and trying to make sense of scientific papers on birds of prey.

I volunteered my time to look after injured and orphaned birds, built my own aviaries, and helped others do the same. I was inspired to get heavily into fieldwork, with the large predatory birds being my greatest passion. My home in Launceston was a gift for any raptor enthusiast. A peregrine falcon's nest was located just a few hundred meters from my parents' back door. Each afternoon I spent hours down in a makeshift hide on a rock ledge, building up my observation skills watching peregrines. As fortune may have it, I was introduced to Penny Olsen, one of Australia's leading raptor researchers (and author of the chapter in this book on wedge-tailed eagles), based at the Australian National University. Penny gave me the opportunity to work on peregrines for six years, which later led me to my own studies on white-bellied sea eagles on the Tamar River.

The Tamar is a 70 km (43.5 mi) estuary lined mostly with introduced rice grass with occasional stands of dry eucalypt forest. While clearing for housing and agriculture has decimated much of the best eagle habitat, the river is still a picturesque place to work. Superb blue wrens dance along the rice grass–curtained banks. Flotillas of black swans snake their heads deep in the river. Choruses of yellow-tailed black cockatoos often sound through the day. Frequently, mist moves down the river. Pockets of eucalypt trees are only recognizable by an occasional lone stag tree. The reflecting colors of the river merge with the sky to provide an indiscernible horizon.

We—two colleagues and me—would slip the boat in before dawn. It was typically cold, and several layers of clothes never seemed enough insulation; the extremities were perpetually numb. Navigating by feel, we would motor into the mist, with our cargo of dead fish and a few lengths of string. Arriving at the bay, the goose-like honk of the sea eagle grabbed my interest. Eventually we saw two white figures within the dissipating mist, sea eagles high on a roost. The male, the smaller of the two, had pinned a long lifeless figure beneath its talons, a short finned eel. That was bad news, as we were here to do one thing—to capture the pair and attach a color band and radio transmitter so I could learn more about their habitat preferences along the river. If only we had arrived earlier to offer the male the noosed fish. It would appear that we had probably come for nothing, as there was little chance now of enticing the pair if they had already eaten.

It was early in the season. The pair had not yet laid an egg in their nest, which towered some 60 m (197 ft) high in a white gum, a stone throw from our "tinny" (boat). If it had been later in the season, we would have had a much greater chance of capturing a bird, as the food requirements of the chicks would certainly have inspired an attack on practically any lure offered. Feeling like our attempts at capture would be futile, we nevertheless decided to run with our plan. Few people had successfully captured white-bellied sea eagles because the techniques used on other species simply didn't work, and we wanted to try out our new technique. My colleague started the motor, and exhaust fumes spluttered into the murky inward tide. This bay on the river was full of snagging obstacles, such as submerged rocks covered with oysters. The silted muddy lining of the riverbed was no kinder because it could choke the motor and leave a distracted or unsuspecting navigator stranded on soft mud. Patience would then be tried while waiting for the rising tide to unlock the ensnared craft. As the revs of the motor increased, the muddied water cleared and we glided through closer to the ghostly figures looking down from above. It was important that the eagles not associate the offering of the fish with us, a potentially dangerous animal. We wanted to offer the mullet lure in a fashion that would make it look like we had stirred up a dead fish from the deep waters. Noting both eagles tensing and ready for flight, we took a wider berth to appear less threatening. Like a pickpocket in a crowd, we slipped the fish into the water without the pair noticing. The fish, now discretely left behind in the water, was followed by a long line attached to a small weight acting as an anchor to the riverbed. If the sea eagle took flight with the snared fish, the drag and weight of the anchor would eventually bring it down to a watery capture. Well, that was the theory.

Quietness settled on the river. The motor had been extinguished for us to play the waiting game. We opened a thermos—the aroma of tea spilled out—and we filled our nervous stomachs. With the mist gone, the sun now gave us warmth. The valley was coming to life; the drone of distant traffic mixed with the lap of water against our small aluminum vessel. Swallows darted out from the forest edge, flying low over the water to catch insects on the wing. Despite the traffic and the obvious signs of human disturbance, the Tamar is a beautiful place. "Its head is bobbing!" exclaimed my assistant. Sure enough, the female seemed unconvinced that her partner was intent on sharing his prized eel, and she had taken an interest in our fish bait. "Something always happens when I pour a cup of hot tea," I complained. We watched the female sea eagle appear from the cover of the trees with closed wings. She approached the water rapidly, outstretched wings curving the dive into a graceful glide. The water erupted into a shower of beads as her talons struck at the surface. The snakelike figure of an eel appeared, writhing, clutched in the powerful kneading of talons. The lure hadn't worked, and both eagles had eel for breakfast.

"Well, bugger it! Let's just wait and see what happens." My assistant offered the hot tea flask, which I accepted, resigned to patience or going home empty-handed. Both birds ate their eels, as we ate cupcakes and drank tea. Talk of eagles, ideas, and tactics filled the small boat as we drifted gently around the bay. Unbelievably, only minutes after the pair had finished their meal, the male emerged once again from the tall gum diving toward the bait. The stealthy blow seemed to take a second, but the line attached to the anchor trailed for what seemed like eternity. The sea eagle's flight was cut short by an ever tightening leash as the male collapsed into the water.

Navigating the boat slowly up on our "first male" required due care. We didn't want to unwittingly cut the line that held the eagle. An eagle freed with a nylon noose would be an entangled eagle, one that would die from exhaustion or starvation. Our gaff hook was quickly deployed to capture the line beneath the water's surface. It was important to maintain tension as the nooses could easily slip. The enraged bird attempted a jumping flight endeavoring to free itself. The eagle fought valiantly, only to be clutched in the water by my cold hand, feeling quickly for his rough legs. The bird came dripping into the boat, and I quickly immobilized the taloned feet, the most dangerous part of the bird. With the bird's back against my chest in a firm embrace, I stretched my neck away from its beak. Most raptors have comparatively weak bills, but sea eagles have formidable beaks capable of tearing a strip of flesh from a naked neck. I had learned this lesson some years before, when not paying attention with an injured eagle.

The bird quivered with growing intensity as its capture ordeal continued. Who knows what raptors think when they're held? For most animals, being grasped by another animal would inevitably mean that you were about to be eaten. Feeling compassion for our wet prize, we placed a loose sock over the eagle's hackled head, dulling the stress on the bird. Having poked, prodded, measured, and weighed him, our team was glad to release the male, complete with some new jewelry. A radio transmitter and identification band would later provide valuable information. A sense of achievement was felt by the team as grins became big smiles telling a story of their own.

Two months had passed before we attempted to capture the second bird, the female. It was another cold morning, felt by all with the telltale red nose. The sky was clear except for the soft haze of wood smoke wafting from a thousand household chimneys. The white-buffed figures we were searching for were not in sight as we passed their roost high on the skyline. Now that one of the pair had a radio transmitter, finding the birds was not so hit and miss. The suggestive beep from the tracking antenna indicated they were on the other side of the bay. Sure enough, there we found the pair sun bathing on a large rock exposed by the low tide. They appeared not unlike a cluster of oysters. Raptors are more nervous when perched low. We kept well back, and with the noosed fish in place we motored back around the point. The wait was short enough to be remarkable. One of the eagles rose to the air with powerful thrusting wings. We sat motionless as the bird approached in a large yet gentle arc. Disappointingly it was the male, already adorned with transmitter and identification band. It dropped from the sky with increasing speed and struck the slippery lure. More to luck than good management, the nooses, which appear invisible to the eagle, slipped between its talons, the fish tearing from its tether. The male received a free feed and we relaxed, not having to put the bird through the stress of recapture.

We set another lure, hoping the free meal for the male would entice the female. Like a spiritual ritual, we laid the offering into the silky brown water. As if the bird was trained, the female took to the air and homed in on the barely perceptible lure. This was it! She hit the lure with hungry intent. The nooses tightened and a watery capture became inevitable. She was much stronger and heavier than her partner, who watched disinterested while dismembering his mullet. She struggled more than the male, but it wasn't long before the three of us had her back in the late-morning air, complete with the second transmitter. At last we had captured our first pair! Many subsequent mornings and evenings were spent tracking the eagles along the estuary, learning where they spent their time. We gathered information on roost locations, territories, and favorite hunting grounds. Management plans for the species could now have more than an anecdotal basis, and the eagles' habitat could be better protected.

Eagle protection is, however, more than just a management plan. Not long after the trapping days, I visited an aunt who knew of my passion for eagles. She had news of an incident that churned my stomach and left me feeling both angry and scared. My aunt and her husband were keen sailors and also knew the Tamar eagles well. At a local pub, she overheard a policeman telling friends about the eagle he blamed for taking his poultry and the shot that brought it down. It seemed unbelievable but it appeared to be true; in a sick ironic twist, the female had fallen victim to an act the law considered a crime. A few days later the lifeless eagle was handed to wildlife authorities; the cause of death, a .22 caliber bullet.

22

Martial Eagle

COMMON NAME: Martial eagle

SCIENTIFIC NAME: *Polemaetus bellicosus*

OTHER NAMES: Martial hawk eagle

IUCN CONSERVATION STATUS: *Near Threatened (population declining)*

DESCRIPTION: An enormous eagle with long broad wings, a longish tail, and a short crest that is only sometimes visible. Martial eagles are brown above and light below, although their head and neck are dark like the back and the breast is spotted. Legs are extremely long and well feathered to the feet. Juveniles are white with gray upperwings, mantle, and nape.

SIZE: Length: 78–96 cm (31–38 in); Wingspan: 188–227 cm (74–89 in); Weight: 3.0–6.2 kg (6.6–13.6 lb)

THREATS: This species faces threats from direct persecution by humans (shooting and poisoning), collision with power lines, drowning in steep-walled reservoirs, and habitat degradation from overgrazing, afforestation, and development.

DISTRIBUTION: Sub-Saharan Africa, except tropical rainforests and thorn-scrub

MOVEMENTS: Nonmigratory; juveniles and immature may disperse long distances and appear nomadic.

HABITAT: Light forest to open Karoo, probably favors well-wooded savanna. As is noted in the story below, has taken to nesting on power pylons in many areas.

DIET: Large to medium-sized mammals, birds, and reptiles. Mammals range in size from squirrels to small antelope, and birds as big as young ostrich may be taken. Monitor lizards may be taken in large numbers.

NOTES: The Martial is among the largest of the African eagles.

Author's Biography

ANDREW JENKINS
searching for raptors at
Blyde River Canyon,
Mpumalanga, South
Africa. Photo courtesy
of the author

   As a 10-year-old with a passing interest in natural history and a developing passion for birds of prey, Andrew Jenkins emigrated with his family from the United Kingdom to South Africa in the late 1970s. Too young for politics and too old for Action Man, he was rapidly seduced by the sunshine, the diversity of wildlife, and above all the impressive array of African raptors. As a schoolboy in Johannesburg he spent all his spare time watching Verreaux's eagles in the nearby Magaliesberg Mountains. After receiving his BSc (Honours) degree at the University of Natal, he moved to Cape Town and began an MSc study, based at the Percy FitzPatrick Institute of African Ornithology, University of Cape Town, on the factors limiting the peregrine falcon population in South Africa. This project was upgraded to PhD research and was finally completed as a comparison of the behavioral ecology of peregrines and lanner falcons in 1998. Since then, Andrew has remained at "The Fitz," first as a postdoctoral researcher, then as a research associate, and more recently as a contracted research biologist. He leads the Western Cape Raptor Research Program, which is the administrative umbrella for a number of raptor-focused research and conservation projects, including work on black harriers as flagships and indicators for the conservation of threatened vegetation in the lowlands of the Western Cape, and on the management of martial and other large eagle nests on electrical utility structures. He has also continued his work on peregrines, in the form of a decade-long color-marking study of the population demography and dynamics of this species on the Cape Peninsula.

MARTIAL EAGLE, SOUTH AFRICA

Andrew Jenkins

"N-I-G-R-I-N-I!" pronounced Chris Nigrini, loudly and proudly, with a challenging sparkle in his eyes, as I was introduced to him on the front step of his farmhouse in the vast, semi-arid heartland of South Africa known as the Karoo. This spelling out of his surname, he alleged, was the sum total of his command of English. Otherwise, he is as fundamentally Afrikaans as *biltong* (salted, air-dried meat) and *boerewors* (spicy sausage)—two unique and staple components of the Afrikaners' frighteningly carnivorous diet. With humor as dry as his rolling acres of ranchland, Chris was keen to remind me that English-speakers or *Engelsmanne* were a rarity in the Karoo, and that I was well out of my comfort zone. This done, he promptly insisted that I take a seat under the palms growing in his incongruously verdant back garden, and attempted to ply me with alcohol and great chunks of cooked meat, fresh off the *braai,* or barbecue. I looked anxiously at my colleague, Koos de Goede, for assistance. A leathery old Afrikaner himself, Koos intervened in what ultimately became a protracted negotiation with Chris on exactly how we were to spend our afternoon. He explained to Chris that, much as we might like to while away the rest of the day in drunken oblivion, we were actually there to check the eagle nest on his farm. After some deliberation, the two reached a happy compromise. Koos and I would first drive out to do our eagle fieldwork, and then return to the house to enjoy some much-deserved Karoo hospitality. This decided, we got back into Koos's vehicle and rattled off down the dusty track that led from the cool, shady surrounds of the farmhouse, and out into the searing hot veld of the Nigrini property (rather optimistically named Springfontein, or "spring-fountain"). As we got clear of the farm outbuildings, Koos stepped on the gas—the deal with Chris included congregating with his family to watch the South Africa–Australia rugby match on TV, and it was due to kick off in only a couple of hours.

Koos and I were in the Karoo collecting data for the Eskom Electric Eagle Project, or the EEEP as it has become affectionately known. This is a collaborative initiative involving applied conservationists (such as Koos), a research biologist (me), and field and office staff of Eskom, South Africa's primary electricity supplier. The main objective of the EEEP is to resolve an "industrial dispute" between Eskom and a population of large eagles. The eagles—mostly martial eagles, with a few pairs of Verreaux's and tawny eagles—had assumed squatters' rights on the pylon structures supporting Eskom's network of high-voltage transmission lines. The 30 m (98 ft) high steel pylons were evidently preferable to the short and brittle acacia trees that the eagles normally use as nesting sites. In the 20 to 30 years since they were first erected, the lines of pylons that crisscross the Karoo have effectively sucked in much of the breeding eagle population from the surrounding countryside. The EEEP covers some 1400 km (870 mi) of pylons, which support about 90 pairs of eagles. The birds build massive stick nests in the upper reaches of the pylons and spend much of their time either tending these structures (during the breeding season) or else perching and roosting high in the lattice work, above the high-voltage power lines that are generally suspended below the pylon cross-beams. This is where the problems arise.

As particularly large birds, eagles are capable of producing, several times each day, very long jets or "streamers" of excrement. These liquid streamers, which can be up to 2 m (6.6 ft) long, are good conductors of electricity! When emanating from a bird perched at a nest or roost directly above the power lines, streamers can fall in such a way that they span the protective air gap between the lines and the pylon, causing the electricity to arc across from the intended conductors to the steelwork in an explosive "flashover" or fault. In such instances, the sudden and dramatic release of 400,000 volts into the immediate vicinity of its perch doubtless comes as a startling surprise to the freshly relieved eagle, but otherwise the birds are generally unharmed. Ironically, the news for Eskom is not so good. Because the high-voltage lines in the study are vital links in the national power grid, these dips in power can destabilize the system and can even result in localized or regional blackouts. At best, they translate into upsets on electronic production lines and the like, and generally inconvenience Eskom's big-paying industrial customers, costing the company at least SAR60,000 (US$10,000) per flashover.

Obviously, although the people at Eskom are generally happy to accommodate their big, feathered tenants, they are very keen to minimize the substantial financial implications of their toilet arrangements. This is where the EEEP comes in. Our brief has been to develop a management strategy to reduce the frequency of eagle-related flashovers to tolerable levels, and in so doing secure the welfare of the eagle population into the future. Much of the initial foundation work on the project involved basic survey and monitoring of the eagles' nests, allowing us to examine the spatial relationship between eagles and faulting, and pinpoint the particular problem lines, pylon structures, and nests that contribute most to the problem. In order to cover the big distances encompassed by the project, we do an annual helicopter survey of all the nests. We follow that up with more intensive work in selected areas, to verify the accuracy of the observations made from the chopper and collect useful additional data and material.

A little earlier in the year we had flown along both of the big transmission lines that cross this area, and were now back on terra firma to confirm that a martial eagle nest recorded as empty from the helicopter was still vacant. Once we had traveled the 10 km (6 mi) or so from the house to the pylon line, we turned off the relatively well-used farm road onto the Eskom track. Theoretically, these maintenance roads allow one to drive under the entire length of all the bigger power lines. In practice, they are generally overgrown or badly eroded, and at best permit bone-jarring progress, at a snail's pace, to only the flatter sections of the lines. As we bumped along over the rocky and deceptively undulating terrain, which is typical of the central Karoo, our nest emerged on the skyline ahead of us, in the top of a pylon about six spans, or 1.5 km (1 mi) away. We rattled up to the nest tower, keeping a careful look out for any eagle activity in the area, but saw nothing. Except for the sinister crackling of high voltage, everything was quiet as we stepped from the truck, and there was little in the way of droppings or prey remains around the tower base that might have suggested that the eagles were in residence. Just to be sure, we walked up a small, stony koppie that was conveniently situated right next to the nest pylon, to get closer to level with the top of the nest and make sure it didn't contain an incubating eagle. Surprisingly, as we peered through the spotting scope at the spiky branches that fringed the top of the nest, we spotted a brown, slightly crested head and a beady yellow eye staring back at us. The bird, probably a female, was lying as flat as she could in the hope that we wouldn't see her. This is a standard response for an incubating martial eagle, and we felt good that we had spotted her, and updated and corrected our nest records for the year, which made the trip to Springfontein worthwhile. Job done, we scrambled down to the vehicle and sped off back along the servitude. Beer and rugby beckoned.

As we arrived back at the farmhouse, hot and thirsty, we saw immediately that circumstances there had changed somewhat. Chris's entire extended family and circle of friends had evidently arrived for a social, and were encamped on the step and in their host's custom-built bar area, like vultures around a carcass. Even more alarming, the carcass was clearly all but consumed—everywhere we looked there were empty or half-empty glasses, plates smeared with grease and vestiges of sauce, many of them stacked with steak and chop bones, but no signs of any leftovers. Just large, recumbent aunts and uncles with distended guts, replete, smiling faces, and damp, sweaty clothing, straining at the seams. As we were about to collapse in a heap of disappointment, Chris emerged from the fray, shirtless, more than a little tipsy, and even more insistent that we join the party. This was the invitation we'd been looking for, and only minutes later, after gorging on a surfeit of hot food and cold booze, we too were belching and beaming, our eyes lacking focus, and our top lips beaded with sweat. We weren't allowed much time to bask though, as the Springboks were about to take on the Wallabies, and we were ushered into the gloomy interior of the house and sat before a giant TV. Ninety minutes, several beers, and much agitated shouting later, we were back out on the step, exhausted by our heroic endeavors—we'd won! As the excitement of the match abated, the sun sank away into the cool of evening, and many of the assembled guests drifted back to their farms, an awkward silence descended. As yet, Koos and I had made no plans for the evening, and we shuffled uncomfortably in our seats, in preparation for a reluctant departure. Just in time, Chris and his wife, Alida, declared that we would, of course, be staying over in their guest cottage, and that preparations for dinner—unbelievably, another dose of barbecued beef—were already well under way. With even quantities of relief and gratitude, we settled back into our deck chairs, just as a fresh round of drinks arrived.

After all the chaos of the afternoon, it was good to be able to sit quietly and chat a little with our hosts. They were very interested in our eagle work, and keen to understand exactly what it all entailed. The situation clearly called for an impressive story or two, and with a few brandy-and-Cokes under his belt, Koos stepped into the breech. He began by describing the aerial survey work that we had been doing, going back to the early days of the study, when a lack of finances forced us to fly the lines in small, fixed-wing aircraft rather than helicopters. This opened the way for him to describe some of the scarier moments we'd experienced on these flights. For example, once, we narrowly avoided a head-on collision with a soaring martial eagle that swept past so closely over the cockpit of the plane that both Koos and the pilot had ducked for cover behind the control console. On another occasion, as we banked to land at the airstrip outside Beaufort West in the center of the study area, the front passenger-side door flew open, and we had to hold it closed until we landed safely. Even scarier was another landing at Beaufort. This time, just before we arrived over the airport, we had seen a martial eagle, carrying a hare, fly across in front of the aircraft. This interesting sighting obviously distracted the pilot, and as we came in to land we got lower and lower over the gravel landing strip, an emergency signal started blaring, and we touched down in the shortest, noisiest, and strangest landing I have ever experienced. The plane came to a halt in a storming cloud of dust and pebbles, and even as the air cleared, we still seemed to be much too close to the ground. "Oh fiddlesticks!" said the pilot (or words to that effect). "I forgot to put the wheels down!"

Koos saved the best (or worst) story for last, and clearly enjoyed regaling Chris and Alida with the intricate details of his closest-to-death flying experience. This time he and his pilot (I had sensibly found an excuse not to go along on this flight) were only 30 minutes or so from home on their way out to the Karoo when they started to experience engine problems. Unfortunately they were flying low over the huge range of mountains that separate Cape Town from the interior, and they searched and searched in vain for somewhere flat enough to put the aircraft down as the engine got closer and closer to finally expiring. Just in time, they found a short length of gravel track and careered down onto it, not quite stopping before the end of the improvised runway, and finishing with the plane nose-down in a thorn bush. Luckily, both occupants emerged in one piece. Understandably, Koos has now given up on fixed-wing flying.

With rufous-cheeked nightjars "churrring" in the distance, our tummies once again tanked up with excessive amounts of protein and carbohydrate, and the coals of the *braai* fire finally starting to cool and fade, we unanimously decided to call it a day. Koos and I were shown to our commodious cottage and were wished a very good night. As I settled down to sleep, I mulled over the events of the day, marveling at the incredible warmth and hospitality of the Nigrini family, and the richness of the peripheral experiences to be had by a couple of raptor biologists working in the austere vastness of the Karoo. I dropped off with two nagging questions on my mind: Would our eagle management scheme prove to be effective, and would there be bacon and eggs for breakfast . . . ?!

23

White-tailed Sea Eagle

COMMON NAME: White-tailed sea eagle

SCIENTIFIC NAME: *Haliaeetus albicilla*

OTHER NAMES: White-tailed eagle, white-tailed fish eagle

IUCN CONSERVATION STATUS: *Least Concern (population increasing)*

DESCRIPTION: A large, bulky sea eagle with squarish wings, a short tail, and a large yellow bill. White-tailed sea eagles are brown above and below, with only a white tail and a very gray head. Because of the large bill and thick neck, the head can appear very small. Juveniles are darker than adults and become progressively paler as they mature.

SIZE: Length: 74–102 cm (29–40 in); Wingspan: 193–250 cm (76–99 in); Weight: 3.5–7.2 kg (7.7–15.8 lb)

THREATS: Historically DDT caused thinning of eggshells of this species. More recently populations have recovered strongly, although shooting, poisoning, habitat loss, and collision with trains, power lines, and wind turbines are all significant causes of mortality.

DISTRIBUTION: White-tailed sea eagles are distributed across the Palearctic, from Scotland, through Scandinavia, and throughout Russia, Mongolia, and much of Kazakhstan. They also occur in Greenland and in Japan and coastal China. Have not yet recolonized or been reintroduced to the Iberian Peninsula or other regions of the Mediterranean.

MOVEMENTS: Northern populations are largely migratory; to the south where food is available year-round, populations are nonmigratory. Juveniles are highly dispersive.

HABITAT: Highly variable. Most often associated with water and regularly found in coastal areas or near large lakes, reservoirs, and rivers. However, in central Asia is often found nesting far from water in trees large enough to support its enormous nest.

DIET: When found near water, white-tailed sea eagles take large numbers of fish and aquatic birds. Marine mammal carrion can also be important to their diet during winter. When breeding far from water, rabbits, ground squirrels, marmots, and even other birds of prey may make up a significant part of their diet.

NOTES: White-tailed sea eagles are remarkable generalists, in habitat and diet. Although typically associated with aquatic habitats, they are also found in some of Eurasia's driest areas, in mountains and in dense forests.

Author's Biography

JUSTIN GRANT descending
a cliff in western Scotland
to reach a white-tailed sea
eagle's nest. Photo by
R. A. J. Beaton

Growing up in a somewhat turbulent family environment, Justin Grant was academically unsuccessful at school and left at age 17, having just managed to pass one "A" level examination. Always an active outdoor type, he spent a year dairy farming in Australia before returning home and attending the Scottish Agricultural College in Ayr, in southwestern Scotland. After gaining a Higher National Diploma in agriculture, followed by the College Diploma in agricultural engineering, he had a succession of farming jobs, worked as a District Council mechanic, an agricultural engineering lecturer, and then a truck driver in London. With such "nonstandard" qualifications, it took three years of persistence to gain a university place, during which time Justin used the University of London's Department of Extra-Mural Studies as a stepping stone, passing exams covering the archaeology of Paleolithic and Mesolithic man and environmental archaeology. Relevant fieldwork included supervising the excavation of a Late Stone Age rock shelter in Swaziland. During time off from that, Justin worked as a tour guide in southern Africa, specializing in archaeology and wildlife tours. Finally, in 1986, he managed to get into Edinburgh University to read ecological science. Wildlife, and avian predators in particular, was an increasing interest, and after emerging four years later with a BSc (Honours) in wildlife management, Justin spent 14 years engaged in fieldwork across Scotland for the Royal Society for the Protection of Birds (RSPB), studying common buzzards, hen harriers, and red kites, but particularly golden and white-tailed sea eagles. When not watching eagles, Justin is likely to be found paddling his sea kayak somewhere off the west coast of Scotland. He may, of course, be watching eagles at the same time!

WHITE-TAILED SEA EAGLE, SCOTLAND

Justin Grant

There are run-of-the-mill jobs, and there are jobs that you hope you never have to do again. What I had to do on the Isle of Skye in early July 2003, on the first day after a vacation, came fairly and squarely in the second category. Thinking back, of course, the situation was my own fault to begin with, for not being sufficiently on the ball earlier in the year. I thought I knew what was going on, and it turned out that I didn't.

Where white-tailed sea eagles on the Isle of Skye were concerned, it was my responsibility to know what was what, as I was employed as the RSPB's Sea Eagle Officer. I was expected to know how many territories there were, the age of the adults, the location of their nests, how many young they were rearing, and so forth. Well, as far as possible, I was expected to know everything about them. And I had to do my best to protect them from the illegal egg-collecting that, unbelievably, was still practiced, threatening our tiny reintroduced Scottish population. Later in the year it was my job to mark the young with colored wing-tags, which enabled us to study their dispersal and movements while they were maturing and looking for territories of their own. I felt very privileged to be contributing to a project dedicated to re-establishing a species that had been irresponsibly exterminated only a few generations ago, and I took my job very seriously.

So it was always exciting to find a new territory, and this particular pair of white-tailed sea eagles was undoubtedly new in the area. I had found them the previous spring, mucking about on a vegetated crag. She was a subadult, her exact age and provenance known because of the luminous green wing-tags she wore, and I could see from his plumage that he was an adult, but I didn't know exactly how old. I had watched them around their nest site throughout March, bringing in sticks and clumps of grass, but when, by the second week of April, she hadn't laid any eggs, I knew they weren't going to breed that year.

One year on and here I was, back in the same observation position, my hopes for their breeding bolstered by time. What a fabulous place for watching them, I thought, sitting in the surrounding forest where I'd found a gap in the trees through which I could see the nest with no chance of disturbing the pair accidentally. But as March slid quietly into April, and one by one my other four territorial females had begun incubating their eggs, I had seen less and less of my new eagles around their nest. Even the local ravens had been completely unchallenged when they brazenly stole sticks off it, and that really was a bad sign. I knew the eagles were about; I had seen them flying wingtip to wingtip over the nearby sea cliffs, and then occasionally I'd observed them perched together on an outcrop. She still had her flashy green epaulettes, and he looked neat and tidy sitting slightly smaller beside her. Okay, so last year's nest for some reason was unattractive and they had built a new one; the problem was, where was it? The possibilities were either somewhere out on the 7 km (4.3 mi) stretch of magnificent coastal cliffs, in the forestry plantation, or out on the nearby islands. I quailed at the thought of the islands. They would be much safer from egg thieves out there, but since it was my job to find and watch the eagles without disturbance, such a location would pose quite a problem for me. I knew also that, particularly with a newly established young pair, they may give up early or not breed at all, and I could spend lots of time looking for . . . well . . . nothing!

Observing this whole area effectively was impossible, and I knew from years of experience that even these huge eagles could be good at sneaking in and out of nest sites undetected. By the end of April I had walked the entire length of the cliffs and looked at every nook and cranny that I could find. I had searched the forestry plantation long and hard, knowing that a big tree with solid supporting branches could be just as attractive a proposition to this pair of white-tailed sea eagles as a windy ledge on a huge sea cliff. But the more I had looked at the plantation, the more I'd thought there was only one word to describe it: unsuitable. The trees were too young, too small, too closely spaced, too . . . *unsuitable!* White-tailed sea eagles are massive, and when they are nesting, an enormous tree is required to support their large nest. I had stared out through my high-powered telescope at the small group of low-lying islands where gulls, geese, and seabirds nested. Well, the eagles wouldn't have to go far to hunt, but nesting there, with all those squawking gulls hassling them continuously? No, they would have a nice comfy nest on a ledge sheltered by an overhang on the big sea cliffs. Obviously, I had just overlooked them.

Throughout May and June I had been busy doing other things, and besides, I'd spent most of April looking for them unsuccessfully. To be honest, I'd pretty much given up and was resigned to the fact that they weren't ready to breed this year either. In fact, I had intended to have just one more look— but it was always a case of, "I'll do it next week." By the end of June it was bothering me more and more. I was due a week's holiday and was looking forward to spending it in Yorkshire ringing woodland birds with a bunch of friends. But these eagles—how sure was I that they were not breeding this year? Not so sure that I was going to give up without just one more look. So, the day before I was due to go on holiday, I walked the entire stretch of coastline again. I saw only one adult white-tailed sea eagle distantly to the north and was just about to give up when right below me on a grassy knoll I spotted a characteristic pile of white feathers where an eagle had plucked a gull or fulmar prior to eating it. Walking toward it for a closer look I saw another pile and then another. Suddenly the picture had changed. With no seabirds breeding along that piece of coastline, the eagles had to be hunting somewhere else and bringing their prey back to the cliff-top. That could only mean one thing; they had a nest somewhere that I just hadn't found yet. By the end of the day I had finished searching the cliffs again, only this time knowing for certain that there was something to find.

All that happened between March and late June. By now it was early July and on the first day back after my week's holiday I was straight back on the case. Well, after you've searched the likely places and found nothing, you have to search the unlikely places; in this case it was the apparently "unsuitable" forestry plantation. I stared at the area and decided to begin by walking through the plantation from my vehicle to the area of cliff where all the feathers were, and from there search the more open forest areas and ridges methodically. They would be on a small crag or in a tree with big enough branches along a stream somewhere. I had gone only 200 m (219 yd) when, as I pushed my way through the branches into a clearing, I smelled the unmistakable odor of fulmars, the medium-sized seabirds that were one of the eagles' favorite prey. I looked up and there, almost immediately above me, was a very big nest in a very small tree. Peering down at me with their wings outstretched in threat were two large white-tailed sea eagle chicks. I stared at them and immediately noticed how well grown they were. It was a well-established practice not to approach chicks of this age, in case they were frightened enough to jump out of the nest, whereupon they would need to be picked up and put back—which could be difficult, and risky for the birds. I turned to retreat, glad that I had found the nest but annoyed that I had not done so three weeks previously. But just as I moved, one of the youngsters launched itself from the nest rim and made its first unexpected, ungainly, and unwanted flight, landing with a thump in the bracken 40 m (44 yd) away. I stared in complete horror, knowing that I would need to put it back and that while doing so the other one would inevitably come out as well. And every time I replaced one, the other would jump again. It didn't bear thinking about; I tried not to.

The immediate and crucial decision to make was whether I could manage this by myself or whether I should call in reinforcements. It was one of those jobs that with one chick, a straightforward climb, and an easy tree to work in, I could manage by myself quite easily—not that one ever did a climbing job solo nowadays. But even if nothing went wrong, it was always so much easier with an assistant. I dug out my mobile phone: it had no signal whatsoever. Even if I could get hold of someone reasonably local, it would take at least an hour and I would need to go and let that person through the locked forestry gate. Okay! I'd cope on my own. Expecting the other chick to jump as well, I quickly caught the escapee and settled it down in a hollow tree root away from the nearby river. Fifteen minutes later, and back at the car, I stuffed the necessary ringing and climbing equipment into a large holdall. If I had to handle the chicks, then they were each going to have their proper identification. I forced myself to slow down and check that I had everything I needed. Back at the tree the grounded chick was still where I had left it, so I "processed" it quickly, starting by fitting it with a stainless-steel leg ring, taking leg and beak measurements, then a tiny feather sample. Finally, I fitted the two colored wing-tags that would enable members of the public to identify it and report back information on its whereabouts in subsequent years. The easy part done, I lifted the chick carefully into the holdall and zipped it up securely.

Looking at the tree and then at the nest itself, I sized up the climb and planned how I was going to replace the errant youngster. It was instantly obvious that this was not going to be easy. The ascent was not going to be straight up and there were lots of branches in the way. Therefore, I would need to climb up, tie myself on safely, lift and reposition my rope, descend to tie it on to the holdall, and climb once more to haul the bag up. I resolved not to think about how much easier this would be with an assistant. As I started to climb I could see the other chick through the foliage. It was impossible to climb such a small tree without shaking it, and as I did, the other eaglet sidled out along the one good branch that stuck out horizontally from the nest. I watched it carefully as I climbed, and froze as it spread its wings and leaned forward. Besides all the extra work I would have if—or rather when—it jumped, if it landed in the nearby fast-flowing stream I would need to do an emergency descent from the tree to rescue it, should it not be able to get out. Although I thought this scenario fairly remote, it was still a possibility and I didn't fancy the prospect at all. After a few seconds the chick folded its wings and relaxed, enabling me to continue upward. This sequence was repeated over the next 20 minutes or so, but at last I was below the nest and had tied my rope on, and the second chick was still there. Repositioning the rope where I wanted it, I slowly and carefully lowered myself down to the ground, keeping out of sight of the eaglet in the nest. After tying the hold-all on to the rope end, I started to climb the tree again. Once again, what should have been a 5-minute climb took a good 20 minutes due to the necessity of playing "grandmother's footsteps" with the teetering figurehead on the end of the branch above me. Tied on safely once more below the nest, and having had a 5-minute breather to settle down a bit, I pulled the eaglet in the bag up to join me, all the time watching its balancing sibling with wings outstretched a few meters away. With the heavy bag in both arms I waited until the other chick had folded its wings for what seemed the hundredth time, and then inched the holdall up over my head and slid it very slowly on to surface of the nest. Maneuvering it onto its side I quietly unzipped it, fully expecting that the indignant occupant would pop out and instantly make another bid for freedom, or startle its sibling into premature flight—or if I was really unlucky, both might happen. The tagged chick peered out, and I worked the bag backward and forward a bit to encourage it out. It stepped out, turned around, stretched its wings, and hissed in my face. Slowly pulling the bag down toward me, I cowered below the rim of the nest, trying to hide from the two chicks even though one was so close I could have touched it. After untying all my extra safety ropes, I descended the main climbing rope, praying—to any fieldwork god that might be listening—that the two eaglets had had enough adventures for one day and would stay put. Back on the ground, I hastily gathered all my ringing and measuring equipment and sneaked quietly off, dripping in sweat, into the forest. A quick glance over my shoulder showed the two large and somewhat feather-ruffled eagle chicks glaring at me from their rickety home. And then just as I got back to the car, I heard the unmistakable yelping call of an adult white-tailed sea eagle overhead. Thank goodness the parents had been away hunting while I was struggling with their offspring. Of course, had I found the nest in April, as I *should* have done, I would not have ended up struggling with them at all.

Driving home half an hour later with waves of relief washing over me, I was struck by a thought. I had come very close to not finding the nest at all, in which case the new pair would have reared their brood completely undetected. I clearly needed to be a bit more careful in the future when classifying areas of forest as being *unsuitable* for these big eagles.

Author's Biography

BJÖRN HELANDER on the Baltic coast of Sweden, holding a half-grown white-tailed sea eagle chick to be ringed, sampled, and then returned to its nest. Photo by Kurt Elmquist

Björn Helander's interest in eagles started when he was 12 years old, after he came across the book *The Last Eagles*, by the Swedish photographer and author Bengt Berg, in the local school library. He began to track down eagle sites in published material and soon also in the field. In 1964, he volunteered on the Swedish Society for Nature Conservation sea eagle survey, conducted in response to local reports of poor breeding success on the Baltic coastline. Björn took responsibility for the national sea eagle survey in 1968, and as eagle reproduction continued to deteriorate, he became leader of Project Sea Eagle from its conception in 1971. After completing his MSc degree at the University of Stockholm in 1971, Björn worked for seven years on the sea eagle project before undertaking his PhD research on white-tailed sea eagles, graduating in 1983. During his PhD studies he was also acting head of the Swedish Bird Ringing Office from 1981 to 1983. From 1985 to 2004 he divided his time between the Swedish Society for Nature Conservation and the Contaminant Research Group of the Swedish Museum of Natural History, studying sea eagles and grey seals as bio-indicators in the Baltic Sea ecosystem. Björn's work on the Swedish Project Sea Eagle has also included establishing an international color-ringing and genetic sampling effort, and in celebration of the thirtieth anniversary of Project Sea Eagle, he organized an international conference, SEA EAGLE 2000, in Sweden. In 2002 he was appointed by BirdLife International as compiler of an international white-tailed sea eagle Species Action Plan, and he has received the Swedish Ornithological Society badge for merit and four different awards for his eagle work. In 2005, Björn accepted a post as full-time senior scientist at the Swedish Museum of Natural History, Contaminant Research Group, where he is still responsible for the annual monitoring of white-tailed sea eagle reproduction and population trends within the national Swedish Environment Monitoring Program.

WHITE-TAILED SEA EAGLE, SWEDEN

Björn Helander

The year 1964 was a special one in my life. Not only was it the year of Bob Dylan, the Beatles, and the Rolling Stones, and the year I turned 18, it was also a special year for white-tailed sea eagles. The relevant events of that year happened in two different sea eagle territories on the Swedish Baltic coast, which we named B13 and C4.

Searching for eagle nests had become my favorite activity in my early teens, but still four years after I had located my first nest, in 1960, I had not seen a nest with young. One special day, I was searching for a nest that I had heard of, but I knew only vaguely of its location. As I slowly drifted through the forest, I suddenly spotted the nest—at the same moment as an old, grayish sea eagle, with an almost ivory-white head and neck, took wing nearby and sneaked away between the trees. My heart was beating fast as I approached the nest-tree and found the ground underneath covered by white droppings—Yes! This looked good. It was near the end of May when nestlings should be about a month old.

I had volunteered that year for a survey of sea eagle nesting and breeding success, so it was my job to climb to nests to verify the eagles' reproductive status. In the cup in the center of the huge nest I had found was an egg! A single, stained, but whitish egg. The eagles had apparently incubated long past the time of expected hatching. In my disappointment I reached out to feel if the egg was still warm, but it was cold. I lifted up the egg and it weighed next to nothing! But the shell was intact, no cracks. I had no idea what was going on—was the egg empty? As it turned out, the answer to that question was "Yes"—the egg content was almost completely dehydrated. Although I did not understand the significance of it then, this was my first encounter with the reproductive anomaly that soon came to be recognized as a gigantic problem for sea eagles, falcons, and other raptors around the world: malfunction of the eggshell gland, as a result of poisoning by the pesticide DDT.

In early May of that same year I had found another occupied site (C4) in a then remote place on the mainland coast. I saw the anxious eagle flying low over the forest canopy before I saw its nest, and I instantly turned back to avoid disturbing the breeding birds. On 23 June, my father drove me all the way from Stockholm to check the nest (I was still too young to have a driver's license). There were no adult eagles at the site when we approached. The nest was about 18 m (59 ft) up a huge pine tree, with the first branches some 12 m (39 ft) up. This was way before climbing equipment came into my world, but a spruce tree standing close enough made it possible to climb up and cross onto the nest-tree a few meters below the nest. I climbed to a spot just beneath the nest and still there was no adult around, but there were lots of white eagle droppings on the branches. Why was it so silent? I would have anticipated the presence of a parent bird, or some sound from the nestling, if there was one. As I slowly heaved up and lifted my head over the rim of the nest, I peered straight into the eyes of a fierce-looking, black-headed juvenile sea eagle. The young eagle was lying down in the nest with its head lifted, motionless except for the quick, intermittent movement of the nictitating membrane over the eye. This was a great moment; after four years of effort, I'd finally seen my first sea eagle chick. Today, some 3000 nestlings later, this first chick at territory C4 still holds a golden place in my memory.

On the Swedish Baltic Sea coast before the 1950s, each pair of white-tailed sea eagle produced on average about 1.3 young annually. In the 1970s during the DDT era, productivity was down to 0.3 young annually—a reduction of nearly 80%. DDT is changed into DDE by birds, and levels of DDE can then be measured in their eggs. Our research team has estimated that at DDE levels of more than 100 µg per gram of yolk fat, sea eagle reproduction begins to be impacted. As the concentrations approach 1000 µg per gram the effect is complete and there is no reproduction at all. In the 1960s and 1970s, the average concentration of DDE in the egg lipids in this population exceeded 800 µg per gram! In many territories the eagles did not produce any young at all from the 1960s to the mid-1980s. Other pairs managed to produce a nestling about every second or third year, and a few did even better. One pair that did better than most started breeding when a new female entered territory C4 in 1978.

From 1964 to 2006, territory C4 was continuously occupied. Four female and four male sea eagles have been present in different combinations over this 42-year period. In no case so far were both mates of a pair replaced at the same time—the survivor teamed up with a new partner. The third female in this succession was a remarkable bird. She was not ringed, but her plumage as she entered the territory in 1978 indicated that she was born in 1973, or possibly 1974. This was an unusually big eagle—she really dwarfed her mate, the widower occupying the territory. She also proved to be totally dominant over all other eagles that came to the nearby feeding station we set up every winter in this region.

In addition to her being large, her breeding record was remarkable. Starting off with two fledglings from her first breeding attempt, she produced a total of 27 young in the 25 years from 1978 to 2003—an average of 1.1 per year. She failed to produce fledglings only seven times—four years as a result of disturbance at the nest from human activities, and two years when males were replaced. She had three mates in her time—her first was replaced in 1985 by a ringed male born in 1980, and a ringed male born in 1989 took over nine years later, in 1994. In 2003 her last breeding attempt failed, and in 2004 the nest was refurbished but abandoned in early April. In 2005 there was a new female present at the same nest.

Such disappearance of a bird from a territory usually indicates that the missing bird has died, especially when that bird was old. But new interesting evidence shows that this is not always the case. In 1984 a color-ringed male born in 1976 mated with a color-ringed female born in 1979. This pair was only successful in 5 out of 19 breeding attempts. In 2003 the female paired up with a new, unringed male, and the old male, with ring number H8007, was assumed to have died. However, in April 2004, a hunter spotted a sea eagle with a green color-ring feeding from bait that he had put out to shoot foxes. The local observer from our eagle project put out a provisional hide there and soon realized that this bird was the old H8007 male that we had assumed had died! Not only was the bird alive, he was accompanied by a gorgeous female in subadult plumage, ringed as a nestling on the Finnish side of the Baltic in 1999. Not bad for an "old man" of 27! This pair was also observed together in April 2005. Apparently the male had been kicked out of his original territory, and he had set up a new home some 30 km (18.6 mi) away. Alternatively he may have left his old home for a new territory and mate. We can only guess at which of these explanations is actually correct.

I find these long-term studies very rewarding. With long-lived creatures like eagles, it is especially interesting when you can follow individual birds over their lifetime. Similarities, as well as differences, among individual birds emerge as you watch them from year to year. As an eagle watcher you soon learn that different birds are unique—despite all natural similarities and stereotypical behavior, eagles have real personalities. They also learn to know you. During the annual nest checks I often get the feeling that I am recognized by the adults—they sometimes meet up at a long distance and keep an eye on me as I approach. One female certainly recognized me and my old boat. Once, as I went out fishing, I saw her come up from her island in the distance and head for me, wings slightly bent and motionless as she swept through the air as if drawn by an invisible string. There were other boats out there fishing but she paid no attention to them—she came right for me, apparently to check what I was up to this time. It was clear that she knew me. I was the guy that used to come once a year and harass her family at the nest—all in the best interest of her kin, but how would she know!

The first real sign of an improvement of the reproduction in this heavily contaminated sea eagle population came in 1986, as the percentage of successful breeding attempts suddenly jumped up to 43% from the stable 20% to 30% level that had prevailed for two decades. And there was more to come. The late 1980s and 1990s have been happy times with our sea eagles; the improvement has continued and since the year 2000, reproduction is almost back at the pre-1950 level. As a result, this population has increased nicely: from 65 pairs in 1985 to about 325 in 2005. A fantastic development that by far surpasses what we dared to hope for when we started our national sea eagle project.

This also means that these are now busy times for eagle watchers—the length of the season for checking nests and ringing the nestlings is still the same as before. Some years back, bald eagle researcher Bill Bowerman visited and joined us during 10 days of intense fieldwork. This was in the 1990s, when I still did all the ringing of sea eagles in Sweden by myself. The white-tailed sea eagle had been adopted by the national Swedish Environment Monitoring Program as an indicator of environmental pollutants in the Baltic Sea. Our goal that year was to take blood samples from nestling eagles as a mechanism for monitoring contaminant levels in the eagle population. With his long experience of taking blood samples from bald eagle nestlings, Bill was of great help as instructor and advisor in this matter. The blood samples, drawn from a large vein in the wing, had to be kept frozen, and since we were on the road for days and weeks between visits back to my institution, we kept a 25-L (6.6 gal) bottle of liquid nitrogen in the back of my car to store samples. We also carried along an inflatable rubber boat with an outboard engine, in addition to a pile of other necessary field equipment.

In one instance we left for a two-day tour with a bigger, hired boat and had to leave the car parked by the pier. After a successful odyssey to nine nest sites in the archipelago, we came back to the mainland. Immediately as I spotted my car I saw that the back window had been smashed. An outboard engine had been stolen, and my good old tent was gone. (I grinned as I saw that the central tent post was still left there.) But thank goodness, the nitrogen bottle with all our samples, the most important thing we carried, was still there. We called for the police to come and register the break-in. The police officer who arrived was a bit of the local kind—like taken out of an old-time movie. In his official way, he asked some questions and took some notes—and then frankly told us that, "This must be old Johnny again." Apparently, this Johnny was a local no-good and a notorious thief. We suggested that we should go and see Mr. Johnny, in the hope of getting our things back, but our police officer said that this was not possible, since there was no real evidence that Johnny was the culprit. And of course, he was right. So the officer left with his notes, leaving us little hope that we would recover our equipment.

A while later, we took the blood samples from the boat trip out of the field icebox for storing, and as they dropped into the nitrogen, one by one with a sizzle, Bill reflected, "I bet Johnny must have been curious about this bottle. He moved it, see? Maybe he thought it was booze in it. Maybe he even put a finger down there to taste it." That would have been something—a finger stuck into liquid nitrogen probably would have frozen and possibly even fallen off! "Johnny Thief Nine Fingers," we started to call him—and we joked about bringing this tip to the police to check out. But we decided to just let it be. It was a new morning and we were already on our way to the next nest.

Author's Biography

JOHN A. LOVE with a young white-tailed sea eagle prior to its release on the Isle of Rum, Scotland. Photo courtesy of the author

John Love was born in Inverness, Scotland, and joined the local bird club as a schoolboy in 1958. He enjoyed weekend trips visiting island seabirds and listened to evening lectures by illustrious golden eagle researchers such as Seton Gordon and George Waterston. John trained as a bird ringer and spent several school holidays as a volunteer helping to protect what were at the time Scotland's only pair of nesting ospreys. He graduated with a BSc in natural history from the University of Aberdeen and did three years of postgraduate research on bird predators of bivalve mussels. In 1975, John moved to the Isle of Rum, where he worked as the project officer on Scotland's Sea Eagle Reintroduction Project. John released a total of 82 Norwegian sea eagles and wrote a book about the project, *The Return of the Sea Eagle*, which was published in 1983 by Cambridge University Press. As the Scottish sea eagle population has grown, John has remained on the UK Sea Eagle Project Team, and has lectured widely about his experiences on what was, at the time, an ambitious and pioneering wildlife management strategy. John recently retired from his post as the Outer Hebrides Area Officer for Scottish Natural Heritage, although he still lives in the outer islands and helps to monitor several breeding pairs of sea eagles. John has written and illustrated several other books on eagles, penguins, and sea otters, together with a detailed human history of the island of Rum. He is currently updating the sea eagle story.

WHITE-TAILED SEA EAGLE, SCOTLAND

John A. Love

"Would you like to go to Norway for a couple of weeks, and then go to the Hebrides for a month?" I was asked. "It's to bring back young sea eagles for release on the Isle of Rum."

Well, who wouldn't jump at the chance? Only I could not have known then that the month on the Isle of Rum would turn into a decade, and sea eagles would still remain part of my life 30 years later.

I had first encountered young sea eagles a few years earlier, in 1968, when three were brought to Fair Isle (a tiny island off the north Scotland coast) as part of what was then considered a bold innovative reintroduction attempt. I was a zoology undergraduate at that time, on holiday at the famous bird observatory. A small aircraft had just landed on Fair Isle's makeshift airstrip, all the way from Norway. In addition to a pair of eagle biologists, on the plane was the precious cargo of three young Norwegian sea eagles (a fourth was to follow later). I suppose the Nature Conservancy Council (NCC) was uncertain whether this new, 1975 shipment of four young sea eagles to the Isle of Rum would be sustained in future years. Perhaps this was why I took only a small rucksack to Rum. Ten years later I had to hire a boat to transport my accumulated gear back to the mainland.

So the lessons from this tale are to "take the opportunity if it arises" and "be optimistic." These early tentative attempts were some of the first, and of course, similar projects with threatened birds of prey are now commonplace all over the world.

In 1975 we opted not to use Loganair's small *Islander* aircraft since we were able to convince the RAF (Royal Air Force) to fly the birds in for us, direct to Kinloss Air Station on the Moray Firth. As planned, we had collected four young sea eagles. The Norwegian Air Force kindly put me up for the night at their Bodø airbase, and I was allowed to install my four well-grown charges in the shower next to my room. Their talons clanked around the marble floor all night, and they beat their wings constantly to exercise and rid themselves of their itchy down feathers. Unfortunately I did not realize that I shared the shower with the man in an adjacent room, and he got quite a shock when he went for his morning shower. When I apologized over breakfast, he merely shrugged off the experience as though it happened every day.

Not quite the reaction that I got from the crew of my RAF Nimrod. At first they naively assumed that the first meter-square cardboard box I loaded onto the plane housed all four eaglets, and were dismayed to discover that it contained only one. The bird inside stood about half a meter (20 in) off the ground and weighed 3 to 4 kilos (6.6 to 8.8 lb). The aircrew were even more astounded when I opened it to show them. But imagine their dismay when I told them that, on this occasion, the Ministry of Defence in Whitehall had declined me permission to accompany them on the flight. The thought of four escaped eagles rampaging through the aircraft over the middle of the North Sea quite horrified them.

Having reassured the apprehensive aircrew that the eaglets would lie quietly in their boxes, I watched them take off before returning to the staff quarters. My next task was to scrub the shower walls of the fishy feces that had been produced overnight. It is surprising how high their smelly squirts can reach!

Within two hours the eaglets landed in Kinloss, and it took only another six or seven hours for them to be driven to meet the NCC boat in Mallaig on Scotland's west coast and be transported across to their cages on Rum. I, on the other hand, took fully two days to make the journey by scheduled flights and public transport.

No sooner had I arrived on the island when a press photographer telephoned to ask if he could come over to take photos. "Perhaps I could take a snap of you, with one of the chicks sitting on your finger?" he inquired. I replied that he was quite welcome to come, but had to explain in words of one syllable why I would certainly not risk losing a finger for his photo shoot. Even the vets who came to examine the birds prior to their release were reluctant to enter a cage with such "monsters." Their size was impressive enough, but their obstreperous behavior left little to be desired. We had carefully avoided the birds becoming used to human presence so that they would adapt to the wild more easily.

The Isle of Rum, 24 km (15 mi) off the Scottish west coast, was not a bad place to live. It was a National Nature Reserve owned since 1957 by the Nature Conservancy Council, now Scottish Natural Heritage. I first visited the island on a student field trip in 1969, the year after I had met the sea eagles on Fair Isle.

Having been there once before, I already knew of its disadvantages—only a couple of dozen human inhabitants for company; ferry boats running only four days of the week, weather permitting; at least 250 cm (98 in) of rain a year; and, perhaps worst of all, the biting insects—blood-sucking ticks, ferocious horse flies (clegs), and last but by no means least, the tiny, persistent, and unimaginably numerous midges.

A rugged and mountainous terrain covering 140 km^2 (64 mi^2) might seem small by some standards, especially when occupied by only half a dozen families. But it was soon apparent from the abundant ruins that this unforgiving landscape had once supported many more people. I became intrigued by its human history, discovering that about 400 souls had been "cleared" from its shores in 1826. Offered no option, all but one family were shipped out to Canada so that a grasping landlord could replace them with sheep and red deer, increase profits, and thus support his lavish lifestyle. I eventually came to write the human history of the island, and it was while scrutinizing old records that I discovered some interesting details about the island's eagles.

It was said that five pairs of eagles bred on Rum, both golden and sea eagles. This is the only place I knew of then in Scotland where, early in the nineteenth century, a brood of three sea eagles had been found in the one nest. Sadly they were all shot by a local shepherd. In the year 1866 alone, the island's gamekeeper destroyed no fewer than eight sea eagles. As late as 1907 another keeper took two eggs from a nest and shot one of the adults; two years later he shot two adults. This was one of the last nests in the whole of Britain. So it seemed that Rum was a pretty good place to start reintroducing the species, in a more enlightened era, albeit seven decades later.

My initial field surveys revealed that during the late 1970s—just as a hundred years ago—there were still four or five pairs of eagles nesting on Rum, but all were golden eagles. It was while investigating one of these eyries on a sea cliff, being used as a roost in 1976, that I discovered an old gin trap on the ledge, rusted solid in the set position. This very rock face appeared on maps in Gaelic as "Sron na h-Iolaire" (The Eagle's Nose), so it had obviously been in use by one species or the other for a very long time.

At another eyrie, several kilometers to the west, a piece of rusty fence wire hung from a rock above, to make it easier to climb into the nest. The late George MacNaughton, then the nature reserve warden, revealed that it was he who had put it there in the 1930s when he had been employed as the estate gamekeeper to destroy the resident golden eagles. He was astonished that my climbing companion had deemed it far too rusty to take his weight but had got into the precarious eyrie nonetheless.

George also remembered his father telling him about one of the sea eagles shot in 1909—it had been nailed to a barn door to show off its impressive 2 m (6.6 ft) wingspan. He also joked that he was too young to have ever had the chance of shooting a sea eagle; maybe now he could. But he was to prove genuinely sympathetic to my reintroduction efforts.

At least three distinct eyries were on sea cliffs, with two further territories inland, in the mountains. From the situation of the eyries I surmised that in former times the island could have easily supported three pairs of sea eagles and a couple of pairs of golden eagles.

Sea eagles are much more sociable creatures than golden eagles and frequently interact together. One adult released as a fledgling five years earlier began to return to the cages at each fresh import of juveniles (we released birds on Rum for 10 consecutive years). For days she would sit on the cage above her adopted brood. Once she even brought them a dead fulmar—she obviously failed to get it to them through the wire netting. But at least she could teach them a useful lesson for the future: she demonstrated how to pluck and eat the fulmar herself.

Later that season, when all the birds had been released, I saw a record seven sea eagles all in the air together. Flying birds might turn over to present talons to an attacker, sometimes even grappling in the process. One day I watched as one juvenile bird flew low along the shore, being dive-bombed occasionally by a sibling. Finally, it flipped over on its back to defend itself but unfortunately forgot that it was only a meter off the ground. Of course it quickly lost height and crash-landed rather ignominiously in a heap of feathers!

Attacks between sea eagles frequently happened if one bird was carrying food in its talons. Swooping up from below the other bird might succeed in grabbing hold. Then both birds, reluctant to give up the prey, would tumble out of the sky, just like the talon-grappling display described for related *Haliaeetus* species, whether bald eagles in America or fish eagles in Africa. I soon began to wonder if this spectacular interaction among our sea eagles was more a simple dispute over food, or between rivals, rather than courtship.

The time of release was always an exciting moment. All that is, except for the very first eaglet in 1975. I first removed the wire from the front of its cage and retreated to watch the spectacle of a sea eagle spreading its wings over Rum for the first time in 70 years. Unfortunately the bird chose to remain firmly anchored to its perch for several hours before it finally flitted down and calmly walked out through the open door. It then proceeded to walk uphill and install itself on a rock knoll, where it steadfastly remained for several hours more. It was only when I returned at dawn the next day that I first witnessed its maiden flight.

Since that day, over the next 10 years, I was responsible for 82 young sea eagles spreading their wings over Rum, from where most dispersed to check out neighboring islands. In the 1990s, 56 more were released on the Scottish mainland, beside Loch Maree in Wester Ross. So many people have assisted the project over the years—from bemused aircrew on both sides of the North Sea and helpful fishermen anchoring in Rum overnight to offer fish for "my" eagles, to scientists studying the diet of the birds in the wild. The modest cast of characters at the outset has now increased to a stage of hundreds. And central on that stage, and stars of the show, are the sea eagles themselves. Some of the 146 set free died before maturity, as we had predicted. But on the whole, survival has been encouragingly high. Many have matured to nest successfully and contribute progeny to the breeding population. One of the first breeding pairs nested on Rum, on the very ledge where I had found the rusted gin trap, thus once more justifying its ancient Gaelic place name. In 2009, our population now stands at more than 44 pairs, with more than 300 young known to have fledged in Scotland since the project's inception. In 2007, a new five-year project began on the east coast of Scotland, where 15 young eaglets are translocated from Norway each year. With this new project, and the success of the established west coast eagles, we are confident that the population will continue to go from strength to strength. All from a casual offer of six weeks' employment on a lonely Hebridean island.

24

Black-and-chestnut Eagle

COMMON NAME: Black-and-chestnut eagle

SCIENTIFIC NAME: *Spizaetus (Oroaetus) isidori*

OTHER NAMES: Isidor's eagle, Isidor's crested eagle

IUCN CONSERVATION STATUS: *Near Threatened (population trend unknown)*

DESCRIPTION: A large stout eagle with broad wings, a relatively long tail, and a crest. Adults are uniformly dark above, with a glossy head and a rich chestnut below. Tail is light underneath with a dark terminal band, and legs are feathered. Preadults are much lighter, showing considerable white below, although the general color patterns are similar.

SIZE: Length: 63–74 cm (25–29 in); Wingspan: 145–166 cm (57–65 in); Weight: unknown

THREATS: This species is one of the world's least known eagles, and threats are not well understood. Habitat loss is likely impacting their populations, since they appear to occur only in undisturbed primary forest.

DISTRIBUTION: Western South America, in a narrow elevational band in the Andes Mountains from Venezuela through Colombia, Bolivia, and into Argentina.

MOVEMENTS: Apparently nonmigratory; nothing known of juvenile movements

HABITAT: Dense, humid montane tropical forest at midlevel elevations in the Andes Mountains

DIET: What is known of this species suggests that it feeds primarily on large to medium-sized arboreal mammals and birds, including squirrels and guans.

NOTES: One of the world's least known eagles, only five nests have ever been described.

Author's Biography

URSULA VALDEZ atop a
canopy-high tower in the
Peruvian Amazon. Photo
courtesy of the author

Ursula Valdez decided to become a biologist at an early age, after becoming fascinated by plants and animals during numerous family trips throughout Peru. While she was an undergraduate student at the Biology Department of Universidad Nacional Agraria La Molina (Lima, Peru), Ursula fell in love with field ecology, and then raptors, after observing a laughing falcon catching a coral snake in the dry forest of northern Peru. She decided to study the breeding biology and diet of laughing falcons and crested caracaras for her undergraduate thesis. In 1999, she completed her MSc degree at North Carolina State University, studying raptor communities in the Manu Biosphere Reserve (Peru). Ursula then worked in southern Spain monitoring raptor migration as part of a collaboration between Doñana Biological Station and Hawk Mountain Sanctuary (where she previously was an intern). A few months later she was back in the tropics teaching tropical ecology in Costa Rica and in mid-2000 started working for The Peregrine Fund. She was assigned to search for the little-known black-and-chestnut eagle (also known as Isidor's eagle) in southern Peru, where she spent several months in one of the most fascinating and least explored montane ecosystems, the "cloud forest." At the end of this project, she fulfilled the ultimate dream of any Neotropical raptor biologist: to work with harpy eagles. For that she moved to Panama and worked as a field biologist and Director of the Neotropical Environmental Education Program of The Peregrine Fund. Ursula obtained a PhD from the Biology Department of the University of Washington in 2009, and her dissertation research focused on the habitat use and ecology of forest-falcons in the Peruvian Amazon.

BLACK-AND-CHESTNUT EAGLE, PERU

Ursula Valdez

I vividly remember the morning I saw a pair of black-and-chestnut eagles circling together high in the sky, then locking talons and descending, cutting through the fog in coordinated and acrobatic spirals until they reached a treetop. The female perched on a high branch while the male soared up, calling constantly. Soon he descended again to join the female and mate with her. Moments like these make an eagle watcher's day: it no longer matters how much daily frustration one has suffered to get to that point.

When I was hired to study black-and-chestnut eagles, I knew very little about them. More than a decade earlier, while driving through a montane forest in southeastern Peru, I had seen an adult black-and-chestnut eagle attending a chick at a nest, and since then I had twice spotted eagles in that area. Therefore when my new boss asked if I could find the eagles and where I would go to do so, unhesitatingly I answered, "Yes . . . in Peru!" I was filled with so much energy and excitement, not only from taking on the challenge to study this rare eagle but also because it gave me the opportunity to do fieldwork in my home country again.

I went back to the Cosñipata Valley, where I had seen the eagles before, and with the help of a field assistant, I established a campsite in San Pedro, a spot in the middle of well-protected cloud forest in Manu Biosphere Reserve. At San Pedro, the only human-inhabited structures were an ecotourism lodge and a small hut. At the lodge, the staff provided us with a tent platform, a small kitchen area, and a bathroom with a shower fed with invigorating Andean glacier water! In good weather, getting to San Pedro meant spending seven hours on a narrow and infamously dangerous dirt road that connects Cuzco (the major Andean city in Peru and center of the old Inca Empire) to Atalaya (a small village in lowland rainforest). During the rainy season, landslides are common along the route and the 161 km (100 mi) journey could take days. The steep local topography was a major headache for road builders, and it became one of the main challenges to our ability to explore for eagles. Massive rocky hills covered by lush forest and narrow valleys dominate the landscape, and steep vertical drops are common on the narrow one-way road. Traffic is only allowed to go one direction each day, but it is not uncommon to find a big truck breaking the rules, creating a hair-raising driving experience and sometimes even causing fatal accidents.

Several weeks passed before we saw our first black-and-chestnut eagle soaring above the Cosñipata Valley, but our efforts paid off. We found two pairs and at least one juvenile using the area. Having confirmed the species occurred there, in the following months we collaborated with many others to collect a considerable amount of behavioral and ecological data. Most exciting of all, we observed courtship and mating behavior, indicating that the eagles may be nesting in the area. But how to find an eagle's nest in the steep and dense forest? Our best option seemed to be to capture an adult eagle, fit it with a radio transmitter, and let it guide us to its nest.

To try to trap eagles, we built bal-chatri traps, often called "BCs." A BC is a wire cage covered with monofilament nooses. A live animal is placed inside and moves around, which attracts the attention of the raptor. When a raptor lands on the cage to try and capture the animal, its feet get caught in the nooses, leaving the raptor trapped and the bait unharmed. Building BCs did not take long, but finding live bait was not as easy. We had not seen many hunting events yet and were not certain about the eagles' diet in our area, but monkeys and chickens had been mentioned as possible prey in other areas. Because of reserve regulations and limitations on my research permit, however, we could not trap wild animals other than eagles. That meant that the only possibility was to use domestic animals. The few times we had recorded black-and-chestnut eagles pursuing prey, they were always hunting just above or below the forest canopy, and therefore we felt we needed to place our BCs near the top of trees. It took some hours to find the right tree, and then using a slingshot, we installed a cord system to raise and lower the BC. Then the day to attempt a capture arrived, and after an early-morning coffee we went to the wider part of the valley favored by one of the eagle pairs. We set up a couple of BCs in treetops that we could monitor with spotting scopes from strategic road viewpoints. The BCs were placed about 20 m (66 ft) high and the bait (chickens) cooperated by moving around regardless of their unusual situation.

Observing the eagles frequently in this part of the valley had familiarized us with their behavioral patterns. This focal pair usually started their soaring activity between 7 to 8 a.m. Around 8:30 a.m. we saw one black-and-chestnut eagle soaring above the valley ridge and then, five minutes later, gliding slowly toward a BC. A few meters before hitting the trap the eagle pulled back and started to ascend. Three more times the bird flew close to the trap, but it did not attempt to catch the chicken. We tried more times that week, and every time at least one eagle flew just above a BC but never hit the trap. I was disappointed. Were the eagles not that interested in chickens? Were the slip nooses too thick and obvious? Was the chosen branch too exposed? We needed to improve the methods and to keep trying.

One day Abel, the caretaker's son, mentioned that a couple of years ago while he was walking on the road with his small dog, a large dark eagle had tried to grab the dog. Abel turned around just in time to scare the eagle and save his loyal friend. "Well," I thought, "let's try finding a small mammal for bait." Abel no longer had dogs but the neighbor did. The neighbor had already turned down our request to buy his chickens, and when I tried asking to borrow his small dog, his expression clearly told me that this was out of the question.

The best next option was the guinea pigs that Jose and Brian, my field assistants at the time, had found in the village two hours down the road from the campsite. We tried for another week with a combination of guinea pigs and chickens inside the BCs. The chickens, which by then probably were used to the protocol, seemed really bored, and similarly the guinea pigs did not move much either. The eagles did not show any more interest than before. What else could we try?

One afternoon we drove up to higher-elevation forest and visited a couple who owned a tiny lot with an excellent view of the hills and valleys below that we hoped to use as an observation point. I showed them a picture of a black-and-chestnut eagle and asked if they had seen it. The man nodded and said that he had seen one soaring around frequently and was afraid the eagle wanted the house pet. The woman went into their hut and returned with Christian, a male brown capuchin monkey that did not hesitate to jump on my head, pull my hair, and play with my earrings. A pet monkey, hmm, what a coincidence! Just a week before, I had seen for the first time a black-and-chestnut eagle taking a monkey. I was observing an eagle flying above the river when I heard woolly monkeys calling from the treetops. I shortly noticed the eagle gliding down toward the monkeys. However, monkey alarm calls alerted the troop, which immediately disappeared into the vegetation, and I saw the eagle perch inconspicuously under the canopy. When the calm returned to the troop, the eagle dived and seized an infant while the rest of the monkeys screamed and dropped from the branches. As I had just confirmed that black-and-chestnut eagles eat monkeys, why not try using a monkey to capture one? Technically my permit allowed me to use Christian, an authorized house pet, as eagle bait.

When I mentioned to the couple the possibility of using Christian to catch eagles, I explained in detail how the BCs worked and how there was little chance that he would be injured. To my surprise they happily agreed to let me use Christian for my research. The next morning the man arrived with Christian at the campsite. The man said that I could let Christian run free, but he gave me a leash and cord just in case, and tied Christian to a pole on our platform. He decided to leave quickly, and I was afraid that Christian would be sad to see him leave, so I went to grab an apple to give to the new team member. What a surprise when I returned and all I found was the leash and the cord on the ground. Christian had managed to untie himself and was gone. I totally underestimated the ability of monkeys' hands! As fast as I could, I reached the road just in time to catch the man, who was about to climb into a truck. While I was asking him not to leave, we saw Christian happily jumping among the branches of a bamboo patch. The man said I shouldn't worry, just to call the monkey by its name and it would return. Then he left despite my begging him to stay. We spent the rest of the afternoon and the next two days wandering and calling for Christian, whom we saw only a couple of times. After three days, I knew Christian was gone for good. Of course I was blamed for losing the monkey; it did not help at all to remind the man that I had asked him to help us that day. I felt really badly and offered my deepest apologies, but only when we mentioned money did things get settled. In the end we left the man five chickens, two guinea pigs, and 50 soles (about US$15), and suspected that this couple did not care much about Christian.

That night we shared a candle-lit dinner with Florencio and Antonia, the lodge caretakers, and they told me that the couple was known for mistreating Christian and he probably was happier in the woods. I felt a little better but still guilty because the poor thing would have a rough time in the woods. But when Florencio mentioned that in the village down the road the local doctor also owned a monkey, my eyes got bigger, as my hopes to catch an eagle with a BC returned.

The next day we visited the doctor at the village health center. After helping his two patients, the doctor asked what he could do for us. He listened carefully as we described our research on the black-and-chestnut eagle, but looked concerned when I mentioned using his pet as eagle bait. After I finished, he remained silent for a moment and said that he and his family loved their brown capuchin, Monito, but added that Monito was driving them crazy and sending him on a short vacation might not be a bad idea.

This time, no more tied monkeys and no risks of losing another one. Jose had prepared a secure cage in which we could keep Monito, who seemed to like both us and the cage. After giving us instructions on how to keep Monito happy with his favorite blanket and popsicles, the doctor's family waved good-bye and wished us luck.

The next morning, we raised Monito in the BC, and at around 8:45 a.m. Jose spotted a black-and-chestnut eagle. Eight minutes later the eagle started descending toward the BC, while I kept fingers and toes crossed hoping this time we would catch the eagle. But Monito realized what was going on and quickly covered himself with something that was inside the BC. Believe it or not, none of us had realized that the favorite tiny blanket had gone with him into the BC! Two eagles soared above that BC for another 30 minutes but then flew toward the mountain ridge and disappeared behind it. Monito did not move for the next hour, although I could see him peeking out from underneath the blanket. I was certainly disappointed at not capturing an eagle, but at the same time totally fascinated by monkey behavior.

On our drive back to camp, a pickup truck caught up and the driver started blowing the horn. We stopped our truck when we recognized the doctor and his family. They had come to visit Monito. The doctor's daughter took a popsicle out of a little box and said, "Is for Monito." I turned to grab Monito from the cage and before I finished opening the door, he was in the girl's arms and she was kissing and hugging him. I did not try to convince the doctor to leave Monito for longer; I knew perfectly well that he would not do it. The doctor said that they did not expect to miss Monito that much and his kids were sad. I was sure that was not all; he must have heard about the crazy woman who borrowed pet monkeys and never returned them.

After this I took a break trying to capture eagles. I did not feel that I had failed, but I still needed to learn lots more to better understand the eagles' behavior and be better prepared to trap them. However, I learned that to be a raptor biologist takes more than an interest in a magnificent study species. I certainly want to succeed in collecting information that produces good scientific contributions, but the combination of social relationships, running after chickens or "wild-but-domestic" monkeys, and many other crazy experiences are what makes the hundreds of hours spent observing or trying to capture raptors worth every minute of my life as an eagle watcher.

25

Philippine Eagle

COMMON NAME: Philippine eagle

SCIENTIFIC NAME: *Pithecophaga jefferyi*

OTHER NAMES: Philippine monkey-eating eagle, great Philippine eagle, Haring Ibon (Tagalog)

IUCN CONSERVATION STATUS: *Critically Endangered (population declining)*

DESCRIPTION: An enormous eagle, dark above, very light below, with a large erectile crest. Body shape typical of large tropical raptors—wings are relatively short and rounded, tail extremely long. Bill is exceptionally tall and narrow, making this bird unusual in profile or head-on. Similar to the harpy eagle, feet are massive.

SIZE: Length: 90–100 cm (35.5–39.4 in); Wingspan: 184–202 cm (72.5–79.5 in); Weight: 4.7–8.0 kg (10.3–17.6 lb)

THREATS: Persecution by humans limits survival of immature and adult Philippine eagles. Habitat loss limits their ability to reproduce and exposes them to human persecution. A lack of knowledge of the ecology of this species limits conservation.

DISTRIBUTION: Endemic to the Philippines. Largest populations are on the southern island of Mindanao. Luzon also likely supports stable populations. Birds have recently been reported from Samar and Leyte.

MOVEMENTS: Nonmigratory. Juveniles are somewhat dispersive.

HABITAT: Tropical rainforest, especially primary dipterocarp forest. As habitat has been cleared, the species has been observed nesting in highly disturbed areas (see Hector Miranda's story for details) and on steep uncleared slopes.

DIET: Mammals, birds, reptiles. On Mindanao, this species takes many flying lemurs and palm civets. However, preliminary research suggests that diet on other islands is different (there are no flying lemurs on Luzon).

NOTES: The Philippine eagle is one of the world's rarest bird species. If it will survive the current extinction spasm, it will be primarily because of the actions of the Philippine Eagle Foundation.

Author's Biography

HECTOR C. MIRANDA JR. holding a juvenile Philippine eagle, one of seven trapped for radio-tracking from 1998 to 2001 on the island of Mindanao, Philippines. Photo courtesy of the author

   Hector Miranda grew up in Manila in the Philippines, and received his BSc in biology from the University of the Philippines at Los Baños (UPLB), right at the foot of the rainforest-covered Mount Makiling. After college, Hector joined the World Wildlife Fund (WWF)–supported Philippine Eagle Conservation Program under the aegis of the Haribon Society, and for two full years he and a team of international biologists studied the natural history of the eagles in Mindanao and surveyed the islands of Leyte and Luzon. At the end of the WWF support, Hector went back to UPLB to study for an MSc in zoology, where he also became a junior faculty member. He moved to the United States as a PhD student at the University of Cincinnati and worked on the molecular systematics of owls under the supervision of Professor David Mindell. He was awarded his degree in 1997 and undertook postdoctoral work at the University of Michigan and at the Human Genetics Division of the Children's Hospital Memorial Center in Cincinnati. In 1998 Hector returned to the Philippines and joined The Peregrine Fund–supported Philippine Eagle Foundation as the Science Director, where he led a team of young local naturalists to study the eagles. Looking for opportunities to get back to the cutting edge of scientific research in molecular evolution, Hector went back to the University of Cincinnati in 2002 for a National Science Foundation–supported postdoctoral position on rodent systematics, before becoming a visiting assistant professor at Rollins College in Florida for a year, where he taught courses in conservation biology, evolution, and bioinformatics. He recently joined the faculty of Texas Southern University as an assistant professor. Hector has written numerous papers on the ecology, evolution, and conservation of raptors and Philippine birds and is a coauthor of *A Guide to the Birds of the Philippines*. He continues to be involved with work on the eagles as an advisor for the Philippine Eagle Foundation.

PHILIPPINE EAGLE, PHILIPPINES

Hector C. Miranda Jr.

I saw my first wild Philippine eagle on May 14, 1981. It was a sunny day in eastern Mindanao, a beautiful island in the south of the Philippine archipelago in Southeast Asia. It was our second day in the field. At around ten o'clock in the morning, a pair of Philippine eagles appeared from the canopy, soaring together, circling each other like aerial "skaters" while riding the thermal updraft. I stood there in the middle of the jungle transfixed and mesmerized, watching the pair through my binoculars until they disappeared beyond the tropical horizon.

A week before that, I'd had a job interview with Dr. Robert (Bob) Kennedy, Scientific Director of the Philippine Eagle Conservation Program; Dr. Dioscoro Rabor, a noted Filipino naturalist; and Edgar Buensuceso, the President of the Haribon Society (one of the Philippine's largest nongovernmental organizations). After the interview I was browsing through the May issue of *National Geographic* and the article on the Philippine eagle by Bob, dreaming about what it would be like to be in the jungles. A week after my interview, Bob called and gave me a one-way ticket to Bislig, Surigao province, on the island of Mindanao. I was soon joined by Marlo Caleda, another Filipino naturalist, and a couple of other naturalists from England and the United States.

Even as a young child, I was always fascinated with the Philippine eagle and the jungles of Mindanao. However, having spent most of my 21 years in the city of Manila, I had no distinct idea of what that world was really like. In 1981, fresh out of college from Luzon island, I couldn't wait to leap into this world that beckoned to me. The religious conflict between Muslims and Christians was brewing, and the growing communist insurgency gave the place a reputation ranging from frightening to terrifying. I was undeterred. I was living a life that seemed to have jumped out of the pages of that *National Geographic* magazine.

The area around Mount Agtuuganon was the largest piece of virgin lowland rainforest remaining in Mindanao; it was scheduled for logging in two years. It was not the impenetrable jungle that I thought it would be. The forest floor was clear and open, wide enough to play a game of tennis. Hues of earth-brown decomposing leaves carpeted the floor, which was sprinkled with a few saplings and some small understory trees. Enormous trees commonly called "lauans" loomed high and dominated the forest, some reaching 2 m

(6.6 ft) or more in diameter and 50 m (164 ft) high. It was relatively cool but not windy, a little dim, with rays of bright sunlight peeking through the cracks of the canopy and penetrating the forest floor. It felt like being inside a magnificent cathedral, in another world. There was something about this landscape that stirred within me a sense of the profound and the spiritual. This vision of the rainforest at Mount Agtuuganon, and the breathtaking initial sighting of a pair of soaring Philippine eagles, are perhaps the most indelible images in my mind from that first field season. It was also a bird-watcher's paradise. I thought that if there were a birder's Garden of Eden, this place would be it. Every now and then, like jewels that dazzle, birds with blinding colors became visible. There were birds I often heard but seldom saw. In time, however, I developed a keen birder's ear and was able to memorize birdcalls and bird names.

I found simple joy in waking up before daybreak to make a robust cup of coffee and to hear the ensemble of birdcalls. The birds seemed to be most active before sunrise and during daybreak. The daily musical act was opened before sunrise by the raucous hornbills. These large colorful birds wore "casques" on top of their large beaks and gave calls that resonated throughout the jungle. Several other species of different sizes had their different calls, ranging from that of a trumpet to that of a clarinet. The "gang" of hornbills foraged from one mountain ridge to another. Once I counted 50 of them in one flock foraging together. Added to this symphony were the melodious squeals of the blue-crowned racquet-tails; the rhythmic, staccato calls of the coppersmith barbet; the deep resonating hoots of the yellow-breasted fruit-doves; and the faint marimba-like sounds of the tailorbirds and flame minivets—all providing the musical background. Listening to this "orchestra" was the greatest joy of my young life.

Before the 1970s little was known about the life history of the Philippine eagle. Questions abounded: When and where do they breed? What do they eat? How large was the remaining population? How large was an eagle's territory? Answers to these key questions were vital in conservation work for the eagles. Dr. Kennedy's research in 1978 pieced together basic information on the eagle's life history, but many more questions remained unanswered.

When I was hired, it was the start of the breeding season. Our field team split up, positioned at several vantage points to track the eagles when they appeared. On a typical sunny day, we would see a pair of Philippine eagles soaring together in a graceful aerial "dance." Other raptors would also show up as a supporting cast to this wonderful daily drama of life. The serpent eagles, Philippine and changeable hawk-eagles, rufous-bellied eagles, and honey buzzards afforded endless pleasure with their accompanying acts.

Finding an eagle nest in the rainforest was a daunting task, like "finding the needle in the haystack." We were determined to focus our observations in one area where the birds were seen soaring together on a daily basis.

By October of that year, we had found a nest by following one of the birds. It happened late in the afternoon one day when we saw and heard the pair calling and circling around an area midway from the top of the ridge. While we were watching the eagles, Marlo saw one bird, its beak clutching green sprigs. It landed on a towering, 300 m (100 ft) tall lauan tree, its nest below, resting on a large platform at the fork of the tree's main branch. There was jubilation in the camp that night. This was the fourth Philippine eagle nest ever found since the pioneering studies by Filipino naturalist Rodolfo Gonzales in the early 1970s.

The pair seemed to spend a great deal of time arranging the green sprigs on the nest, much as expectant parents devote their time and effort preparing a nursery room. For the next month the female stayed around the vicinity of the nest while the male hunted most of the time. They would also regularly indulge in their majestic soaring "dance," delighting those of us fortunate enough to be watching them. For a birdwatcher, there is no other sight more grand and spectacular to look at.

When carrying food, the male usually announced his arrival with a series of sharp whistle-like *whee-whee-whee* calls. The female would usually reply, and the pair would meet on the nest tree and copulate. We recorded several copulations per day for a full month after the egg was laid in early November, whenever the male brought food to the nest. The only time that the pair did not copulate was when the male came with a small bat. The female was obviously unimpressed with this offering.

Once the egg had been laid, the female did the majority of the incubation, but the male also took his turn sitting on the egg to keep it warm. Incubation went on for two months, then, around four o'clock on a chilly November morning, the parent eagles started calling nonstop for hours. We knew something momentous was going on. We raced to the observation blind even before daybreak and discovered a little downy eagle chick on the nest! The team was in high spirits. It felt like a new member of our family had been born.

A few weeks after the eaglet hatched, reports from the loggers reached us about an active nest with a chick at Road 7, about 5 km (3 mi) away from the first nest. In reality, this translated into a four-hour drive back to the city of Mangagoy and then another five-hour drive to the site. Although the roads were wide enough to accommodate the monstrous logging trucks, driving was perilous since the roads were marked with steep ravines and falling boulders. The large logging trucks made the trip even more dangerous because they always claimed the right-of-way since braking downhill was difficult for them.

Together with a colleague, I drove to the new nest site. Just less than a kilometer (about half a mile) before the logging road ended, down on the ridge, was a nest with a 4-week-old chick. Trees were falling around the nest since the company was logging in the area at the time it was discovered. The loggers' curiosity seemed to be more about my American colleagues than the birds themselves. Perhaps driven by this curiosity, when we decided to make a tree blind close to the nest, the loggers took no time in getting 21 m (70 ft) up to construct a tree blind in less than an hour. This was where I would be spending the next seven months of my life, watching this family of eagles.

With two known active nests and two other pairs whose nests we were still trying to locate, the team was spread thinly. Every week, I hitchhiked on logging trucks going down to Mangagoy and came back up after getting fresh field supplies. I spent most of every day in the field, getting up before daybreak, climbing up to the tree blind, and observing and recording the eagles' daily activities. During this time, I grew closer to the local loggers, who, from time to time, climbed up to the tree blind to see what I was up to. Soon afterward, they were climbing to the tree blind to bring me food.

The weather in the mid-elevation jungles of Mindanao was pleasant and cool, but during the wet season, from November to March, it was also *really* soaking wet. It rained for weeks and months without end, and when it wasn't pouring hard, it was foggy. The fog got so thick that visibility was poor beyond 3 m (10 ft). The end of that particular year's wet season was marked by an unusual entomological phenomenon that happened once every 15 years—a cicada hatch. In a week's time, the sounds of these insects went from nonexistent to unbearable, and I had severe headaches almost every day.

Throughout the rain and the cicadas' racket and the loggers' visits, I kept a daily log of the eagles' activities. By March the eaglet was as big as the adults, and the parents spent less and less time in the nest. There were some differences in how this particular family of eagles behaved from the first pair we had observed. The parents did not call to "announce" their arrival to the nest, nor did they deliver food as frequently as the first eagle pair we had found. Probably this had something to do with the pounding noise from the calamitous logging activities nearby. Every time a giant tree fell, the earth shook, and the tree "bulldozed" every living thing along its path down the mountain ridge.

At the time when it was supposed to fledge, the eagle chick started to reject prey brought in by the parent eagles. I knew something was wrong, but there was nothing I could do and soon the eaglet died. After watching this eaglet every day for five months from my vantage point 21 m above the ground, I felt a deep sense of loss. Later I was to find out that soon after I had left the first nest, the eaglet there also died.

At that juncture of our research, when nesting by both pairs had failed, armed groups started appearing at our camp in Mangagoy. Their increasing presence forced us to move to Mount Apo, another area of good forest closer to the city of Davao. The following year we investigated several other pairs of eagles, but most of those young also died before the end of the first year. I did not know why juvenile mortality was so high among the birds we studied, and on several occasions I have wondered whether deforestation directly affected their population and survival.

I left the Philippine Eagle Conservation Program in 1983, after two years of work, and went back to graduate school, carrying memories that would last a lifetime. Several years after we left Mount Agtuuganon, gold was discovered in the area. The gold rush that ensued further devastated the whole area. My memories are about all that remains of the eagles of this remarkable area.

Almost two decades later, armed with a PhD from the University of Cincinnati and after many years as a graduate student in the United States, I decided to haul my family back to Mindanao to re-experience the paradise the forest had imprinted in my mind, and live it, perhaps for the last time. Leading a group of young Filipino naturalists, we studied several active Philippine eagle nests, all of them in severely degraded landscape. We trapped and radio-tagged Philippine eagles and tried to seek answers to deeper questions about the eagles that had haunted me for years.

Strange and sad as it may seem, on this second venture into the forest I never again heard the symphony orchestra of the hornbills and the racquet-tails, or saw the majesty of the giant lauan trees. Most of what I had seen was now a shadow of the past. I never realized that the forest could all disappear so soon. It is hard for me to imagine how this magnificent bird, which has been called "the Hope Diamond of the ornithological world," could recover when the evolutionary forces that took millions of years to create it are almost gone. The reality of what the naturalist Charles William Beebe once said, and was so often repeated by my mentor, Bob Kennedy, has now dawned on me: "When the last individual of a race breathes no more, another heaven and another earth must pass before such a one can be again."

Appendix
Conservation Status of the World's Eagles

The International Union for the Conservation of Nature (IUCN) assesses the conservation status of plants and animals on a global scale, to highlight the species that are threatened with extinction. Species are assessed by analyzing the latest scientific information on specific qualitative criteria, namely, distribution, population status or trend, habitat(s), and perceived threat(s). Once the scientific information has been assessed, each species is categorized into one of the following levels of threat on the IUCN Red List as an indication of its risk of extinction:

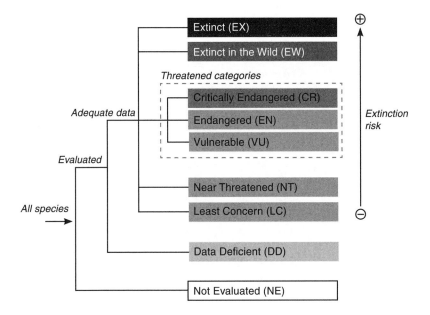

The Red List classification method is useful for highlighting species that are most threatened with the risk of extinction, and scientists use the Red

List to help inform their decisions on which species need the most urgent conservation action (i.e., those listed as Critically Endangered, Endangered, or Vulnerable). However, the list is only as good as the data on which it is based. There are many limitations to the Red List approach, principally concerning data paucity (e.g., data are rarely available for the whole range or population of a given species). For further information, please visit http://www.iucnredlist.org.

Below, we have listed the 2009 IUCN conservation status of the world's eagle species, based on the most recent updates that were announced in February 2009.

Appendix
IUCN conservation status of eagles, 2009

English name	Scientific name	Region	IUCN conservation status
Flores Hawk-Eagle	*Spizaetus flores*	Asia (islands only)	Critically Endangered
Madagascar Fish Eagle	*Haliaeetus vociferoides*	Africa (islands only)	Critically Endangered
Philippine Eagle	*Pithecophaga jefferyi*	Asia (islands only)	Critically Endangered
Crowned Solitary Eagle	*Harpyhaliaetus coronatus*	South America	Endangered
Javan Hawk-Eagle	*Spizaetus bartelsi*	Asia (islands only)	Endangered
Madagascar Serpent Eagle	*Eutriorchis astur*	Africa (islands only)	Endangered
Beaudouin's Snake Eagle	*Circaetus beaudouini*	Africa	Vulnerable
Eastern Imperial Eagle	*Aquila heliaca*	Europe, Asia, and Africa	Vulnerable
Greater Spotted Eagle	*Aquila clanga*	Europe, Asia, and Africa	Vulnerable
Indian Spotted Eagle	*Aquila hastata*	Asia	Vulnerable
Mountain Serpent Eagle	*Spilornis kinabaluensis*	Asia (islands only)	Vulnerable
New Guinea Harpy Eagle	*Harpyopsis novaeguineae*	Asia (islands only)	Vulnerable
Pallas's Fish Eagle	*Haliaeetus leucoryphus*	Asia	Vulnerable

English name	Scientific name	Region	IUCN conservation status
Philippine Hawk-Eagle	*Spizaetus philippensis*	Asia (islands only)	Vulnerable
Sanford's Sea Eagle	*Haliaeetus sanfordi*	Asia (islands only)	Vulnerable
Spanish Imperial Eagle	*Aquila adalberti*	Europe	Vulnerable
Steller's Sea Eagle	*Haliaeetus pelagicus*	Asia	Vulnerable
Wallace's Hawk-Eagle	*Spizaetus nanus*	Asia	Vulnerable
Andaman Serpent Eagle	*Spilornis elgini*	Asia (islands only)	Near Threatened
Bateleur	*Terathopius ecaudatus*	Africa	Near Threatened
Black-and-chestnut Eagle	*Spizaetus isidori*	South America	Near Threatened
Crested Eagle	*Morphnus guianensis*	Central and South America	Near Threatened
Gurney's Eagle	*Aquila gurneyi*	Asia (islands only)	Near Threatened
Grey-headed Fishing Eagle	*Ichthyophaga ichthyaetus*	Asia	Near Threatened
Harpy Eagle	*Harpia harpyja*	Central and South America	Near Threatened
Lesser Fishing Eagle	*Ichthyophaga humilis*	Asia	Near Threatened
Martial Eagle	*Polemaetus bellicosus*	Africa	Near Threatened
Solitary Eagle	*Harpyhaliaetus solitarius*	Central and South America	Near Threatened
South Nicobar Serpent Eagle	*Spilornis klossi*	Asia (islands only)	Near Threatened
Southern Banded Snake Eagle	*Circaetus fasciolatus*	Africa	Near Threatened
African Crowned Eagle	*Stephanoaetus coronatus*	Africa	Least Concern
African Fish Eagle	*Haliaeetus vocifer*	Africa	Least Concern

(*Continued*)

English name	Scientific name	Region	IUCN conservation status
African Hawk-Eagle	*Hieraaetus spilogaster*	Africa	Least Concern
Ayres's Hawk-Eagle	*Hieraaetus ayresii*	Africa	Least Concern
Bald Eagle	*Haliaeetus leucocephalus*	North and Central America	Least Concern
Black-chested Buzzard-Eagle	*Geranoaetus melanoleucus*	South America	Least Concern
Black-chested Snake Eagle	*Circaetus pectoralis*	Africa	Least Concern
Black Hawk-Eagle	*Spizaetus tyrannus*	Central and South America	Least Concern
Black-and-white Hawk-Eagle	*Spizastur melanoleucus*	Central and South America	Least Concern
Blyth's Hawk-Eagle	*Spizaetus alboniger*	Asia	Least Concern
Bonelli's Eagle	*Hieraaetus fasciatus*	Europe, Asia, and Africa	Least Concern
Booted Eagle	*Hieraaetus pennatus*	Europe, Asia, and Africa	Least Concern
Brown Snake Eagle	*Circaetus cinereus*	Africa	Least Concern
Cassin's Hawk-Eagle	*Spizaetus africanus*	Africa	Least Concern
Changeable Hawk-Eagle	*Spizaetus cirrhatus*	Asia	Least Concern
Congo Serpent Eagle	*Dryotriorchis spectabilis*	Africa	Least Concern
Crested Serpent Eagle	*Spilornis cheela*	Asia	Least Concern
Golden Eagle	*Aquila chrysaetos*	North America, Europe, Asia, and Africa	Least Concern
Indian Black Eagle	*Ictinaetus malayensis*	Asia	Least Concern
Lesser Spotted Eagle	*Aquila pomarina*	Europe, Asia, and Africa	Least Concern
Little Eagle	*Hieraaetus morphnoides*	Australia	Least Concern

English name	Scientific name	Region	IUCN conservation status
Long-crested Eagle	*Lophaetus occipitalis*	Africa	Least Concern
Mountain Hawk-Eagle	*Spizaetus nipalensis*	Asia	Least Concern
New Guinea Hawk-Eagle	*Hieraaetus weiskei*	Asia (islands only)	Least Concern
Ornate Hawk-Eagle	*Spizaetus ornatus*	Central and South America	Least Concern
Philippine Serpent Eagle	*Spilornis holospilus*	Asia (islands only)	Least Concern
Rufous-bellied Eagle	*Hieraaetus kienerii*	Asia	Least Concern
Short-toed Snake Eagle	*Circaetus gallicus*	Europe, Asia, and Africa	Least Concern
Steppe Eagle	*Aquila nipalensis*	Asia and Africa	Least Concern
Sulawesi Hawk-Eagle	*Spizaetus lanceolatus*	Asia (islands only)	Least Concern
Sulawesi Serpent Eagle	*Spilornis rufipectus*	Asia (islands only)	Least Concern
Tawny Eagle	*Aquila rapax*	Africa	Least Concern
Verreaux's Eagle	*Aquila verreauxii*	Africa	Least Concern
Wahlberg's Eagle	*Hieraaetus wahlbergi*	Africa	Least Concern
Wedge-tailed Eagle	*Aquila audax*	Asia and Australia	Least Concern
Western Banded Snake Eagle	*Circaetus cinerascens*	Africa	Least Concern
White-bellied Sea Eagle	*Haliaeetus leucogaster*	Asia and Australia	Least Concern
White-tailed Sea Eagle	*Haliaeetus albicilla*	Europe and Asia	Least Concern
Bawean Serpent Eagle	*Spilornis baweanus*	Asia (islands only)	Not Evaluated
Central Nicobar Serpent Eagle	*Spilornis minimus*	Asia (islands only)	Not Evaluated
Mentawai Serpent Eagle	*Spilornis sipora*	Asia (islands only)	Not Evaluated

(*Continued*)

English name	Scientific name	Region	*IUCN* conservation status
Natuna Serpent Eagle	*Spilornis natunensis*	Asia (islands only)	Not Evaluated
Nias Serpent Eagle	*Spilornis asturinus*	Asia (islands only)	Not Evaluated
Ryukuyu Serpent Eagle	*Spilornis perplexus*	Asia (islands only)	Not Evaluated
Simeulue Serpent Eagle	*Spilornis abbotti*	Asia (islands only)	Not Evaluated

Further Reading

Books

The following is a chronological and annotated list of books about eagles. Several are now out of print but secondhand copies can usually be found.

General Eagle Books

Ostling, Bruce, and Staffan Soderblom. 2008. *The Kingdom of the Eagle*. London: A&C Black. *Compiled by a wildlife photographer and natural history writer, this book centers around stunning photographs of golden and white-tailed sea eagles. For a nonspecialist audience.*

Helander, Björn, Mick Marquiss, and Bill Bowerman (Editors). 2003. *Sea Eagle 2000: Proceedings from the International Sea Eagle Conference in Björkö, Sweden, 13–17 September 2000*. Stockholm: Swedish Society for Nature Conservation. *Edited by three leading eagle biologists, this book contains more than 50 technical research papers, mainly on the white-tailed sea eagle. Aimed at a scientific audience.*

Savage, Candace. 2000. *Eagles of North America*. Vancouver: Greystone Books/D&M Publishers. *Written by an accomplished nature writer, this book provides a general account of the lives of bald and golden eagles. For a general audience.*

Ueta, Mutsuyuki, and Mike McGrady (Editors). 2000. *First Symposium on Steller's and White-Tailed Sea Eagles in East Asia*. Tokyo: Wild Bird Society of Japan. *This is a compilation of a dozen scientific papers. For a specialist audience.*

Grambo, Rebecca. 1999. *Eagles*. Osceola, Wisc.: Voyageur Press. *Written by an accomplished natural history writer, this book provides a general introduction to eagle natural history, with a focus on bald and golden eagles. For a general audience.*

Grambo, Rebecca. 1997. *Eagles: Masters of the Sky*. Osceola, Wisc.: Voyageur Press. *This book contains a blend of eagle natural history, folklore and photography. For a general audience.*

Meyburg, Bernd, and Robin Chancellor (Editors). 1996. *Eagle Studies*. Berlin: World Working Group on Birds of Prey & Owls. *This book, edited by a leading scientific authority on eagles, is a compilation of more than 60 scientific papers on eagles, with an emphasis on the white-tailed sea eagle and* Aquila *eagles. Aimed at a specialist audience.*

Olsen, Jerry. 1995. *Some Time with Eagles and Falcons*. Blaine, Wash.: Hancock House Publishers. *This book contains anecdotal stories of time spent in the field in the United States, Australia, and the Solomon Islands. Written for a general audience.*

Love, John. 1989. *Eagles*. Yatesbury, Wiltshire, UK: Whittet Books. *Written by one of the United Kingdom's leading eagle fieldworkers, this general book focuses on the golden and white-tailed sea eagles. Aimed at a nonspecialist audience.*

Burton, Philip. 1987. *Vanishing Eagles*. New York: Dodd Mead. *This book provides text and artwork on several eagle species around the world. For a general audience.*

Brown, Leslie. 1976. *Eagles of the World*. Cape Town, South Africa: Purnell. *This popular science book about the biology and ecology of eagles worldwide, but with a particular focus on African species, is written by one of the world's leading eagle biologists. Suitable for both a specialist and general audience.*

Steyn, Peter. 1973. *Eagle Days: A Study of African Eagles at the Nest*. Sandton, South Africa: Sable Publishers (PTY). *In its day, this was a groundbreaking book about the behavior and habits of breeding African eagles. Written by an accomplished raptor researcher and photographer, it is suitable for both a general and specialist audience.*

Brown, Leslie. 1970. *Eagles*. London: Arthur Barker Limited. *This book is an introduction to the natural history of eagles, written by a man who spent most of his life devoted to their study. Suitable for a general audience.*

Brown, Leslie. 1955. *Eagles*. London: Michael Joseph. *At the time of its publication, this book was one of the first to introduce the natural history of eagles to a general audience.*

Bald Eagle

Breining, Greg. 2008. *Return of the Eagle: How America Saved Its National Symbol*. Guilford, Conn.: Lyons Press/Globe Pequot Press. *Written by a nature writer, this book documents the bald eagle recovery effort in the post-DDT era. Suitable for a general audience.*

Carrick, Douglas. 2008. *Eagles of Hornby Island*. Blaine, Wash.: Hancock House Publishers. *This book tells the story of one man's observations of a pair of bald eagles breeding on his property. For a general audience.*

Hancock, David. 2007. *Bald Eagle of Alaska, BC and Washington*. Blaine, Wash.: Hancock House Publishers. *This introduction to bald eagle ecology and conservation was written by a leading bald eagle field researcher. Aimed at a general audience.*

Tekiela, Stan. 2007. *Majestic Eagles: Compelling Facts and Images of the Bald Eagle*. Cambridge, Minn.: Adventure Publications. *A broad overview of bald eagle information, this book was compiled by a nature photographer. Suitable for a general audience.*

Anderson, Cary. 2004. *The Eagle Lady*. Anchorage: Eagle Eye Pictures. *This illustrated biography is about Jean Keene, famed for feeding a congregation of up to 300 bald eagles for over 30 years. Aimed at a general audience.*

Hutchinson, Alan. 2000. *Just Eagles*. Minocqua, Wisc.: Willow Creek Press. *This general book is on the natural history of the bald eagle. Aimed at a nonspecialist audience.*

Beans, Bruce. 1997. *Eagle's Plume: The Struggle to Preserve the Life and Haunts of America's Bald Eagle*. Lincoln: University of Nebraska Press. *These anecdotal stories are about some of the people involved in the post-DDT recovery period. Aimed at a general audience.*

Rennick, Penny, and Cary Anderson (Editors). 1997. *Alaska's Magnificent Eagles*. Anchorage: Alaska Geographic Society. *This photographic essay is on bald eagle behavior, folklore, and preservation. For a general audience.*

Wolfe, Art, and Donald Bruning. 1997. *Bald Eagles: Their Life and Behavior in North America*. New York: Three Rivers Press/Random House. *Compiled by a wildlife photographer, this book provides a general introduction to the natural history of the bald eagle. For a general audience.*

Anderson, Cary. 1995. *Valley of the Eagles*. Anchorage: Fathom Publishing. *The focus of this book is on the large gathering of eagles at Alaska Chilkat Bald Eagle Preserve. Aimed at a general audience.*

Nielsen, Scott. 1994. *A Season with Eagles*. Osceola, Wisc.: Voyageur Press. *This book documents a researcher's observations at a bald eagle nest. Written for a general audience.*

Tucker, Priscilla. 1994. *Return of the Bald Eagle*. Mechanicsburg, Penn.: Stackpole Books. *The author discusses how various policies have helped the bald eagle to recover from the DDT era. For a general audience.*

Leeson, Tom, and Pat Leeson. 1990. *The American Eagle*. Hillsboro, Ore.: Beyond Words Publishing. *This is a general book on the natural history of the bald eagle. For a nonspecialist audience.*

Hancock, David. 1989. *Adventure with Eagles*. Blaine, Wash.: Hancock House Publishers. *A wildlife biologist shares his eagle field stories. For a general audience.*

Gerrard, Jon, and Gary Bortolotti. 1988. *The Bald Eagle: Haunts and Habits of a Wilderness Monarch*. Washington, DC: Smithsonian Institution Press. *Written by two accomplished wildlife biologists, this book includes general and anecdotal information about bald eagle ecology. Written for a general audience.*

Stalmaster, Mark. 1987. *The Bald Eagle*. New York: Universe Books. *This comprehensive overview of bald eagle biology and ecology is written by a leading authority on this species. Suitable for a general and scientific audience.*

White-tailed Sea Eagle

Love, John. 1983. *The Return of the Sea Eagle*. London: Cambridge University Press. *This detailed account of the reintroduction of the white-tailed sea eagle to western Scotland is written by the man who ran the project. Suitable for a scientific and general audience.*

African Fish Eagle

Brown, Leslie. 1980. *The African Fish Eagle*. Folkestone, South Africa: Bailey Bros. and Swinfen Ltd. *This species monograph was written by an eagle biologist who had studied the species for more than 20 years. Suitable for a scientific and general audience.*

Golden Eagle

Preston, Charles. 2004. *Golden Eagle: Sovereign of the Skies*. Portland, Ore.: Graphic Arts Center Publishing. *This book is an account of the natural and cultural history of the golden eagle. Aimed at a general audience.*

Crane, Ken, and Kate Nellist. 1999. *Island Eagles: 20 Years Observing Golden Eagles on the Isle of Skye*. Isle of Skye, Scotland: Cartwheeling Press. *Written by two eagle fieldworkers, this book provides anecdotal information about the natural history of the golden eagle. Suitable for a general audience.*

Campbell, Laurie, and Roy Dennis. 1997. *Golden Eagles*. Grantown-on-Spey, Scotland: Colin Baxter Photography. *This is a photographic essay on the natural history of the golden eagle. Aimed at a general audience.*

Watson, Jeff. 1997. *The Golden Eagle*. London: T. & A.D. Poyser. *This scientific monograph on the golden eagle is written by one of the leading authorities on this species. Aimed at a specialist audience.*

Tomkies, Mike. 1994. *On Wing and Wild Water*. 1987. London: Jonathan Cape. *This book follows on from where his earlier book ended. Aimed at a general audience.*

Tomkies, Mike. 1982. *Golden Eagle Years*. London: Jonathan Cape. *This is an intimate account written by a naturalist who spent many years observing golden eagles in a remote corner of Scotland. Aimed at a general audience.*

MacNally, Lea. 1977. *The Ways of an Eagle*. London: Collins & Harvill Press. *These anecdotal accounts on the natural history of the golden eagle are written by an accomplished eagle field researcher. Aimed at a general audience.*

Olendorff, Richard. 1975. *Golden Eagle Country*. New York: Knopf. *This book is an overview of the natural history of golden eagles, written by a leading wildlife biologist. Suitable for a general audience.*

Murphy, Robert. 1965. *The Golden Eagle*. New York: E.P. Dutton & Co. *This book contains anecdotal stories about the species' natural history. For a general audience.*

Gordon, Seton. 1955. *The Golden Eagle: King of Birds*. London: Collins. *This early account on the natural history of the golden eagle is written by an accomplished fieldworker. For a general audience.*

Gordon, Seton. 1927. *Days with the Golden Eagle*. Caithness, Scotland: Whittles Publishing (reprinted in 2003). *These anecdotal field stories are written by a man who spent decades watching eagles in Scotland. Aimed at a general audience.*

Macpherson, H. B. 1909. *The Home Life of a Golden Eagle*. London: Witherby & Co. *This book is one of the first published accounts on the natural history of this species, written by a man who studied a pair of breeding eagles in Scotland. For a general audience.*

Wedge-tailed Eagle

Olsen, Penny. 2005. *Wedge-Tailed Eagle*. Victoria, Australia: CSIRO Publishing. *Written by a leading authority on this species, this book documents the natural and cultural history of the species. For a general audience.*

Spanish Imperial Eagle

Ferrer, Miguel. 2001. *The Spanish Imperial Eagle*. Barcelona: Lynx Edicions. *This scientific species monograph is written by a world authority on this species. Aimed at a scientific audience.*

Black Eagle

Gargett, Valerie. 1993. *The Black Eagle*. London: Academic Press. *Written by an accomplished eagle biologist who spent many years studying black (Verreaux's) eagles, the book provides a detailed account of this species' biology and ecology. Suitable for a scientific and general audience.*

Harpy Eagle

Tufiño, Paul. 2007. *Cunsi Pindo: The Mistress of the Monkeys.* Quito, Ecuador: SIMBIOE.
  This is a bilingual (Spanish/English) book documenting the first seven years of a harpy eagle field research project in Ecuador. Suitable for a general and scientific audience.

Web Sites

The following Web sites, listed alphabetically, provide information about current eagle research projects.

Aguila Harpia Panama (in Spanish)
http://www.aguilaharpia.org
Project on the harpy eagle (Panama)

Asian Raptor Research and Conservation Network
http://www5b.biglobe.ne.jp/~raptor/
Compilation of information on eagle research in Asia

Center for the Study and Conservation of Birds of Prey in Argentina (in Spanish and English)
http://www.cecara.co.ar
Project on crowned eagle (Argentina)

Doñana Biological Station (in Spanish and English)
http://www.ebd.csic.es
Projects on Spanish imperial eagle and Bonelli's eagle (Spain)

Eagle Conservation Alliance
http://www.eagleconservationalliance.org
Compilation of information on all of the world's eagle species

Endangered Wildlife Trust
http://www.ewt.org.za
Projects on African fish eagle, Verreaux's eagle, and martial eagle (South Africa)

Global Raptor Information Network
http://www.globalraptors.org
Compilation of information on all of the world's eagle species

Golden Eagle Trust
http://www.goldeneagle.ie
Projects on golden eagle and white-tailed sea eagle (Ireland)

HawkWatch International
http://www.hawkwatch.org
Projects on bald eagle and golden eagle (United States)

Highland Foundation for Wildlife
http://www.roydennis.org
Projects on golden eagle and white-tailed sea eagle (Scotland)

National Aviary
http://www.aviary.org
Projects on golden eagle (United States and Kazakhstan); Philippine eagle (Philippines); white-tailed sea eagle and eastern imperial eagle (Kazakhstan)

Natural Research
http://www.natural-research.org
Projects on golden eagle and white-tailed sea eagle (Scotland); Steller's sea eagle (Russia); Madagascar fish eagle (Madagascar); grey-headed fishing eagle (Cambodia)

Neotropical Raptor Network
http://www.neotropicalraptors.org
Compilation of information on eagle research in Central and South America

Norwegian Institute for Nature Research (in Norwegian and English)
http://www.nina.no
Projects on white-tailed sea eagle and golden eagle (Norway)

Percy FitzPatrick Institute of African Ornithology
http://www.fitzpatrick.uct.ac.za
Projects on martial eagle and African fish eagle (South Africa)

The Peregrine Fund
http://www.peregrinefund.org
Projects on harpy eagle and black-and-chestnut eagle (South America); Madagascar fish eagle and Madagascar serpent eagle (Madagascar); Philippine eagle (Philippines); New Guinea harpy eagle (New Guinea); African fish eagle (Kenya)

Philippine Eagle Foundation
http://www.philippineeagle.org
Project on Philippine eagle (Philippines)

Polish Eagle Conservation Committee
http://eagle.free.ngo.pl/
Projects on white-tailed sea eagle, golden eagle, lesser spotted eagle, and greater spotted eagle (Poland)

Rocky Mountain Eagle Research Foundation
http://www.eaglewatch.ca
Projects on bald eagle and golden eagle (Canada)

Royal Society for the Protection of Birds
http://www.rspb.org.uk
Projects on white-tailed sea eagle (Scotland); imperial eagle (Bulgaria)

SIMBIOE (in Spanish)
http://www.simbioe.org
Project on harpy eagle (Ecuador)

Sociedad Española de Ornitología (in Spanish)
http://www.seo.org
Project on Spanish imperial eagle (Spain)

Society for Research of the Golden Eagle (in Japanese and English)
http://homepage1.nifty.com/srge/
Project on golden eagle (Japan)

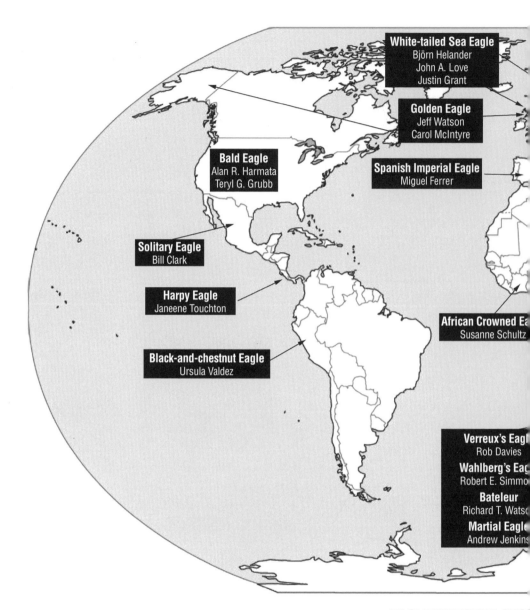

White-tailed Sea Eagle
Björn Helander
John A. Love
Justin Grant

Golden Eagle
Jeff Watson
Carol McIntyre

Spanish Imperial Eagle
Miguel Ferrer

Bald Eagle
Alan R. Harmata
Teryl G. Grubb

Solitary Eagle
Bill Clark

Harpy Eagle
Janeene Touchton

Black-and-chestnut Eagle
Ursula Valdez

African Crowned Ea
Susanne Schultz

Verreux's Eagl
Rob Davies

Wahlberg's Eag
Robert E. Simmo

Bateleur
Richard T. Watso

Martial Eagl
Andrew Jenkins

EAGLE WATCHER STO